Quest

Leading Global Transformations

The IMD Guide to the Seven Journeys
Reshaping Corporations Today

N. Anand
Jean-Louis Barsoux

Chemin de Bellerive 23
P.O. Box 915
CH – 1001 Lausanne
Switzerland
Tel: +41 21 618 01 11 – Fax: +41 21 618 07 07
www.imd.org

Typeset in Sabon®, a font designed in Basel, Switzerland by Jan Tschichold. Sabon is a trademark of Monotype Imaging Inc. registered in the U.S. Patent and Trademark Office and may be registered in certain other jurisdictions.

ISBN 978-2-940485-05-5
Designed by Yves Balibouse, BBH Solutions Visuelles, Vevey, Switzerland, www.bbhgraphic.com.
Printed in Switzerland by PCL Presses Centrales SA, Renens, www.pcl.ch.

Contents

Foreword

"Business as usual" is a thing of the past. In the last four decades we have witnessed unprecedented and accelerating shifts in the business environment. Globalization has imposed profound changes on business models in corporations across all industries. And these sweeping transformations are creating complex and demanding leadership challenges.

IMD aspires to be the best in the world at enabling the development of successful global leaders – individuals, teams and organizations. To live up to this ambitious vision, IMD continuously strives to be at the cutting edge in helping individuals and organizations to lead global transformation efforts.

IMD's world-class faculty members combine thought leadership and practical experience. They interact constantly, not just with one another but also with more than 8,000 global executives from over 98 countries who attend IMD programs each year. This book captures the richness of the faculty's experience, expertise and insight on a diverse set of themes relating to successful transformation journeys.

I am delighted to introduce this book, which distills the collective intellectual capital developed at IMD since its inception in 1990. This guide will help global leaders to navigate their transformation challenges effectively.

My particular thanks go to Dominique Turpin, President of IMD, who served as the key sponsor of this initiative, and to Professor Anand Narasimhan for orchestrating this collective contribution with the help of colleagues at IMD.

I wish you an enjoyable reading experience.

Peter Wuffli
Chairman of IMD Supervisory
and Foundation Boards

Acknowledgments

IMD is truly an exhilarating and fulfilling place to work. Every day we have the privilege of engaging with colleagues and executives about all aspects of leadership in organizations and corporations. This book very much embodies the distinctive interdisciplinary and problem-driven discussions that connect and animate the faculty at IMD. We therefore extend a heart-felt thank you to our faculty colleagues for their input and support throughout this project – in multiple conversations as well as helpful feedback on drafts of each chapter.

We are grateful for the many quotes from the global leaders interviewed by our colleague Paul Hunter as part of IMD's exclusive Corporate Learning Network. We also owe thanks to a small team of dedicated individuals who brought the project to fruition. Marco Mancesti put together and led the cross-functional team to produce the book. Michelle Perrinjaquet worked tirelessly on editing the manuscript, with the help of Lindsay McTeague. Laure le Hardy de Beaulieu coordinated the project in meticulous detail, including liaising with the designer, acquiring images and clearances, and keeping everything on track. Vincenzo Palatella coordinated the printing and the e-versions of the book and Yves Balibouse, of BBH Solutions Visuelles, was responsible for the design.

Introduction: The Quest for Transformation

THE TRANSFORMATION IMPERATIVE

In creating corporations, people have bestowed on them the gift of life. It is now customary to think of corporations as "artificial persons," having life beyond that of their founders. The world's oldest surviving joint-stock corporation, Stora, dates back more than 700 years. Looking forward the same length of time, how many of today's corporations will still exist? Even among the biggest, which of these would we predict, with any degree of assurance, to be active seven centuries from now?

Perhaps the one thing we can predict with relative confidence is that corporations will continue to play an ever-expanding role in people's lives.[1] The pervasive presence of corporations has reached deeper, not only into our working lives but also into our private lives. Corporate organizations have become indispensable partners in many of our leisure activities, from entertainment to exercising and vacationing. Corporations have even seeped into parts of our lives that used to be intimate and personal, such as dating, friendships and even our own genealogy.

Corporations have also become the dominant drivers of innovation. The big scientific and technological breakthroughs were once engineered by lone geniuses, either acting on their own or sponsored by a monarch or nation-state. Their names are legend. Gutenberg's movable type presses democratized the distribution of knowledge. Watt's steam engine powered the industrial revolution. Bell's telephone ushered in the era of instant virtual communication. Babbage's mechanical calculator foreshadowed the modern information age. Diesel's internal combustion engine got us moving as never before. The Wright brothers' airplane propelled us into the jet age. Fleming's discovery of penicillin transformed healthcare. And Watson and Crick's DNA model sparked the biotechnology revolution. Yet, scanning the list of innovations since the 1950s, fewer and fewer can be attributed to individuals.[2]

In future, great changes to society will most probably be pioneered by corporations. They are not going to come about because of acts of genius alone, but because of incremental advances on an epochal scale happening within companies all the time.

To continue to be part of that future, established corporations will have to excel in one domain above all – they will have to master the art of transformation. To endure, corporations will have to constantly pursue the quest for transformation, as demonstrated by Stora over the course of its extended history.

The transformations of business: Stora's story

Stora started out life in Sweden as a copper mining concern. A deed of exchange signed in 1288 is one of the earliest documented stock transfers. The mine went on to dominate the European copper market, becoming the engine of Sweden's rise to prominence as a European power from the 16th to the 18th centuries, easily as important to the country's economic wellbeing as any of today's companies. Stora merged with a Finnish firm in 1998 to become Stora Enso and is now headquartered in London, not Sweden. It is a leader in paper products instead of mining, with operations in 35 countries (including China, Brazil and Russia) and it boasts "annual sales that are larger than the GDP of almost a hundred countries."[3]

Still trading: Stora's first stock certificate (1288)

The foundations for Stora's longevity were laid in 1347 by the delivery of a royal charter and a mining statute that dispersed power among a group of master miners. The end of the Swedish crown's direct authority over the mine in 1862, and the adoption of limited liability status in 1885, signaled the company's conversion from servant of the state to an independent agent. These key shifts – relating to the "artificial person," the ability to trade ownership shares and limited liability – are now understood to be defining characteristics of the modern corporation.[4]

In parallel, Stora underwent a number of key conceptual transformations. Its journey to automation began as far back as 1556 with the invention of a pump driven by a water wheel, which gave the mine a new lease of life. In 1648 Stora's expansion into wood-trading activities to fuel the copper smelters marked the start of its long diversification journey and its gradual shift from mining to forestry activities. The company's internationalization journey started in 1838 when it expanded into central Europe, before establishing its first overseas presence, initially in North America in 1891, and later in South America (1973) and Asia (1998). The purchase of another large Swedish company, Skutskär Sawmill, in 1885 set it on a journey of acquisitive as well as organic growth. Stora's past transformation journeys are not so different from the current journeys of many corporations. The big difference is that several of Stora's formative journeys lasted decades, if not centuries.

Today, corporations no longer have the luxury of time and must shorten their transformation journeys. In recent years, Stora Enso has been forced to undergo some heavy restructuring, divesting its North American operations in 2007 and closing down some of its mills in Finland, Sweden and Germany. The current CEO, Jouko Karvinen, has been at the helm since 2007 and acknowledges the complex, ongoing transformation challenges, "The first years were horrible for our people because we had restructure after restructure after restructure. We don't argue anymore about whether the world is changing or not. It has already changed. Now it's about getting ahead of the curve."[5]

> *We don't argue anymore about whether the world is changing or not. It has already changed. Now it's about getting ahead of the curve.*

The roots of global business

Although the world's oldest corporation is seven centuries old, the origins of global business stretch back a lot further. Today's corporations can be regarded as the direct descendants of two pre-existing entities: multinational trade networks and international empires.[6] Many of the global transformational challenges tackled by corporate executives today, including international expansion, strategic and operational agility, value creation and capture, capability building and renewal, supply chain security, dispersed innovation and distributed leadership, already challenged their forbears. The dual forces of exchange and war have not only shaped the global competitive landscape in which today's corporations operate but they have also influenced *how* they operate.

Empires and conflict have taught us about competition for resources, the role of leadership and the principles of strategic thinking, as well as the importance of logistics for feeding our troops. Indeed, the language of war continues to permeate and frame the way we think about global business. The rise and fall of the great powers also reminds us of the importance of renewal for today's corporate powerhouses in order to ward off complacency and decline.

Trade and exchange, by contrast, have taught us the language of collaboration and co-creation; the challenge of developing control structures and systems to influence the behavior of distant agents (without physical coercion); the importance of networks, flexibility, speed and information in international business; and the notion of win-win.

The historical examples discussed at the start of each chapter are intended to underline the endemic nature of certain corporate challenges, reaching back to the earliest international conquests and trading exchanges. We often overrate the novelty of contemporary dilemmas.[7] Professor Carlos Braga notes, "Many of the globalizing forces are not new, and some have been present for centuries. What has changed is the way they have come together in a kind of perfect storm for business. Things are changing rapidly and will continue to change. So even companies or economies that currently have a strong competitive advantage may not be as competitive tomorrow."

The storm created by the "flattening" of the business world puts pressure on long-established companies to reinvent themselves in order to survive and prosper. By contrast, companies from some of the fast-growing economies are often more accustomed to dealing with flux.[8] Professor Martha Maznevski comments, "Volatility has been a staple feature of several South American economies for decades. Executives from those countries fully understand the need for flexibility and contingency plans. They know that you need to devolve responsibility to teams so that they can respond quickly. In the more stable economies, we're still inclined to reason in terms of multi-year plans."

Appreciating the scope and speed of the disruption is a vital preliminary step to managing it. Much has been written about the megatrends that are transforming our economies and societies – from outsourcing to connectivity, from global financial markets to trade agreements. This big picture focus stresses the need for businesses to adapt – the *why* of change – but does not address the specific challenge facing global executives, namely *how* to respond. Other writers, taking the organizational perspective, have focused on the mechanics of corporate transformation.

The business of transformations: Selling change

Research on corporate transformations has grown out of previous works on organizational development, change, corporate turnarounds, restructuring and reengineering in the 1970s and 1980s. The concept started to gain real traction in the mid-1990s, particularly through the work and advice of John Kotter on transformation failures,[9] Tom Vollmann on the process of transformation[10] and Robert Miles on orchestrating transformation efforts.[11]

The "transformation" concept had broader appeal than its forerunners. It was not just about responding to crisis. Transformation was a proactive and uplifting term that could apply to a wide array of corporate situations: it was reinvention for companies that were still healthy and wanted to become more competitive, and could even be extended to the "transformational" leaders driving the changes.[12]

What distinguishes a transformation effort from other large-scale changes is its emphasis on establishing new ways of perceiving, thinking and acting throughout the organization. The litmus test of a successful transformation effort is whether we have achieved broad-based behavior change, not just improved performance results.[13] According to Professor Robert Hooijberg, "Transformational change means reinventing the corporate business model and the culture."

Embarking on any transformation journey, we have to accept two realities: first, that it will be much easier to launch than to complete; and second, that it will not be a one-off. Modern executives, like the traders and warriors of former times, can expect to set out on one quest after another.

As the shelf life of business strategies grows shorter, success is increasingly tied to change. Renewal is something we not only have to accept but also have to become good at.[14] As Professor Bala Chakravarthy puts it, "Corporate transformation is not a new phenomenon, more of a new label. What Alfred Sloan did decades ago at General Motors to establish a multi-brand strategy and divisional structure was corporate transformation. But we hear the term more often today because the phenomenon is more pervasive. Also, the clock speed for change has accelerated. Corporate transformation is continuous."

We no longer live in a "one change at a time" environment. Numerous necessary changes jostle for our attention. The transformed global marketplace demands faster expansion, more customer focus, more agility, more innovation, more collaboration, better value capture and more attention to sustainability – sometimes all at once.

The central challenge is therefore *what* to change or, more particularly, what to change *first*. A key limitation of the corporate transformation research is that it tends to frame transformation as a generic challenge, implying that the *goal* of the transformation and its *content* have little bearing on the process.

Yet, a corporate transformation does not take place in a vacuum. Different transformation goals generate different challenges, constraints and priorities that influence the way the process unfolds. We indicate where the transformation impetus has come from and what type of companies should be most concerned by it, then discuss the main points of leverage and the chief hazards associated with each type of journey.

A map for transformation journeys

This book has been written for those of us confronting the challenges of global transformation on a daily basis. Depending on the type of transformation, there are different things we need to *think about, do* and *avoid*. And this is the simple framework that has been applied to each of the transformation journeys.

The book is intended as a map for global executives with a mandate for corporate change, transformation and learning. It draws on insights from leading companies and proposes lessons for leading transformations. More specifically, it is meant to help us better understand and address the seven journeys reshaping corporations today. These transformations are referred to as "global" not only in the sense of applying to businesses worldwide but also in the sense of all-encompassing, that is, involving the entire organization.

To reflect this sense of shared challenge, the pronoun "we" is used throughout the book. This is how IMD professors address executives in the classroom and it reflects their deep experience as participant-observers in the process of leading strategic and organizational change.

The book integrates and builds on the collective experience and learning of the professors, who work directly with many firms and observe their transformation struggles at close range. It is a broad-based search for knowledge that is problem-driven and that cuts across academic specialties. To illustrate the points, we leverage IMD's extensive collection of case studies, featuring companies from across the globe, focusing not only on transformations that have succeeded but also learning from those that did not go according to plan. The resulting propositions, models and frameworks have been repeatedly "reality-tested" with thousands of executives both in the classroom and in consulting assignments. The concepts presented here are those that make most sense and that have proved most useful to participants.

We believe in scholarship from the ground up. The research and thinking are both inspired by and designed for our interactions with global executives. The same is true of the choice of transformations. The quests were identified in trends that we have observed in our research and teaching work, and were validated through surveys with senior executives from the world's major corporations attending IMD programs. These journeys turned out to be the challenges that preoccupy global executives right now. But they are by no means permanent. They are of great significance today, but may not be a decade from now.

A generation ago, other quests would have dominated the list, relating to quality, safety, empowerment, lean manufacturing, business process re-engineering, outsourcing and offshoring, and customer-centricity. The corporations still thriving have completed those journeys. Those differentiators are now givens, fully integrated into their way of working. Excellence on these dimensions once provided a competitive edge, but now they are prerequisites for competing in the global arena.

Global executives are the unsung agents of globalization. It is their day-to-day actions that precipitate the ongoing process of globalization, and it in turn reshapes them. This book celebrates their work – in transforming companies, global executives transform our very world. Tomorrow, global executives will be on another quest and the journeys charted here will no longer have the same allure. The quest for transformation is the sum and substance of executive action.

The quest for transformation is the sum and substance of executive action.

1

The Quest for
Global
Presence

" Once you start thinking globally, it brings you
a lot of value. However, it also brings you a lot of
challenges: challenges of coordination, challenges of
clarity, challenges of how you make sure people are
really driving the mission that they are supposed to;
as well as rewarding the right behavior, promoting the
right people – who may not be technically superior,
but are fantastic at bringing teams together and
getting the best out of people across the globe... "

Adel Al-Saleh, Chief Executive,
Northgate Information Solutions.[1]

Prince Henry the Navigator: The Original Blue Ocean Strategist

LESSONS FROM CIRCUMNAVIGATION

The lure of the ocean has long been the key driver of globalization. Take the case of Portugal, the world's first naval superpower. In 1433, it was the last stop on the Spice and Silk Road, hemmed in between Spain and the Atlantic Ocean. Things changed that year as a result of Prince Henry the Navigator's initiative to build up the country's expertise in navigation and shipbuilding, with the eventual aim of monopolizing a sea-based trading route.[2] The initiative was a spectacular success – of the 770 recorded transcontinental sea voyages between 1500 and 1600, 705 were Portuguese.[3]

However, Portugal's advantage in creating global presence proved temporary. Naval talent migrated out of Portugal – Ferdinand Magellan being the most notable case. When Portugal showed a distinct lack of interest in his proposal to seek a westward route to the Spice Islands, Magellan successfully sought sponsorship from King Charles I of Spain.[4] On 10 August 1519 Magellan's fleet of five ships, with a multinational crew of 237, set sail in a bid to stamp Spain's presence on the globe.

The state of the world has not been quite the same since Magellan's voyage. In the new geographies, Europeans encountered many novel flora and fauna.[5] Their attempts to make sense of these discoveries transformed the nature of knowledge from that revealed in the Bible to one based on empirical observation, leading eventually to the scientific method.[6] The limitations of existing technologies of shipbuilding and mapmaking became exposed. Magellan, for example, had miscalculated the distance to his destination by over 110 degrees, which proved fatal for himself and many of his crew. Just 18 sailors returned to Spain in a single battered ship laden with spices after circumnavigating the globe.[7] An accumulation of the knowledge of mechanics in subsequent years, especially through the design and fortification of ships, eventually led to the industrial revolution.[8]

In parallel, the nature of the funding model for expeditions also changed. Magellan's expedition was funded by the House of

Fugger, a family business based in Augsburg, Germany. Although the spices from that investment provided a handy return, subsequent voyages failed and stretched the finances of the Fugger family. Commercial advantage migrated once again, away from Spain and toward the Netherlands and Britain following the creation of the joint-stock East India companies, which pooled and limited the risk of underwriting multiple merchant ship voyages.

The history of the journey toward global presence is very revealing of the temporary nature of commercial advantage, as well as the early mobility of talent, and the developments in science, technology and business that underpin this quest.

Global grasp

Global aspirations are a running theme through this book. As will become clear from the chapter headings, "global" can take on multiple meanings. This can cause problems, especially when we talk loosely about "going global."[9] Professor Phil Rosenzweig explains, "The word global is an adjective, so what is the noun that is being modified? Is it a global strategy, a global mindset, a global workforce, a global product? You can have a conversation in which people are using the word global to mean different things." Indeed, in some people's minds, going global is still just shorthand for "we want to sell to China, secure a low-cost workforce in India or cheap commodities from Brazil."

In some minds, going global is still just shorthand for "we want to sell to China, secure a low-cost workforce in India or cheap commodities from Brazil."

When the term "global company" first gained currency – with the wave of mostly US-based multinational corporations post-1950s – the definition was straightforward. It was based on the percentage of sales outside the home country and the spread of international operations. It did not really matter whether companies did the same thing everywhere – to leverage economies of scale and scope – or whether they did things differently in every country, to meet local customer needs and gain market penetration. High foreign direct investment meant they were global.

The relative merits of centralization versus decentralization were hotly debated until the late 1980s when Bartlett and Ghoshal came up with the "transnational solution."[10] This was based on the recognition that competitive pressures increasingly demanded *both* global integration *and* local responsiveness.

"Think global, act local" became a kind of mantra for companies expanding internationally – which later gave rise to a more compelling axiom, "learn local, act global."[11] Professor Kazuo Ichijo elaborates, "Becoming a global company used to mean building a network of production, sales and service operations able to deliver to markets around the world. Today, the challenge is not just to push but also to pull – to learn from the world, from our partners and from our operations in far-flung locations, in order to share the local learning globally."

> *Today, the challenge is not just to push, but also to pull – to learn from the world, from our partners and from our operations in far-flung locations.*

This thinking has been accompanied by a critical shift in our definition of the global company. Rather than emphasizing *where* a firm operates, we are now more concerned with *how* it manages and structures its worldwide activities.[12] Professor Michael Wade observes, "The distinction today is really about how we use our global operations to be competitive, not only internationally but also in our domestic market. It's about using our global reach to develop new business models and mindsets, which then feed back into our system. Many companies are missing the boat because they are entering these fast-growing economies in order to leverage what they already know."

Our understanding of what it means to be "truly global" has therefore evolved and continues to do so with the accelerating shift of economic activity from Europe and North America to markets in Africa, Asia and Latin America (see **Figure 1**).

Conventional View		Emerging View
Managing expatriates	➔	Managing global talent
Centralized or decentralized	➔	Integrated
Single HQ	➔	Virtual or multi-polar HQ
Dominant nationality	➔	United nations
Teaching mode	➔	Learning mode
Hub and spoke relations	➔	Networked

Figure 1: Going global   Source: Adapted from Phil Rosenzweig

Why go global?

Companies are going global because they *can*. Deregulation, trade liberalization, improved communications and technology have opened access to markets we would not have taken seriously a decade ago. The conventional reason for expanding internationally is to find new growth markets. Another driver is the possibility of following in the slipstream of global customers, which has the advantage of removing concerns about whether we will find local customers.[13] The case of the Danish cleaning company ISS is a good example.[14] Professor James Henderson remarks, "It transformed itself into a global powerhouse by leveraging the demand for integrated facility services – including cleaning, catering, security, office support and landscape services – from multinational companies."

In other cases we are not pulled abroad by customers, but pushed by competitors. It is more a case of expanding geographically because we *must*. Many of the same global trends that create opportunities also constitute threats.[15] The rapidly falling boundaries between industries, organizations, regions and markets and the dispersion of valuable knowledge are among the factors creating new competitive threats – stimulating a growing sense of "we had better do it to them before they do it to us."[16] This has been a strong driver for many of the former state-owned enterprises, such as the telecom companies.[17]

In addition to the traditional market-seeking and cost-seeking motivations for venturing overseas, there is now a further set of drivers. We need to be where the leading-edge innovation is taking place because there are many examples of leapfrogging in what used to be fringe markets. The entire value chain – the people we need, the insights we need, the technology we need, the connections we need, the customers we need, the consumers we need – can be strengthened by being global. If we are not global, then we are not participating in the markets that matter or tapping into the resources that matter or being exposed to the business models and mindsets that matter.

> *If we are not global, then we are not being exposed to the business models and mindsets that matter.*

Global expansion can yield substantial benefits, but it also creates complications. As Lars Olofsson, former CEO of Carrefour, cautioned, "It's all very well saying, 'Emerging markets are the future.' Actually, emerging markets are the future if you are *good* in emerging markets! Otherwise they are not the future – they are the future problems."[18]

The pressures to go global, whether from competitors or customers or analysts, can lead us to underestimate the difficulties and to overreach. Reflecting on Carrefour's retreat from certain international markets, Olofsson conceded, "We went too fast into too many countries and we didn't have resources to fuel the expansion in each of those countries. If nobody had come after us at that point in time, it would have been an excellent strategy. Now, the world is not like that and we don't have unlimited funds... We spread ourselves too thin."

A more dramatic case, in the banking sector, was that of ABN AMRO.[19] The bank's inability to achieve economies of scale among its international operations ultimately led to the dismantling of its global empire.

The global "imperative" has, to some extent, been oversold. The world remains "semi-globalized," leaving many opportunities for smaller players. Take the example of the logistics industry, dominated by the likes of FedEx, UPS and DHL.[20] Professor Leif Sjöblom observes, "The logistics industry is global, but few players can do full service globally – most companies are regional. But you can even be local. In terms of making money, you don't need to be global. If you are a big fish in a small pond like Swiss Post, you can do very well. The same goes for Flextronics, which focuses on just one industry. In fact, in terms of percentage return, you will probably do better than the bigger players."

The underlying point is that globalization is not for everyone and when we embark on such a journey we should not underestimate the challenges. Just because others are rushing headlong into it does not necessarily mean that it makes sense for us.[21] We therefore have to think through the competitive advantages expected from this strategy – the timeless question being, "How are we going to be better off after the move?"[22] As Professor Martha Maznevski puts it, "The road to globalization holds out the promise of exceptional learning, innovation and opportunities, but it is also strewn with the debris of ill-considered mergers, acquisitions and market entry attempts."

The road to globalization is strewn with the debris of ill-considered mergers, acquisitions and market entry attempts.

When setting off on this journey, there are some things we need to think about, some things we need to do and some traps we need to avoid.

LEARNING MODE   THINK

To think more globally, companies need to abandon their "center-knows-best" teaching mode and focus instead on three aspects of learning: learning from the inside, learning from the outside and learning to manage complexity.

Leveraging what we know

To get the most out of our globalization strategy, we need to harness the best practices and innovations bubbling up across the organization and to invest in the most valuable opportunities. This means thinking about how we allocate our attention to different units and markets worldwide.

We tend to follow the herd into "hot" markets or else let past performance dictate which signals we heed.

If we have a long history of success by focusing attention on our home or regional market, switching attention to a more global level is bound to present problems. Even if we can get over our home base fixation, we may still not give individual markets the attention they deserve.[23] Some markets are simply off our radar, and weak signals emerging from those areas tend to be drowned out by the calls of more established operations. Professor Cyril Bouquet explains, "It's easy to focus too hard on the high profile strategic markets at the expense of opportunities and insights from peripheral markets. We tend to follow the herd into 'hot' markets or else let past performance dictate which signals we heed."

This bias is understandable. The only way to cope with overwhelming amounts of information is to develop mechanisms for structuring and filtering attention. These mechanisms include choices about lines of reporting, what meetings to attend, and who we put in positions of influence.[24] They ensure that we focus on the markets that matter, but in the process we can become hostages to our own assumptions.[25] People in the peripheral markets grow accustomed to the fact that the only attention they get is when there are "nasty surprises." As a result, they stop taking initiatives and try to keep a low profile, making it even harder to identify problems or opportunities.

There is no easy way to devote the right attention to the different sources of information, but we can at least make sure that multiple "attention channels" exist so that important new insights are more likely to come into view.[26]

Another key to picking up on signals that do not fit into our existing grid is mindfulness.[27] Over time, the way we look at markets becomes institutionalized. Consensus builds around where we should be scanning and how. Collective mindfulness reflects our ability to remain alert and responsive to patterns, ideas, threats or opportunities from unexpected quarters. Our top management teams need to retain the willingness to question their assumptions and frameworks and how these may be limiting their thinking.[28]

Professor Ben Bryant comments, "When running a team meeting, we need to manage the tension between focusing and noticing. Some people think that leadership is all about focus – setting a goal and going after it – but that automatically means that we are going to stop noticing. Yet, if we spend all our time noticing, then nothing gets done. So periodically we need to be able to jolt our thinking – by bringing in outsiders, changing the context or the routines, or by creating a space to discuss weak signals – to keep the process of sensemaking going."

> *When running a team meeting, we need to manage the tension between focusing and noticing.*

A good starting point is to establish how much time and effort we allocate to various markets around the world. We then have to establish practices and structures that stimulate more mindful ways of acting, thinking and organizing.

Chasing the global challengers

Established companies in developed markets can learn a great deal from two sets of challengers who are rewriting the rules of globalization.

The first set are the multinationals from emerging markets – not just from the BRIC countries (Brazil, Russia, India and China) with their huge domestic markets, but also from the likes of Korea, Turkey and Mexico. In the early 1990s, it was still difficult for firms "born in the wrong place" to overcome the limitations of their domestic environment.[29] Professor Nuno Fernandes points out, "As emerging markets have become better integrated with the world economy, those firms can now compete with firms in developed markets in terms of attracting debt financing."

Take the case of Argentina-based, La Martina.[30] From a local polo equipment producer, it has become one of the most recognized global brand names in polo and fashion alike.[31] As sales boomed, the founder had the opportunity to pursue fashion-led growth, but chose instead to reinforce the exclusive image of La Martina. So he reduced the number of European distributors, ended the agreement with his Italian partners and focused on high-end stores in prestigious locations. As IMD President Dominique Turpin puts it, "By focusing efforts on protecting La Martina's luxury brand and pursuing 'quality volume,' the company has weathered the economic crisis remarkably well."

The point is that firms from emerging economies are no longer relying on low costs to compete. They can also do quality and they know how to pursue sophisticated and unconventional strategies. Haier, for example, did not tackle the US competition head-on in the household appliances sector.[32] Instead, the Chinese giant bulked up by targeting niche markets overlooked by the major players. It started selling inexpensive mini-fridges that were designed to double as computer desks for cramped student accommodation. It also introduced small refrigerators designed as wine coolers but sold them at a fraction of the price of these expensive specialty items.[33] As Professor Bill Fischer puts it. "By the time US rivals woke up to the threat, Haier had already established both the brand and the links with America's leading retail chains. It had also worked out how to deliver outstanding customer service." Ambitious and resourceful, these emerging giants are no longer content to play a secondary role in their industry.[34]

Firms from emerging economies are no longer relying on low costs to compete. They can also do quality and they know how to pursue sophisticated and unconventional strategies.

The second set of emerging challengers from whom we can learn are the global startups. These flourished thanks to the internet, which suddenly opened up new communication and retailing channels without national boundaries. Take the case of Vistaprint.[35] This company was not "born global" in the strict sense of being active in international markets from day one. For the first years of its life, it was primarily a French supplier of specialized stationery to the small-office market. Then in 2000, its founder decided to switch to a "web-driven" business model – instantly allowing it to reach a worldwide customer base – making it a kind of "born-again global."

Vistaprint developed the technology to enable quality short print runs, such as business cards, from the web design of the cards to their centralized printing on dedicated, fully automated offset printing facilities. In 2005, it went public on the US (NASDAQ) stock exchange, soon becoming the leading online provider of marketing products and services to small businesses around the globe. Today, the company has over 4,100 employees, 13 offices and over 25 localized websites that serve various markets around the world, three state-of-the-art manufacturing facilities – in Australia, the Netherlands and Canada – and has relocated its headquarters to Venlo, in the Netherlands. Professor Benoît Leleux comments, "The context now is that firms can locate pretty much wherever they want. It is even easier to move a firm's head office. If an environment is not particularly favorable or receptive, you no

Firms can locate pretty much wherever they want. Geography is no longer destiny.

longer fight to get treated properly: you simply vote with your feet. Geography is no longer destiny."

Another key lesson for established multinationals concerns the pace at which it is possible to gather critical mass, even when selling a physical product. Creative partnership strategies can make a nonsense of the conventional stage model of internationalization.[36] Professor Howard Yu observes, "We used to have the luxury of expanding internationally on a country by country basis – now we have to think about our expansion strategy from a global perspective."

Established firms in developed economies have to compete against global startups and emerging giants who are prepared to envisage very different routes to globalization.[37]

Comprehending complexity

A key to grasping the challenge of globalization is to understand the sources of complexity resulting from the erosion of boundaries.[38]

There are four basic drivers of complexity in the environment. The first is *interdependence*, the idea that everything is connected to everything else so that along with any desired effect, we are likely to get a raft of side-effects. The second is *variety*, which includes workforce diversity, as well as multiplicity of stakeholders, company strategies, competitor strategies, customer needs and supplier possibilities. The third is *ambiguity* – we have a lot of information but we do not know what it means or which are the causes and which the effects. And the last one is *flux* – even if we understand the first three today, it might all change tomorrow.[39] According to Professor Martha Maznevski, "Complexity is unavoidable, but it can be managed to create better organizational outcomes. The critical question is whether the complexity occurs in areas where it generates value or destroys it. Sometimes we spend so much time trying to manage the complexity inside that we forget about the complexity outside."

Complexity is unavoidable, but it can be managed to create better organizational outcomes.

We must therefore free up time and attention to be able to focus on the right dilemmas. As mentioned earlier, we need to achieve both global integration and local responsiveness simultaneously. This makes it sound as though there is a single point of balance that can be applied across activities. Not so. The trick is to standardize where possible and to allow flexibility where it matters (see **Figure 2**).

Non-authorized Processes and Systems

Authorized Floating Processes and Systems

Fixed Processes and Systems

Data Standards

Governance mechanisms
to correctly allocate
elements as fixed or
floating

Figure 2: Continuous readjustment   Source: Michael Wade and Bettina Büchel [40]

If we look at different activities, back office functions, such as finance, procurement and IT, can be heavily standardized and so belong mostly in the "fixed zone." On the market-facing side – sales, marketing, business development, government relations – we can expect the weight to swing toward the "floating zone," with more localized practices. Yet even at the customer interface, some activities, like brand management, may need to be highly consistent (one color, one logo, one slogan).[41]

This differentiated approach can be pushed deeper. Within any activity, we can look at the processes and systems. Professor Michael Wade explains, "Take the HR chain – from hire to retire – we can break down that sequence into different pieces. Some aspects, like performance appraisal and training, may fit more in the 'fixed zone,' while others, like hiring and compensation, require more local adaptation. So within every set of global processes, whether it's the HR chain or manufacturing, there will be some that are fixed and others that are floating."

This is not a one-off choice, but an ongoing balancing act. Local initiatives or best practices can become part of the fixed template, while systems that we incorrectly thought benefited everyone, could be pushed out into the flexible arena. Professor Wade points out, "This calls for a strong governance process, otherwise the fixed zone gets too bloated, and you get back into bureaucracy – or else the floating zone gets too big, with everyone organizing exceptions and you end up with duplication everywhere."

Within every set of global processes, there will be some that are fixed and others that are floating.

This balancing act does not come naturally. It is a capability that we need to learn. That is why becoming global is so hard. It is a shifting dynamic that must be actively managed.

## ACT AS ONE COMPANY	DO

To optimize the learning from our network, we need to work on four organizational levers: the structure, the people, the systems and the networks.

Redesign reporting relationships

With changes in the range and depth of activities conducted worldwide, we have to restructure the reporting relationships. This means modifying the role and involvement of our headquarters as well as the connections between and within the units.

Going global inevitably raises questions about where decisions are made – routing everything through headquarters no longer makes sense. So we must transfer some functions from the headquarters into the new centers of gravity – either at regional or local level – closer to where the work actually gets done. Dispersing head office functions across different locations around the world is a powerful signal of global intent.[42]

Professor James Henderson explains the reasoning, "Companies create new hubs to help shape their thinking. For example, China is becoming the most sophisticated market for electronics, churning out over 1,000 new mobile phone models per year. Companies that want to stay ahead cannot let their strategic mindset be shaped by mature markets."

Take the case of the Dutch firm Irdeto, a leading player in media content security.[43] Concerned that it was missing out on big opportunities in China, the top team decided in 2007 to create a second head office in Beijing. More significantly, the CEO moved out there with his family, shortly followed by two other top executives.[44] Professor Cyril Bouquet observes, "Creating a second corporate headquarters was a radical move and it immediately forced a change in mindset. It dispelled the 'mothership syndrome,' whereby everything – including customers, product development and employees – was seen from a

Dispersing head office functions across different locations around the world is a powerful signal of global intent.

European perspective. Through structure you create information channels, you create positions, and all kinds of processes and teams that increase the salience of the information located in those different places."

Going global also raises questions about lines of reporting. If our goal is to optimize global standardization, local responsiveness *and* learning across the network, then there is no escaping some kind of matrix organization.[45]

The purpose of a matrix structure is to help us to manage two or more priorities simultaneously, which could include products, geographies, functions, customer segments, channels, brands or other dimensions. But sometimes it creates more problems than it solves, blurring accountability, generating bureaucracy and absorbing a lot of management attention.

These problems are typically rooted in our overreliance on the structure itself and a tendency to try to overcomplicate the matrix. ABB, for example, once had a six-dimensional matrix structure until it dramatically simplified the structure as part of its turnaround.[46]

> *The matrix will generate conflict. That's not a sign that the structure is not working, but it's all about getting conflict into the right places.*

We have to make sure that the matrix design is as simple as it can be. Professor Martha Maznevski clarifies, "The matrix *will* generate conflict. That's not a sign that the structure is not working, but it's all about getting conflict into the right places. The leadership team needs to be clear on which trade-offs it really wants to manage rather than just passing confusion down into the organization."

Another challenge has to do with implementation. We can never design a perfect structure, so we have to make sure that we create coordination mechanisms, such as project groups and steering committees, that compensate for the biases within the structure.[47] Professor Bala Chakravarthy notes, "A structure always exaggerates the decision right. If the matrix structure suggests that the geographies have more power, then we need to have processes that make sure that the global businesses and functions have the corresponding power. We have to generate some tension."

Amend the mindset

To work effectively within an integrated global structure, we need to develop a "global mindset." This elusive concept encompasses both individual and organizational perspectives.[48]

At the individual level, we have to select for and develop two sets of related competencies. First, we need the cognitive abilities to be able to handle complex business dynamics.[49] We have to operate in a matrix that requires us to manage people over whom we have only dotted line authority, and influence others over whom we have no authority. We need to be collaborative but also comfortable with disagreements. As Professor Martha Maznevski puts it, "When we ask executives 'What does globalization mean to you?' the most common answer is, 'It means I am exhausted.' Global responsibilities mean we have to hold conflicting priorities in our minds. So companies need people who not only can deal with ambiguity and complexity but actually like it. It takes a lot of resilience."

The second set of competencies we need to look for and expand relate to cultural competencies. The core elements are cultural self-awareness, openness to and understanding of other cultures, and the acceptance of diversity as

Just because we are good at handling complexity does not mean we can work effectively across cultures.

a source of opportunity.[50] According to Professor Allen Morrison, "Just because we are good at handling complexity does not mean we can work effectively across cultures. Openness and adaptability are mostly developed through international mobility – through exposure to cross-cultural situations, including international assignments, projects and training."

An effective example was the initiative taken by the International Air Transport Association.[51] Twenty change agents, half from East Asia and half from "mature" regions were asked to co-lead 10 teams made up of high-potentials in different locations. Working on real business projects, the co-leaders had to build bridges across cultures and adapt their management styles in order to deliver preliminary results within a six-month time frame. The initiative helped not only to build up the global mindset of the individuals but also to weave global ties across the organization.

At an organizational level, the biggest obstacle to developing a global mindset is the widespread perception that access to opportunities is driven by nationality.[52] New entrants quickly get a sense of "who gets promoted around here." There may be little incentive to try to develop a wider perspective if there appear to be limited opportunities for anyone from outside the parent country or its close neighbors. Professor Stewart Black remarks, "Becoming global as a company increasingly means striving to become 'passport blind.' We must look for the best person for the job regardless of origin. As the company becomes more interdependent, we need to make sure that the competencies match the requirements and that talent trumps passport. That's a huge challenge for most companies."

Becoming global as a company means striving to become "passport blind."

A critical indicator of an organization's global mindset is the level of C-suite cultural diversity. Typically, there is a significant time lag between establishing a global presence and trying to globalize our top team. An interesting counterexample is the Lenovo group.[53] Since acquiring IBM's PC division in 2005, the company has used its multicultural leadership team – seven of Eastern and five of Western origin – to reflect and accelerate its global ambitions. Although founded in China, the PC maker has no official headquarters. Its top team simply gathers wherever it makes most sense, often in the fastest growing markets (recently in South Africa).

Of course, if "passport blind" is the metric, then few companies claiming to be global would even qualify. In reality, the perception of openness to diversity can be achieved with relatively modest levels of overseas representation.[54] Professor Robert Hooijberg explains, "People are looking for evidence of opportunity. If people believe that they can't move up, then we are shooting ourselves in the foot as a company. It's not about building the United Nations but about sending signals to the organization that *anyone* can reach the top."

Building a cosmopolitan top management team sends a powerful message that the center no longer regards itself as the source of all knowledge and influential ideas.

Reassess the systems

Working within a global matrix has strategic implications for two types of systems: HR systems and IT systems.

The big challenge for HR is that prior even to setting out on our globalization journey, we need to look ahead and start preparing for a more interconnected future.[55] Building global leadership must precede the declared organizational need for it. As Professor Stewart Black puts it, "In advance of globalization, we need to set up assessment programs to figure out who could become global leaders, and a repertoire of development programs and international assignments to mature that talent. This cannot happen overnight. It is at least a five-year preparation journey."

The case of Capgemini provides a good example of such anticipatory change.[56] The company's corporate university, set up in 1989, has been instrumental in transforming a federation of national firms into one of the top five global players in its industry. Professor Shlomo Ben Hur comments, "Thousands of employees attended courses at the center to improve their understanding of collaboration, co-creation and their effectiveness as members or leaders of cross-boundary teams."

In a matrix organization, we expect people to work effectively in teams across functional, country and business boundaries. While development programs can help to instill team-based behaviors, they have to be supported by performance management and compensation systems to create a context for knowledge sharing. For example, we need to set up joint performance evaluations by managers on all sides of the matrix as well as systems that reward group efforts. When a collaborative matrix structure bumps up against an individually oriented reward system, the reward system typically prevails.

When a collaborative matrix structure bumps up against an individually oriented reward system, the reward system typically prevails.

We also need to reconfigure our IT-related systems to support our globalization strategy – in pursuit of both business flexibility and business standardization. This was the classic problem faced by ABB, a leading player in the power and automation technology sector.[57] The Swiss-based giant boasted operations in 100 countries worldwide, but suffered from system duplication across markets and high IT support costs.

Besides inflating operating costs, such decentralization puts us at a disadvantage in negotiations with more globally integrated firms. Professor Don Marchand elaborates, "If our suppliers, customers or strongest competitors are global and we are not, then we have an information asymmetry in our disfavor – because they know more about doing business with us than we know about doing business with or against them. They may have a complete file on us – pricing, contracts, volumes – while we continue to do business country by country, which makes us a sitting duck for variable pricing by country."

In response, ABB decided to consolidate its IT infrastructure and internal functional systems globally, while at the same time preserving and enhancing highly distinct business systems necessary for competitive advantage or adapting to regional variation.

Beyond efficiency gains, we need to reconfigure our IT systems to harness the value of globally dispersed knowledge. In many international companies, best-practice sharing is voluntary. It may be encouraged by corporate leaders, but it

IT systems provide transparency on information that may indicate superior practices in unexpected locations.

remains ad hoc. As we transition to a more global approach, best-practice sharing becomes an operational necessity.[58]

The main reason we fail to draw on knowledge residing in other parts of the organization is that we are unaware of its existence. IT systems provide transparency on information – about customers, products, operations and performance – that may indicate superior practices in unexpected locations. The systems enable leaders throughout the organization to look across the company and identify new ideas that work locally and globally.

Of course, locating potentially valuable knowledge is not the same as appropriating it.[59] Professor Kazuo Ichijo expands, "Information is different from knowledge. Knowledge is information filtered through experience. It's often tacit, which makes it difficult to transfer digitally, requiring instead face-to-face communication and direct observation."

In globalizing firms, we too often treat our big data and analytics projects the same as we treat the installation of our enterprise resource planning or customer relationship management systems, paying too much attention to the deployment of technology and neglecting the exploration of information.[60] According to Professor Marchand, "Improving the way we extract value from data requires more than analytical tools. We have to create an environment where people can combine the data and their own knowledge to improve performance." In reality, knowledge management is as much about managing people as managing information.

Knit networks

Matrix organizations run on social connections and relationships.[61] Professor Maury Peiperl notes, "Transnational social links allow us to overcome the rigidities of the structure. They fuel coordination, collaboration and knowledge sharing within the firm's global network."

In most companies, the vertical connections between the head office and subsidiaries are firmly in place. What is lacking are the lateral connections that will help information, ideas, research findings and opportunities to circulate better between business units. To enable that flow, we have to rewire for lateral coordination.[62]

In most companies, the vertical connections between the head office and subsidiaries are firmly in place. What is lacking are the lateral connections.

Building and maintaining global networks is costly and the outcomes are diffuse and hard to measure. Regardless of constraints on travel budgets, the best way to create connections is to bring people physically together.[63] As Professor Martha Maznevski puts it, "Building relationships of trust and commitment is best done face-to-face because it requires dialogue, shared experiences, questions, answers and sharing of personal information. It also requires that people let themselves be vulnerable to each other, so that the trust can be demonstrated."

Two common ways of establishing these connections are through company retreats and executive development programs. Often, these events will incorporate sessions that deliberately mix participants from different parts of the global organization for interactive and action-learning exercises. And there are ways for us to map the breadth and depth of connections among groups – before and after these events – in order to measure the impact on connectivity.[64]

We can also bring people together in a more deliberate way, with specific cooperation objectives in mind. For example, the Swiss food giant Nestlé has set up over three dozen functionally oriented networks, which meet a couple of times a year, with the aim of diffusing best practices across the group.[65] Professor Robert Hooijberg comments, "We can set up conditions so that the social links form in the right places, for example by allowing people to interact around a common set of professional interests, and encourage these communities of practice to raise the bar across the organization. But there is always a fine line between 'promoting' participation and putting people off through too much intervention."

Keeping such global networks alive is a real challenge. Of course, we can schedule meetings where we reconnect periodically, but much harder to reproduce virtually are the casual encounters and information exchanges that do not happen

We need to find ways of helping people to bump into each other electronically.

in planned meetings. So we need to find ways of helping people to bump into each other electronically.[66] Professor John Weeks explains, "We have to use proximity technologies to bring the key populations together. For example, leaving video links and virtual offices open promotes the feeling that geographically distant groups are welcome to engage with each other casually, as they might in a real-world common space. We also have to provide compelling reasons for people to voluntarily engage, otherwise traffic soon trails off."

AVOID   HITTING THE WALL

The experiences of successful and less successful "globalizers" highlight three potential barriers as we try to develop our global presence: "one-way" thinking, neglecting nomads and acquiring weakness.

"One-way" thinking

For many leading industrial companies, years of sustained success based on high quality manufacturing platforms and economies of scale resulted in strong policies and practices, which in turn reinforced the existing business model and generated a certain sense of superiority. Such companies succeeded brilliantly in transferring the know-how needed to produce high quality products on the other side of the world. Internationalization was mostly concerned with initiating foreign workforces to the subtle norms and behavioral expectations of the established approach.[67]

Companies wedded to maintaining "The Way" are less open to modifying it as they grow and become more international.

Yet, Professor Allen Morrison observes, "The way things get done in a company has to change as the company's strategy evolves. And so what leads to the success of the company – 'The Way' – at some point acts a major roadblock or barrier to success going forward. Companies wedded to maintaining 'The Way' are less open to modifying it as they grow and become more international."

Another factor maintaining the dominance of "The Way" is the wide gap in perceptions between parent country nationals and foreign executives. Assessments of our company's global mindset can differ dramatically depending on where in the organization we sit.[68] Home country executives typically overestimate the global mindset of their companies, and downplay the relevance of nationality in managerial promotion decisions. This distortion is more likely in global organizational structures where foreign executives have relatively low voice and weight, making it difficult to challenge the corporate orthodoxy.[69]

Consider the classic case of Daimler-Benz AG.[70] In 1998, when the Stuttgart-based automaker announced its "merger of equals" with the Chrysler Corporation, this heralded an audacious new chapter in the global presence of automobile manufacturers. The combination promised much because the geographic spread and product portfolio of the two companies had very little overlap since Mercedes occupied the upper market segments in many parts of the globe, whereas the Chrysler brands were a strong mid-market presence limited to the US. The globalization attempt seemed to proceed well, with savings of close to $1.4 billion in the first year. However, the marriage eventually soured and Chrysler, valued at $36 billion at the time of the merger, was sold to a private equity firm for $7.4 billion nine years later. One reason for the failure to create value through global presence was the determination of the Stuttgart executives to impose the "Daimler Way" on Chrysler.[71] In one interview given to a German newspaper, Daimler CEO Jürgen Schrempp admitted that the "merger of equals" rhetoric was necessary at the outset but it was never intended to be a reality.[72]

Neglecting nomads

For several decades, Japanese companies were the great overachievers of international business. In 1989, when IMD first published its World Competitiveness ranking, Japan held the No. 1 spot. At a corporate level, Japanese firms dominated the 1995 Fortune Global 500 list, taking the top three places (by revenues) and six of the top ten. IMD President Dominique Turpin notes, "The likes of Sony and Toyota punched way above their weight, investing heavily in foreign operations, moving up the value chain and turning 'Made in Japan' into an assurance of quality, innovation and value for money."

But then Japan, Inc. hit a wall. In the 2012 ranking of World Competitiveness, Japan stood 27th out of 59 countries, below smaller but more dynamic economies like Qatar, Hong Kong and Norway. By 2012 only Toyota remained in the top ten of the Fortune Global 500 list. Professor Stewart Black comments, "For the US and European companies, the Fortune Global 500 proportions have stayed roughly constant over the last 18 years – and looking at individual countries, they have also held pretty steady. The only country that has seriously declined is Japan, mostly replaced by new entrants from the BRIC nations."

One compelling explanation for what went wrong is that Japanese companies resisted the diversification of human capital needed to become global.[73] Despite one or two notable exceptions, their failure to bring foreign executives into the leadership team is well documented. As Professor Jean-Pierre Lehmann puts it, "The trailblazing efforts of Nissan – its alliance with

To a greater extent than their rivals, Japanese companies show extreme reluctance to use third-country nationals.

Renault, the influx of foreign managers at the top and its re-emergence as a global player – occurred over a decade ago, and is now seen as an anomaly, the desperate response of a company on the verge of bankruptcy rather than as a pattern for moving forward as a global company."

Japanese firms are among the least proactive in seeking to globalize their top teams.[74] Securing even regional responsibilities is a major feat for non-Japanese executives, making it difficult to attract or retain local talent. Professor Maury Peiperl remarks, "To a greater extent than their rivals, Japanese companies show extreme reluctance to use third-country nationals. Of course, that makes it more difficult to create lateral networks or to share best practices across organizational units." When Olympus famously promoted a European to the role of worldwide president in 2011, the experience ended badly, with Michael Woodford being fired within six months of his appointment for blowing the whistle on mismanagement and corruption at board level.[75]

More insidious still has been the lack of appreciation for international experience.[76] Professor Turpin observes, "Japanese companies rarely insist on international experience as a necessary condition for promotion to the top ranks, often keeping the best managers in Japan at head office rather than sending them out to work in the most critical markets." That insularity is compounded by linguistic barriers. In a 2009 comparative survey of English-speaking abilities, Japanese test-takers ranked 135th in the world, almost 40 places below isolationist North Korea. In fact, the number of students who study overseas is actually falling, in part because international experience is not especially valued by employers.

Acquiring weakness

Acquisitions are a swift way of increasing global presence. For successful companies in developed markets, acquisitions in emerging markets seem particularly attractive, and vice versa for emerging market companies aspiring to be global contenders. For the top leaders of such companies, cross-economy acquisitions are emotionally laden and may create biases in decision-making, especially through the Halo Effect.[77]

The Halo Effect is a form of bias whereby an observation about one aspect of a company that we seek to acquire leads us to make an impaired judgment about its other aspects. For example, if an emerging market company that we want to acquire seems successful – perhaps because its sales and profits are growing rapidly – we will tend to infer that it also has a sound strategy, a visionary leader, capable employees and efficient organization.

In 2008, leaders at Japanese pharmaceutical company Daiichi set their sights on Ranbaxy, an Indian generic drugs manufacturer with a glowing reputation based on its exponentially increasing sales revenues. The fit between the two companies was great: Daiichi had strong innovative products but lacked growth prospects; Ranbaxy manufactured post-patent generic drugs and had a strong sales franchise in the US.[78] The halo of Ranbaxy's sales record led Daiichi executives to conclude that it was fundamentally a sound organization. Soon after the $4.7 billion acquisition, they discovered that executives at Ranbaxy had cut corners to get approvals for their generic drugs from the US Food and Drug administration. In 2013 Ranbaxy settled with the FDA and paid a $500 million fine to resolve questions about the quality of its products and manufacturing processes. Daiichi did acquire global presence, but it came at a steep price and caused a severe dent to its reputation.

While acquisitions may confer instant global status, it may be a long time before we can claim that our organizational functioning is truly global. In particular, we must not underestimate the difficulties of integrating – or just coordinating – radically different business models. According to Caroline Firstbrook, managing director for strategy at Accenture in EMEA and Latin America, "Many companies now have a foot in the emerging markets and a foot in the developed markets. And that is a very difficult place to be. It is a sort of schizophrenia of management because emerging markets have extremely different customer needs; they are looking for a low-cost, stripped-down product; they have very different distribution environments, very different rules, and you need very different governance to operate there."[79] Global presence through acquisition requires caution and foresight.

> *While acquisitions may confer instant global status, it may be a long time before we can claim that our organizational functioning is truly global.*

TAKEDA'S PRESCRIPTION FOR GLOBAL GROWTH   PAYOFF

When Yasuchika Hasegawa took over as president of Takeda in 2003, the Japanese pharmaceutical company faced very slow growth domestically and the menace of a steep patent cliff, with some of its most lucrative medicines soon open to generic competition. Significantly, Hasegawa was not a member of the Takeda family and had spent over a decade working for the company in Germany and then the US.

Rather than looking to join forces with other Japanese drugmakers, Hasegawa set out to globalize the company.[80] He initiated an aggressive series of acquisitions starting in 2005 with the purchase of two small foreign-based biotech ventures, an unprecedented move for a Japanese drugmaker at the time. Next came the $9 billion acquisition of US oncology company Millennium Pharmaceuticals in 2008. And in 2011, Takeda completed the third-largest overseas acquisition by a Japanese company, paying out $14 billion for its unlisted Swiss rival Nycomed. Hasegawa was very conscious about using these acquisitions not just to plug product and geographic gaps, but also to accelerate the cultural transformation of Takeda into a truly global company, using the four global levers mentioned previously.

Structurally, the acquisitions dramatically shifted the center of gravity of the group. The Nycomed acquisition, in particular, gave Takeda access to more than 70 countries and a strong on-the-ground presence in some of the fastest-growing emerging markets. Hasegawa was especially keen to build on Nycomed's entrepreneurial dynamism and clearly instructed his senior managers not to hamper its nimble decision-making. At the same time, he relocated key business functions to other countries, notably shifting drug development to North America. He also established a Global Advisory Board to bring in insights from experts beyond Japan, including heavyweights from Pfizer, Eli Lilly and GlaxoSmithKline among its members.

> *The CEO even floated the idea of creating dual headquarters to break the Japan-centric culture of the group.*

Hasegawa even floated the idea of creating dual headquarters to break the Japan-centric culture of the group, telling the press, "We may eventually run the company from two headquarters, in Japan and abroad. The most important thing is to change the mindset of our employees. I hope that talented Nycomed personnel will inspire them to become more global minded."[81]

Developing a *global mindset* became a recurring theme in speeches by Hasegawa. It was not just rhetoric. He was surprisingly willing to point out Japanese needs for improvement. For example, he publicly recognized the critical contribution of Millennium's high-caliber executives in negotiating and wrapping up the acquisition of Nycomed, conceding, "The acquisition might have been difficult with Takeda's Japanese staff alone."[82]

To back up these comments, he appointed several non-Japanese managers into key roles, including five of the nine corporate officers and two of the board members. He also insisted that all board meetings be conducted in English, allowing a one-year transition period during which interpreters would be present.[83] It was a huge symbolic change and a measure of his determination to create an environment conducive to doing global business.

The *systems* also had to keep pace, particularly the HR systems. For example, Takeda revised its selection policy, requiring higher standards of English proficiency among hires at all levels, with a special drive to recruit Japanese executives who had studied abroad in English. There was a similar aggressive drive to recruit non-Japanese staff prepared to work for prolonged spells in Japan.[84] These recruitment drives had a knock-on effect on the executive compensation systems, the most glaring example being the appointment of a top executive who earned significantly more than the CEO. Though upsetting to some, the CEO's acceptance of that "disorder" helped to flatten another cultural barrier to globalization, reinforcing the primacy of merit and the importance of attracting top talent.

Takeda also invested heavily in developing global leaders, establishing a three-module leadership program for its executives worldwide, sending a vital signal to current and prospective executives about the company's commitment to global talent development.[85] Professor Stewart Black notes, "The final module has 19 of the senior management there. It's been running for seven years, so we can track what has happened to the early participants. The evidence suggests that they have dramatically accelerated not only their careers but also the development of Takeda as a company. It currently stands as the only meaningful global pharma player left in Japan."

Creating *global networks* has been a big challenge for Takeda. After acquiring Millennium, Takeda engineered an exchange of personnel to facilitate the mutual understanding of their respective corporate cultures. Over the following years, Japanese researchers met several times with their counterparts from Millennium, and these proved uncomfortable but eye-opening encounters. Hasegawa pointed out, "They realized they were no match for the Millennium staff, who presented well-planned, specific measures to win in global competition. The Takeda staff, who lacked in vision and failed to make things clear, eventually accepted proposals made by their Millennium counterparts."[86] Paradoxically, when the periphery is allowed to take the lead, it is a strong indicator of the company's global progress.

Beyond creating internal networks, Takeda faced a broader networking challenge. With drug development increasingly reliant on biotechnology, not just chemical synthesis, pharmaceutical companies have more difficulty managing the whole innovation process within their own boundaries. In response, Hasegawa introduced an "Open Innovation" program, designed to attract top-level researchers from academia and biotech ventures worldwide by providing access to Takeda's state-of-the-art research facilities, including its drug discovery technology.

Though still a work-in-progress, Hasegawa's strategy has seen Takeda rise from 16th to 11th position by sales among drugmakers worldwide, in spite of key patent expiries. More impressive though, is the company's pipeline ranking, where it stands at No. 7.[87] According to the *Wall Street Journal*, "The company has surprised even skeptics with the speed with which it has been planting its seeds, luring talent from overseas and hunting aggressively for technologies that will lift it into the top ranks."[88]

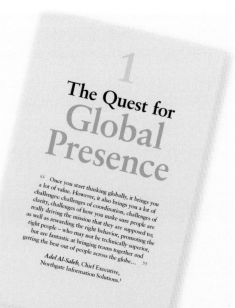

1

The Quest for Global Presence

" Once you start thinking globally, it brings you a lot of value. However, it also brings you a lot of challenges: challenges of coordination, challenges of clarity, challenges of how you make sure people are really driving the mission that they are supposed to; as well as rewarding the right behavior, promoting the right people – who may not be technically superior, but are fantastic at bringing teams together and getting the best out of people across the globe... "

Adel Al-Saleh, Chief Executive,
Northgate Information Solutions.[1]

Where Do We Stand?

1. How global should we be?

2. Are we developing a cadre of global leaders for the next generation?

3. Which globalizing companies are threatening our business?

4. Which of our systems are too standardized? Too flexible?

5. How culturally diverse and internationally experienced is our top management team?

6. What new systems do we have to put in place to manage globally?

7. How can we encourage horizontal interactions between units, especially virtually?

2

The Quest for Global Value Generation

66 We wanted all our people to change their focus to touching more consumers and more customers; touching more bottlers, touching more governments, NGOs, shareholders. You touch… that is how you create value. You don't create value by being inside and meeting internally with yourself. But we had to change the organization architecture; we had to change the way we did things and to simplify our processes; and also how we looked at information. 99

Muhtar Kent, Chairman and CEO,
The Coca-Cola Company[1]

LESSONS FROM CHINA

The Chinese started producing white porcelain china as early as the seventh century. It was the product of an inspired feat of alchemy. Intense heat (around 1300°C) was needed to transform a mixture of clay (kaolin) and powdered rock (petuntse) into a ceramic material that was hard, translucent, nonporous and resistant to thermal shock. These rare properties provided the basis for some of the world's most enduring and emblematic luxury products.

From the 9th century, high-fired ceramic wares were exported to Japan and Southeast Asia, then across the Indian Ocean to Africa and the Middle East. By the 13th century, Chinese potters started introducing new forms and even customizing designs to suit the tastes of foreign dignitaries, as evidenced by large plates with Islamic motifs excavated from ancient Yuan dynasty kilns. It was Marco Polo who first brought word of this exotic material to the Western world and coined the term "porcelain" because of its resemblance to the translucent hardness of cowrie shells (*porcellana* in Italian). Through the 14th and 15th centuries, porcelain items reached Europe, but only in tiny quantities, mainly serving as prestigious gifts to European rulers, such as Lorenzo de Medici in Florence and François I of France.

Realizing the tremendous advantage of controlling the production of highly prized goods, the Chinese emperors of the Ming dynasty (1368–1644) took steps to reinforce that advantage. They centralized porcelain production in Jingdezhen, setting up official kilns to produce wares for the palace and for diplomatic gifts, and banning porcelain production in other parts of China. Jingdezhen offered nearby access not only to the constituent materials but also to pine wood to fuel the kilns and to river transport to ship the finished products. Alongside these official kilns catering for imperial orders, Jingdezhen's private kilns continued to supply the sizable domestic market and the ever-increasing export markets.

The concentration of porcelain production and craftspeople guaranteed that the technique for manufacturing porcelain remained a closely guarded secret. But it also improved both the quality and quantity of porcelain wares. New techniques, glazes and designs were invented and advances in kiln technology made mass production possible, with the biggest kilns capable of firing as many as 25,000 wares at a time. The kilns grew increasingly sophisticated, with multiple chambers and stoke holes in each chamber so that the temperature could be precisely adjusted.

European demand really took off in the mid-16th century after Portuguese ships landed on the south coast of China, and for several decades Portugal leveraged its privileged access to these exclusive goods. But it was the Dutch East India Company, founded in 1602, that really contributed to the explosion in demand for Chinese porcelain and to the evolution in designs to reflect European tastes and table customs.

Porcelain constituted the heart of the Chinese export trade to the West for several centuries, the first truly global luxury product. It became known as "white gold" and European potters naturally looked for ways to replicate it. Some succeeded in producing materials with a superficial resemblance to porcelain, but the pottery lacked the fineness of Chinese porcelain. Even when the

Generating value from clay and powdered rock

porcelain was not from China, it posed as Chinese to maintain its market value. Far from rivaling Chinese porcelain, these poor European imitations only enhanced its prestige and value.

The production of porcelain remained a mystery in Europe until 1708, when the experimentation of a German pharmacist in Meissen finally yielded a similar ceramic. A few years later, the precise ingredients and the elaborate production procedures needed to make Chinese porcelain were revealed in letters sent home by a French missionary – one of the earliest recorded cases of industrial espionage. As a result of this "technology transfer" to Europe, other manufacturing centers emerged and the Chinese porcelain industry progressively lost its dominant position.

English potters did not enjoy the scale of royal patronage common in other countries and were therefore more exposed to market realities. In 1772, in the face of falling sales and mounting stocks, the Staffordshire-based potter Josiah Wedgwood decided to investigate more closely the actual costs of his product lines. That exploration revealed the extent to which special orders added to fixed costs as well as the huge advantages of economies of scale. Armed with a much more sophisticated system of costing – which took into account depreciation, administrative and selling costs, and interest on capital – Wedgwood was able to make much more informed decisions on pricing and manufacturing.[2] For example, he initiated planned production rather than letting it be dictated by demand.

Value creation may be a recent expression, but producers of porcelain have long been aware of its implications. The Chinese clearly understood the extent to which porcelain objects were valued abroad and the importance of remaining the sole source of supply in order to secure maximum gains. Later, Wedgwood's pioneering costing systems helped his company to generate value by capturing a mass market with daring pricing policies and to yield additional savings by identifying and diminishing wasteful uses of labor and materials.

More broadly, the early efforts of Europeans to replicate porcelain helped advance experimental science and laid the foundations for modern chemistry, opening up whole new possibilities of value creation.

The hunt for value

If there is one thing in business we can easily agree on, it is the importance of creating and delivering value. The concept of value creation lies at the very heart of the purpose of the corporation.

Unfortunately, there is far less agreement on what value creation actually means, to whom it applies and how to drive it. When people from different areas discuss value creation, the likelihood is that they are talking about different things and focusing on different constituencies.

> *One thing in business we can easily agree on is the importance of creating and delivering value.*

As Professor Salvatore Cantale puts it, "Finance people have their own way of thinking about value creation, which focuses on shareholders. Marketing people have a different approach that concentrates on customers. And people in strategy have yet another take on value creation, sometimes focusing internally on the top management team and sometimes externally on the alliance partners, suppliers or distributors."[3]

Originally, value creation referred to the economic value generated by firms for their shareholders. It was Michael Porter's work that brought customers into the equation and provided the best-known model for analyzing how value can be created.[4]

His value chain framework divided organizational processes into sequential activities that created value for customers. There were two sets of activities – those that contributed directly to producing and delivering the offering: primary activities like logistics, operations, marketing and sales; and those that contributed indirectly: support activities, including HR, technology and procurement.

Porter maintained that an organization could develop a competitive advantage in any of the primary or support activities, or indeed in managing the linkages between them, and hence boost its margins or "generate superior value." He urged companies to analyze the competitiveness of each link in the chain. For each area, the key question became, "How much value is produced in this area compared to the cost of producing that value?" This conceptualization allowed us to assess which activities we could perform better than rivals and to highlight areas where outsourcing might make sense.

The value chain provided a much needed framework and a language for discussing value. Its influence was reinforced by trends in the business environment, notably the globalization of capital markets. Competition for financial funds became global and grew increasingly intense. Not only did the proportion of stock owned by large investors grow rapidly, but these investors showed their readiness to intervene directly when management was deemed to be underperforming.[5] Professor Leif Sjöblom remarks, "Stock markets became the great arbiters of company performance. The increase in merger and acquisition activity put the spotlight on shareholder value creation. Today, there is hardly a corporate mission that fails to refer to the goal of creating value."

Although Porter's framework covers the value creation and cost reduction aspects of the challenge, it is very much internally focused and tends to neglect who else is competing for that value. Value *capture* is the process through which a firm secures an appropriate share of the value it creates, in relation to partners and competitors. The case of The Coca-Cola Company provides a fitting illustration.[6] Professor John Walsh comments, "Coke does battle with Pepsi and other rivals to capture the maximum value from a market that it created and continues to develop through branding and product development. But Coke also has to make sure that it obtains its fair share from its partners, including the bottlers and the retailers."

Creating value is not helpful to the firm unless it can also capture significant parts of this value as profit. For example, EMI was responsible for inventing the CT scanner. But the firm's inability to profit from this breakthrough led to its takeover, even as the inventors themselves were being awarded the Nobel Prize in medicine. Other companies, notably General Electric, Siemens, Toshiba, Philips and Hitachi, went on to capture most of the revenues. This represents a classic failure to capture value created, sometimes called "value slippage."

Another example is Nestlé's MAGGI instant noodles in India.[7] Although Nestlé created this product category in India, the company struggled for a long time to make money from it. The specially adapted texture of the noodles and the "masala" taste had broad appeal but the growth rates of the product quickly attracted local competitors. As Professor Bala Chakravarthy notes, "The product's low price point and the need to invest heavily in distribution, marketing and innovation meant that it was unprofitable for about 15 years. The company was creating value for the customer but was unable to capture any for itself. But having established a loyal following and reformulated the product to provide health benefits, the company was finally able to achieve the volumes that allowed it to capture some of the value." Part of the confusion surrounding value creation comes from our tendency to conflate value creation and value capture. In broad terms, the value created establishes the size of the pie, while the value captured represents the share of the pie. Professor Albrecht Enders proposes a simple model to clarify the distinction.[8] While value creation is primarily influenced by activities within the company, value capture is mostly dictated by the competitive environment. Professor Enders explains, "It's often assumed that value creation is simply the price you charge less the costs you incur. But actually the value we create is much more. It's just that we don't capture it all, because of competitive forces, and so the surplus goes to the customer and not to us." The more unique the offering – as was once the case with Chinese porcelain, in terms of quality, scarcity, image and so forth – the smaller the competitive discount (see **Figure 1**).

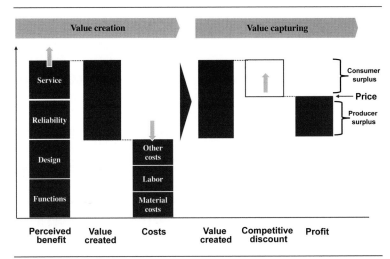

Figure 1: The value process framework   Source: Albrecht Enders, Andreas König,
Harald Hungenberg and Thomas Engelbertz [9]

The hunt for value has become a dominant preoccupation for businesses. It especially concerns traditional businesses, threatened either by disruptive technology or commoditizers. Consider the book publishing industry.[10] Professor Bill Fischer observes, "The growth of internet book retailing and the advent of eBooks have wrought havoc on incumbent businesses, forcing publishing houses and book retailers to overhaul their approach to value creation and value capture in order to stay in business." Barnes & Noble, for example, has repositioned its business from a store-based model to a multi-channel model focused on internet and digital commerce, with its proprietary e-reader becoming the biggest-selling single item for the company.

At the other end of the spectrum, internet-based businesses also need to concentrate on value. While they may boast millions of eyeballs or members, these firms do not always manage to translate customer interest into income. Consider the experience of Twitter.[11] Founded in 2006, the micro blogging site grew exponentially, focusing on increasing its community of users rather than on revenues. By mid-2010 it possessed 160 million user accounts and had raised over $250 million in three rounds of funding, yet it still had not turned a profit. Worse, in fact, its founder admitted that it was struggling to monetize the offering and appealed to its user base to come up with a revenue-generating model. Professor Salvatore Cantale comments, "In the past, you would not create a new business unless you could see the value capture opportunities. But this is no longer true. Facebook and Skype are both examples of businesses that took several years to discover how to capture value from their innovations and popularity, and a host of other internet ventures never made a penny before going bust."

A wide range of companies – from well-established to start-ups – could therefore benefit from sharpening or overhauling their approach to value creation and value capture.

When setting off on this journey, there are some things we need to think about, some things we need to do and some traps we need to avoid.

THINK   DIVERGENT VIEWS ON VALUE

Our understanding of value is multifaceted. How we think about value is also constantly evolving. Consider three developing perspectives on value creation.

The financial perspective: Beyond generating profits

Traditionally, finance has had a very clear view of what value means. Professor Arturo Bris notes, "The starting point in finance is always shareholder value. All of the financial modeling is based on shareholder value maximization. This is taken as a given and is based on the simple logic that if we don't deliver value to shareholders, through dividends and capital gains, we won't be able to raise capital and we will go out of business."

> *If we don't deliver value to shareholders, through dividends and capital gains, we won't be able to raise capital and we will go out of business.*

Within companies, the notion of shareholder value is a bit abstract, so we tend instead to focus on the bottom line. But the idea that our primary role is to generate profits is actually a distortion of the basic objective of creating shareholder value.[12] Professor Nuno Fernandes explains, "We have to dispel the fallacy that value is really just a fancy name for profit. Value creation is not about profits because profits don't take into account the cost of capital and the use of capital. Most of us are used to P&L accountability and to being evaluated according to some metric of profitability, such as EBIT or EBITDA. As a result, we easily forget that we are working for a company that requires capital, and that we have to provide a return to shareholders that is consistent with the risk."

Dell's dramatic impact on the PC industry between 1995 and 2005 underlines the need to factor in the cost of capital.[13] Even if its profits were not that much higher than those of its rivals, Dell created significantly more value because it used less external financing. The company substituted shareholder capital with supplier capital. Most businesses have to pay their suppliers well before they get

Dell created significantly more value because it used less external financing.

paid by their customers. At Dell, it was the other way round. Because of its build-to-order business model, Dell collected cash from customers over a month before it had to pay its suppliers for the components. This generated a huge amount of liquidity that helped to finance the company's growth on the cheap. At the same time, it benefited from much lower risk than its rivals because it produced only what customers actually wanted. By reducing its capital needs and the risk associated with inventory and unwanted goods, Dell was able to squeeze more value from the same revenues. It ran into problems because it relied excessively on its business model to stay ahead of the pack and failed to develop future sources of growth when times were good.

Time is another key difference between profit and value. Professor Bris remarks, "Profit is how much money you make today. Value is how much money you make today and for the rest of time."

The time dimension also helps to reconcile the value claims of shareholders and other stakeholders.[14] Having captured the value, we have to distribute it to the various stakeholders, not just the shareholders and customers but also the employees, suppliers, community, government and so on. The goal of shareholder value maximization has been criticized for failing to consider the interests of these other stakeholders.[15] Professor Fernandes counters, "The dichotomy of shareholder versus stakeholder is true in the short term. In the short term, you may cut back services to customers or fire employees or squeeze suppliers and achieve better results next quarter. But value creation is about the long term. And those kinds of actions won't deliver value over time. So it's a false dichotomy, and if you don't create value for your shareholders, then it's difficult to create value for others."

The strategic perspective: Beyond the value chain

For strategists, the value chain metaphor is not as compelling as it once was. Too rigid and linear, it sits uneasily with a fast-changing competitive environment where many of the conventional ways through which we created value no longer create value. To succeed, we must not just add value, but reinvent it.[16] Professor Allen Morrison comments, "From a strategy perspective, when we talk about value creation, we first have to look at what's changing outside: how markets are changing, how our industry is changing, how our consumers are changing. We develop a view on where the world is heading and how that impacts what we have to do, where we compete, what we don't do, how we operate, how we interact with customers, and who we partner with."

From a strategy perspective, we develop a view on where the world is heading and how that impacts what we have to do, where we compete, what we don't do, how we operate, how we interact with customers, and who we partner with.

The focus of strategic analysis is no longer the company but the value-creating system of which the company is a part. We used to outsource activities for cost-reduction purposes to companies that could perform tasks more cheaply and efficiently than us. But increasingly we are looking to outsource for value creation purposes, to gain access to capabilities that we are unable to develop ourselves.[17]

Take the case of Bharti Airtel.[18] The Indian telecom operator currently boasts the world's fifth largest customer base, with over 250 million subscribers. But back at the start of the millennium, the company was struggling against better-funded competitors. To reduce its dependence on capital, the top management team decided to outsource all functions, except marketing, sales and finance. In 2004, Bharti Airtel entrusted all of its IT services to IBM and tied IBM's compensation to its own growth. The development and management of its network operations were shared out between Ericsson, Nokia-Siemens Network and Huawei. The telecom company also teamed up with SKS, India's largest microfinance institution, to allow customers to pay for mobile phones in small installments. Bharti Airtel even persuaded two big competitors to pool resources in order to share the infrastructure costs of expanding into rural India. Professor Pasha Mahmood observes, "The results were spectacular in terms of both revenue growth and returns on capital employed. But rivals have latched on to Bharti's strategy and the company's growth has slowed, so it has to expand into other sectors and develop newer business models."

This example suggests that value creation is really a moving target, and that the key strategic challenge is to reorganize a shifting constellation of suppliers and partners to seize new opportunities and fill unmet market needs ahead of rivals. A more appropriate metaphor than value chain is therefore value network.

We face an expanded set of possibilities for value creation. Professor James Henderson notes, "Many industries have undergone or are going through transformations and are becoming far more networked. And the more networked we are, the more we are part of a system and the more we can reconfigure that system and charge for that system in a variety of different ways, whether we use an advertising-based model, pay-for-use or some kind of subscription model. There is a much greater scope of choice on the revenue generation side than was previously available."

Yet, the transition from value chains to value networks requires a change of mindset from owning resources to gaining access to them. In many companies, we are still organized around the processes of creating products and services and managing owned resources. Increasingly, we need to pursue the creation of value in new forms with new players. The key words are no longer ownership, control and strength, but access, influence and flexibility. We need to build networks of suppliers and partners that can be remixed to meet shifting and individualized needs.

> *The transition from value chains to value networks requires a change of mindset from owning resources to gaining access to them.*

The marketing perspective: Beyond delivering value

We have grown used to viewing value from the supply side as something produced exclusively by companies. Raw materials are combined and transformed along the value chain, with value being added at each step until the product is delivered to the end user. According to this logic, value creation is the first stage in the sequence, followed by value exchange and then value consumption.

The problem with this perspective is that it cannot easily explain businesses like Facebook, TripAdvisor or YouTube, where there is no value creation in the firm without the customer. Such exceptions alert us to the idea that customers not only claim value but also contribute to the value creation process.

The emerging view among marketers is that the customer is not a passive recipient of value but an active partner in its creation. Indeed, some marketing specialists go as far as to suggest that value is *always* co-created with customers.[19] Professor Stefan Michel elaborates, "A BMW car has no value unless a customer does something. That does not mean I need to drive it. I can just buy it and enjoy it. Owning a BMW may be enough for me. The point is that the value is really not created when the car leaves the factory in Bavaria, but rather in my experience of it."

According to the marketing perspective, our goal is not to make or do something of value for customers, but rather to mobilize them to take advantage of an offering to create value for themselves. As Professor Michel puts it, "What matters is not what we produce for the customer, but rather what the customer *does* with what we produce. The traditional approach views value creation as an activity, whereas the new approach views it as a mindset. It is a fundamentally different way of understanding how value is co-created."

> *What matters is not what we produce for the customer, but rather what the customer does with what we produce.*

This mindset shift has considerable implications for the way we look at customers and how we try to enrich the potential experience of the customer, not simply by offering a wider choice. In the case of BMW, the company now enables customers to design their own BMW on Facebook through an application. In the process, the customer actually co-designs the *exact* car that he or she wants to drive and ends up devoting an average four hours of undivided attention to the brand. The platform serves to provide a richer co-created experience.

Companies increasingly need to view their products as vehicles for services that enrich the interaction, not just in the business-to-customer sector but also in the business-to-business domain. Take the extreme situation in which our company is asked to supply a component with standardized features at a set price. What differentiates our offer and helps us secure preferred supplier status is the buyer's perception of the "relationship value."[20]

Professor Wolfgang Ulaga investigated the multiple facets of relationship value by interviewing purchasing managers, "There are several ways of offering superior value to our customers beyond the product and the price, especially

> *There are several ways of offering superior value to our customers beyond the product and the price, especially through personal interaction and servicing, by shortening go-to-market cycles and by providing access to know-how.*

through personal interaction and servicing, by shortening go-to-market cycles and by providing access to know-how."

The underlying point is that producers and buyers converge in creating and sharing value rather than being on opposite sides of a value equation. This is a critical perspective as our share of revenue derived from services keeps increasing.

These three perspectives – financial, strategic and marketing – have significantly enriched our understanding of value, but we sometimes have difficulty reconciling them. Going back to **Figure 1**, we can see why. Professor Albrecht Enders explains, "People in marketing and product design are mainly looking at the benefits side of the value creation picture, whereas operations people are primarily concerned with the costs side of value creation. Then the finance and the sales people are really concerned with the other side of the picture, and what price they can set to maximize the value captured. Strategy people sit in the middle, trying to figure out how our company can differentiate itself in the marketplace [the value capture side] and how to organize and put together the resources to target new opportunities [the value creation side]. The framework helps us to see where each party is 'coming from' and to have a more intelligent conversation around the whole topic of value."

LOOK IN THE RIGHT PLACES   DO

To boost our value creation and capture capabilities, we need to work on four fronts.

Question costs

The starting point for enhanced value creation is to have a clear idea, as Wedgwood did in the 1700s, of where our costs are incurred and where we make money – which offerings, brands, customers, client groups, distribution channels and markets. In many businesses, profitable accounts subsidize unprofitable ones, and management is blissfully unaware.[21] The quality of cost accounting systems seldom ranks very high on the top management agenda. Yet the information they generate drives our decisions on project investments, customer accounts, pricing, marketing spend, activities to outsource, and hence value creation. As Professor Leif Sjöblom puts it, "We can create more value just by having more transparent data that is structured

> *We have to improve the way knowledge is shared between finance and its internal customers.*

and reported in a way that is useful for making decisions, without spending hours trying to analyze it. Too often, we find brilliant finance people who churn out numbers computed to five decimal places, and business heads who don't understand the numbers produced. So we have to improve the way knowledge is shared between finance and its internal customers."

Beyond improving the quality of the financial information at our disposal, we also need to think more creatively about costs. In established companies, we can learn a lot from low-cost competitors in terms of cutting costs or passing costs on to other players in the value chain, including suppliers and customers.[22]

A prime example is the case of Ryanair.[23] Struggling as a conventional airline, the company decided to adopt the Southwest model, using just one type of aircraft flying point-to-point between secondary uncongested airports, and abolishing in-flight meals, assigned seats and business class. These factors enabled the company to replicate Southwest's impressive turnaround times and aircraft utilization levels, as well as limiting the costs associated with pilot training, the purchase and storage of spare parts, and maintenance. But Ryanair went one better, pioneering the *ultra* low-cost business model and becoming one of the most profitable airlines in the world.

Beyond outsourcing activities such as ground services and maintenance services, the airline's management team also off-loaded costs in unconventional ways, eliminating a free checked baggage allowance and ticket refunds for "no shows." It got rid of reclining seats and seat pockets, which attract clutter, to speed up turnaround times. The airline even insisted that pilots and cabin crew pay for their own training, saving the company money while at the same time testing their commitment to the job.[24] All the frills, including water, "given away" by traditional carriers have to be paid for, and flight attendants also offer high mark-up items for sale, such as digital cameras. Ryanair went as far as to sell the advertising space on its aircraft fuselages and on seat-back trays. In the process, it redefined the economics of the airline business. Its operating costs are so low that it only needs to sell about half of the seats on each flight to break even. Of course, some of the moves have left it open to criticism. But the underlying point is that no cost is left unexamined (see **Figure 2**).[25]

Professor Carlos Cordón observes, "Customers may sometimes complain, but they know what they are getting, and they seem to value punctuality and price above politeness and pampering.

Principle	Examples
Minimize fixed costs	Place bulk orders for planes in a downturn.
Leverage fixed costs	Enable higher aircraft utilization with faster turnarounds, sell space on seat backs and on fuselage to advertisers.
Convert fixed costs into variable ones	Outsource key services like ground services and maintenance services.
Eliminate variable costs	Use online booking and call centers to bypass travel agents, stop issuing paper tickets.
Minimize variable costs	Select secondary airports with low charges for services.
Convert variable costs into revenue sources	Charge for drinks and snacks, and for freight luggage.

Figure 2: Cost innovation at Ryanair   Source: Adrian Ryans and Atul Pahwa [26]

They also get value in that they only pay for what they use, rather than one customer cross-subsidizing another. The goal is not simply to strip costs to the bone, but to rethink the traditional business models and perform some activities in fundamentally different ways."

Create value with data

Many of us still tend to look upon IT as a competitive necessity rather than a serious source of competitive advantage.[27] But it is through information about customers, competitors, operations and products that value is created and performance improved.[28] Professor Don Marchand asserts, "Our information management practices – the way we collect, process, organize and share information – add up to our information orientation. In some companies we have more mature approaches to this, resulting in the more effective use of information by our colleagues, partners and indeed customers, and better business performance."

Take the example of Cemex, the Mexico-based construction company.[29] In a commoditized industry, the company developed its information capabilities to transform the value of its offering to customers. Realizing that the differentiating factor for customers was not the product itself but the deliveries, Cemex focused on getting the ready-mix concrete to sites at the right time so that expensive work crews were not kept waiting and the concrete itself did not spoil. The company built up a digital system that made it possible to track trucks and re-route them in real time to meet unexpected needs. Cemex learned to optimize delivery patterns across each geographic market served. With the new system, 98% of deliveries fell within the agreed 20-minute time slot, in contrast with the previous delivery record where only one-third of orders were on time despite a three-hour time window.

Between 1995 and 2008, these capabilities helped Cemex to outperform industry rivals in terms of share price, operating margins and return on assets, propelling the company into the top three in its industry. While changes in the IT infrastructure made this growth possible, significant changes in mindset and working practices were needed to unlock its full potential. The value of information resides less in the technology than in how we use it – as a means to leverage the knowledge and capabilities of our people. Executives at Cemex conceded that the company's success hinged on a sustained drive to shift attitudes and to promote flexibility, openness to learning, proactivity in meeting commitments, and the improved use of information to serve customers. In spite of all these efforts, the company came close to bankruptcy in the wake of the 2008–2009 financial crisis owing to a large acquisition made with short-term credit, providing a useful reminder that value creation is a multifaceted challenge.

The value of information resides less in the technology than in how we use it – as a means to leverage the knowledge and capabilities of our people.

China's Ping An is another example of a company that has used its information capabilities to achieve accelerated growth and challenge established players.[30] In just over two decades, the company has transformed itself from an entrepreneurial venture selling freight insurance into an integrated financial services group and China's largest insurer by market capitalization. The company embraced the leading practices of overseas companies, partnering with the likes of Microsoft, HP and Intel for its IT needs. Ping An implemented advanced IT platforms to centralize back-office operations and provide consistent service to its 33 million customers. But it also innovated. Its 24-hour customer service call center, initially set up to answer queries, became a growing source of telesales, evolving from a cost center into a profit center.[31] The company developed an online system to enable its 200,000 sales agents to do self-training on all the products they sold, on cross-selling and on how to engage customers. Ping An also developed the first mobile application allowing policy holders involved in car accidents to take pictures of the damaged vehicle and to send them through for rapid approval of repairs.

Professor Winter Nie affirms, "Ping An is very different from most Chinese companies. Peter Ma [its founder and CEO] has worked hard to instill a culture that combines Confucian ideology with a commitment to the best Western practices, emphasizing transparency, mutual respect, learning and merit. As a result, employees have become accustomed to sharing knowledge and using knowledge and information openly – at the operational level, at the customer-facing level and also at the management level."

Create new value space

We can pursue two very different approaches to come up with new value spaces: top-down and bottom-up.

Top-down, we can list the various competitive dimensions of our offering – such as performance, price, reliability, quality, style, customization, convenience – and map out where substitute offerings stand in comparison. This analysis can yield strategic insights, showing us common combinations of differentiators and missing combinations. Uncontested space can indicate counterintuitive opportunities for new value creation, and solution-shaping techniques like "deep dives" can help us to investigate opportunities along with partners from our value network to appeal to customer segments previously overlooked.[32] Some features may need introducing or reinforcing, while others can be reduced or dropped altogether.

Take the case of the Brazilian footwear brand Havaianas, owned by São Paulo Alpargatas.[33] The company used to manufacture flip flops that were cheap, comfortable, durable and available in just five colors. As sales slowed in the mid-1990s, the top team decided to reposition the cheap commodity product as an aspirational product. Repriced at a premium, the flip flops were offered in different styles; enthusiasts could choose between scores of combinations of multi-colored soles and straps to customize their Havaianas. Their availability in Brazil was actually reduced as the company started distributing them through smarter sales channels with more attractive displays at the point of sale. These changes were accompanied by an innovative and consistent communication strategy that showed celebrities wearing the shoes, in an effort to appeal to more affluent customers. IMD President Dominique Turpin observes, "Havaianas transformed the flip flop from a functional item mostly worn indoors into a

> *Havaianas created a new value space that has encouraged a host of sports and fashion players, including Nike and Armani, to jump in with their own versions.*

product with emotional resonance and a fashion accessory that could be worn outside on different occasions. In the process, it created a new value space that has encouraged a host of sports and fashion players, including Nike and Armani, to jump in with their own versions."

Bottom-up, we can create new value spaces by taking the individual customer as the starting point for exploration. The advantage of this approach is that it may reveal unknown needs, not just novel recombinations of known needs. To identify those latent unfulfilled needs, we must spend time with customers. We have to develop a deep sense, through observation as well as questioning, of the customers' priorities and concerns around the experience. Value comes not only from enabling customers to do something but also from relieving them of undesirable activities.[34] As Professor Stefan Michel explains, "When we gather customer intelligence, we have to go beyond traditional surveys and focus groups to include more immersed and holistic perspectives that provide intimate observations of how customers co-create value."

A striking example of profound customer understanding is the case of Disney in China.[35] The company was initially concerned about how it could capture value in a market where DVD piracy was endemic and local competitors could deliver the same content without incurring any of the development costs. The company responded by re-examining the problems that Chinese consumers wanted to solve and re-imagining its own offering accordingly. Professor Howard Yu expands, "Disney recognized that parents who were reluctant to spend money on movies would willingly dip into their private savings in order to secure the best education for their children. So it used the emotional pull of its characters to launch Disney English learning centers." The curriculum, aimed at children under 10, was developed in the US and is taught by native English-speaking trainers. Launched in 2008, the centers proved so popular that within three years there were more than 30 of them around the country, and the business established itself as the most profitable product line for Disney in China.

Disney recognized that parents who were reluctant to spend money on movies would willingly dip into their private savings in order to secure the best education for their children.

Mind the value-critical stakeholders

In many companies, we have a group of rainmakers, reputation drivers or experts without whom the value of our business would fall dramatically. As Bill Gates once said, "Take our 20 best people away, and I will tell you that Microsoft would become an unimportant company."[36]

We tend to devote a lot of top management attention to keeping this collection of individuals happy and committed. Yet this group represents just one of a much wider set of what Professor Paul Strebel calls "value-critical stakeholders."[37] These are the groups whose input, connections or cooperation are essential for our company's long-term value creation.

Value-critical groups are those that have the capacity to boost value or to destroy it. Employees who can easily be replaced would not normally be regarded as value critical. But if they belong to a powerful union, they too become value critical, as British Airways found to its cost when cabin crew strikes caused it to lose its position as "the world's most profitable airline."[38]

Beyond the confines of the firm there are other key relationships within our value constellation that we simply cannot afford to neglect.[39] Professor Strebel elaborates, "We first need to identify which players are going to make and break our strategic initiatives. Is it a critical customer? If we lose that customer, will we go belly up? Is it some NGO that can destroy our reputation? Is it frontline traders in an investment bank or subcontractors managing drilling platforms?" An extreme example is that of Venezuela's Santa Teresa Rum Distillery, which had to manage both squatters and criminal gang members in order to do business in a tricky political and economic environment.[40]

Using existing reports, such as enterprise risk analyses, we can discuss how value creation could be threatened and on whom we depend. For strategic projects or new business initiatives, we have implementation plans that indicate activities along the critical path and specify indispensable internal and external contributors.

Take the case of Sula Wines.[41] Its founder Rajeev Samant set out to create an export quality winery in India. Producing fine wine turned out to be the easy part. Selling and distribution proved the real challenges. Excise duties on the production and marketing of wine were punitively high, reflecting negative social attitudes to alcohol. Also, there was no distribution network for wine and the only existing retail outlets were those specializing in hard liquor.

Once we have identified the value-critical stakeholders, the next stage is to develop communication channels with them and to start establishing goodwill. In the case of Sula Wines, Samant lobbied the authorities to acquire a winemaking license, holding out the promise of rural employment. On the distribution front, he tapped into existing beer and spirits networks, and persuaded

Samant's success in getting winemaking reclassified as agribusiness ended up creating huge value, not only for Sula but also for other grape farmers and for aspiring wine producers in India.

the retailers to provide shelf space alongside beer and whisky. He also linked up with big name spirit makers, such as Rémy Cointreau, that were setting up their own distribution networks direct to hotels and restaurants, offering local knowledge in exchange. Most importantly, though, Samant set about convincing the regulators that wine was primarily an agricultural product and should not be subject to the same high tax regime as hard liquor. His success in getting winemaking reclassified as agribusiness ended up creating huge value, not only for Sula but also for other grape farmers and for aspiring wine producers in India.

Over time, the set of value-critical stakeholders may change as new ones emerge. So we need to review whose ongoing support is essential and continue to reach out to those stakeholders. If they are vital to our survival we may include one of their representatives on the top management team or the board to ensure that their voice is ever present. We can divide up other critical stakeholders between different members of the top team who assume responsibility for engaging with them and monitoring their mood, so that we are not caught off guard by events we could easily have anticipated – what Professor Michael Watkins calls "predictable surprises."[42]

AVOID   VALUE-DESTROYING PRACTICES

It goes without saying that we want to guard against value destruction, but there are three traps that are liable to frustrate our attempts to create or capture value: bad governance, faulty indicators and poor PR.

Bad governance

In recent years, we have seen some spectacular examples of value destruction caused in large part by the failure of boards to curb the excesses of the company's top executives,[43] notably at Tyco, Parmalat, Ahold, Swissair and BP.[44] Professor Arturo Bris observes, "Many boards neglected their control role, their responsibility to challenge or intervene when the top team was getting carried away or becoming overly focused."

Take the case of Home Depot.[45] Under Bob Nardelli, the company's domineering CEO and chair, it significantly boosted both revenues and profits. Yet its stock price stagnated as analysts remained unconvinced by the new strategy. With mounting pressure from shareholders to justify his huge pay package, Nardelli anticipated a confrontational annual meeting and told board members they need not attend; he took questions alone and gave cursory answers. The whole meeting lasted just over half an hour. The predictable backlash only increased the public pressure on Nardelli, and his belated apology did nothing to restore his relationship with shareholders, culminating in his resignation a few months later.

Essentially, the board abdicated its responsibility. Board members could surely see that Nardelli's relationship with shareholders was growing dangerously dysfunctional. They knew that their "no show" was likely to make matters worse. Yet they failed to deter him – not through weakness, but through solidarity. They fell prey to groupthink.[46] Professor Shlomo Ben-Hur remarks, "Groups lacking in diversity – composed only of CEOs for example – are especially prone to groupthink. This makes it hard to slam the brakes on when board–CEO relations become too aligned, because there is no source of independent thought to reassess what is happening."

One way of fighting against such governance crises is through board composition by including board members who are sensitive to the interests of key stakeholders, who have real industry expertise and who are willing and able to devote the time needed for the board's work.[47] As Professor Paul Strebel notes, "The moment of truth for a board comes when management starts destroying long-run value, because it stops adapting to changing conditions, makes decisions that involve large hidden risk, or engages in behavior causing critical stakeholders to withdraw their support. It is at these times that board directors have to be willing to raise the red flag."[48]

Boards are supposed to guard against value destruction. But they also have a key role to play in contributing to value creation.[49] Professor Didier Cossin explains, "Boards can be a competitive advantage for companies. They can provide an outside view, overcome blind spots in strategy, alert the top team to overlooked opportunities, connect with governments, society and other stakeholders, give credibility and build trust in ways that executive teams cannot."

The moment of truth for a board comes when management starts destroying long-run value. It is at these times that board directors have to be willing to raise the red flag.

Leadership teams now have to confront escalating complexity from society, governments, alternative business models and shifts in economic conditions. CEOs, in particular, desperately need sparring partners, who are not beholden to them, to make sense of the challenges and opportunities facing the company. The board must be equipped to provide that peripheral vision.

Faulty indicators

To create value we need to be able to measure it. But the metrics we use can actually interfere with value creation. For example, if we start measuring time-to-market, we may be inclined to look for safer projects, those that we know we can take from start to finish quickly and predictably, meaning projects that do not stretch us or create much value. Professor Salvatore Cantale warns, "We often confuse indicators and value drivers. Value creation depends on value drivers, things like brand reputation, attention to customers and proprietary technology. Then there are the metrics we use to gauge progress, which are the indicators. So, for the three drivers just mentioned, it could be brand awareness levels, customer satisfaction scores and patent awards. But after a while, we start focusing on and trying to influence the indicators and we forget about the drivers. So we have to be careful not to put invalid indicators between us and value creation."

The metrics we use can actually interfere with value creation.

Of course, that problem is exacerbated when we link the indicators to incentives. When we pay people according to these metrics, they realize that it is in their best interest to deliver on the metric, even if that does little to create value, and possibly even destroys it. A classic example is the use of the "average handling time" indicator when assessing rep performance in contact centers, based on the belief that customers are happier if they spend less time on the phone.

Zappos.com, the online shoe retailer, takes a different approach.[50] Top management realized that having reps worrying about how quickly they could get customers off the phone might not promote outstanding customer service. Professor Winter Nie explains, "At Zappos, they dispensed with timing metrics altogether and instead encouraged reps to spend the time required to 'wow' customers. This resulted in incredible word of mouth advertising and fast growth. They figured that if you can make every customer happy, they will tell 10 other people, so that time should be seen as an advertising cost." The aim at Zappos is not to maximize every single transaction, but rather to build relationships that deliver value over time.

Of course, this does not imply we should get rid of indicators. Metrics help us assess if we are making headway, but we must remember that their primary function is to promote organizational learning and improvement. Once they are attached to incentives, they can easily become distorted and drive the wrong kind of behaviors. Periodically, the indicators need to be revisited to make sure that they are truly aligned to value creation and learning.

Poor PR

With the rise of social media, consumers have acquired much more power to destroy corporate value. This has reshaped the way we need to engage with customers.[51] Professor Seán Meehan comments, "It's always been risky for companies to disappoint their customers. But the reach and impact of social media have magnified the damaging consequences of falling short. Just look at the internet-fed criticism of Kryptonite's pricey but easily picked lock and Dell's flammable laptops."

What might previously have remained isolated complaints now gain critical mass and momentum because of social media. A single disgruntled customer can rally like-minded others to his or her cause even, as P&G discovered, when it is unfounded: A mother who attributed her child's nappy rash to the company's more absorbent diaper created a Facebook page to get the product withdrawn. In the weeks that followed, 7,000 parents joined the campaign – and P&G shares fell over 5% before the US Consumer Product Safety Commission established that there was no causal link.

In another high-profile case, United Airlines became the target of a musical rant called "United Breaks Guitars" when it persistently refused to accept responsibility for an instrument damaged in transit. The video went viral, scoring half a million hits in the first week after being posted online, and the airline's stock price plunged by 10% in the same period, costing shareholders some $180 million in value.

The mismanagement of one-off incidents can quickly spiral into a reputation-damaging crisis that spills from online to traditional media. The interconnectedness of consumers and free-flowing exchange of information have radically altered the marketplace.[52] Professor John Walsh observes, "Word of mouth has been turbo charged. Opinions potentially reach billions. Consumers have formed a collective. They have unionized. So we're shifting

Word of mouth has been turbo charged. We're shifting from managing customers to managing communities, and those may vary widely in their perspective and membership, from fan clubs to gripe clubs.

from managing customers to managing communities, and those may vary widely in their perspective and membership, from fan clubs to gripe clubs."

Take the case of Nestlé's response to an attack on its Kit Kat brand.[53] Greenpeace, the environmental protection group, posted a parody on YouTube criticizing Nestlé's sourcing of palm oil. The hard-hitting video features an office worker taking a break by unwrapping a Kit Kat and eating what turns out to be the finger of an orangutan, whose habitats are cleared to cultivate oil palms.

Nestlé reacted swiftly, insisting that the video be withdrawn for breach of copyright. Its heavy-handed response caused outrage, fanning the flames of publicity instead of smothering them. Irate internet users found other ways of spreading the "banned video" and its notoriety grew. As the battleground shifted to other parts of the social media, Nestlé's Facebook moderator reacted angrily to the negative comments. Professor Albrecht Enders notes, "Very soon the furore itself became newsworthy and Nestlé was criticized for its 'snarky attitude' to social networking, which started to impact the share price. At that point, Nestlé understood that its damage limitation strategy was not working and it ultimately switched tack. It managed to retrieve the situation by instituting a sustainable strategy around palm oil sourcing

Managing Employees	Managing Connected Customers
Fairness	Beware of differential pricing which becomes harder to justify with increased transparency.
Communication	Explain when we make changes to the brand. A void leaves space for misinterpretation.
Listening	Monitor consumer blogs and chat rooms for hot issues and deal with them proactively.
Empowerment	Provide a platform to stimulate discussion, on which consumers can create and upload their own content.
Accessibility	Make it easy for consumers to complain or compliment. Reach out to them.
Learning	Take corrective action when mistakes happen and inform consumers of the changes made to prevent it happening again.

Figure 3: Treat customers more like employees   Source: John Walsh [54]

and sustainable sourcing in general, and altering its corporate stakeholder engagement strategy."

It follows that we must develop policies and strategies for monitoring and managing online communities. Indeed, because consumers now talk to each other, there are many parallels between managing customers and managing employees (see **Figure 3**).

ASSEMBLING VALUE THE IKEA WAY   PAYOFF

Value creation and capture can be fleeting advantages before the competition closes the gap or goes one better.[55] But sometimes the coherence of the business model makes it very difficult to emulate. The case of IKEA offers a compelling example.[56] The company has redefined a number of principles and organizational practices in the furniture business. In the process, it changed the industry, creating value for itself, but destroying value for many of the traditional furniture manufacturers. IKEA has managed to create value on all four fronts.

> *IKEA has changed the furniture industry, creating value for itself but destroying value for many of the traditional furniture manufacturers.*

Questioning costs that other manufacturers took for granted has been central to IKEA's disruptive approach. Customers are responsible for locating, collecting, transporting and putting together the furniture kits they purchase. According to Professor Arturo Bris, "This creates substantial assembly and distribution savings for IKEA, but also allows it to pass on a significant portion of those savings to customers. In fact, there is even evidence to suggest that some customers derive added satisfaction from assembling the furniture themselves. So that's the magic formula: a cost efficiency that actually enhances the experience."

Underpinning this business model is a culture that takes pride in eliminating waste, in which frugality has always been a core value, not a strategic drive or cyclical effort. IKEA executives, right up to the CEO, fly economy and obsess about stripping costs out of the value chain: designing products that are stylish but inexpensive; minimizing the volume of their flat-packs in order to cram more merchandise per pallet or shipping container; and maximizing the amount of shelf-ready packaging that can be delivered directly into the store.

Creating value with data and systems at IKEA is primarily a matter of supporting customer self-service. This starts with product design where virtual prototyping technology allows designers, developers and suppliers to collaborate. Professor Ralf Seifert observes, "IKEA is a master of virtual prototyping. It conceives designs that are optimal not only for manufacturing and transporting but also for assembly by amateurs. The ease with which the components and sub-components fit together is validated in a virtual environment before production starts, and the company produces 3D assembly leaflets without a single written instruction to assist the customer."

Another key technology that supports customer self-service is the company's website. Ranked in the top four retailers for speed, the website allows prospective customers to prepare their store visit by checking the availability of specific products at their local store. Customers can also download kitchen planning systems that enable them to experiment and plan their own kitchen designs virtually. They can even upload pictures to show others how they have decorated their homes and why. IKEA makes the same tools available on social networks such as Facebook and Twitter. It supports the idea of integrating customers into the co-creation process.

IKEA supports the idea of integrating customers into the co-creation process.

Creating new value space for IKEA started with the counterintuitive combination of stylish design at low prices. But behind that value proposition was a radical redefinition of the role of the customer in the value-creation process. Instead of viewing customers as mere buyers, IKEA has transformed them into active partners through the self-service and do-it-yourself model. It tries to instill in customers the idea that their role is not to consume value but to jointly produce it.

In comparison with traditional furniture manufacturers, IKEA puts a lot of burden on customers, but it also enables them to take on these tasks more easily. They are supplied with data-rich catalogues and labels, tape measures, writing materials, virtual design facilities to help them make choices without staff assistance, and "room sets" to visualize what they can fit into a standard 12m^2 space. At the same time, it proposes some distinctive relievers that enhance the experience.[57] Professor Stefan Michel expands, "IKEA relieves you of several stressors in terms of co-creation. For example, the fact that it all fits nicely together takes a cognitive burden away from you. Someone else has made sure that the materials and designs match nicely. Then there are services like supervised childcare, playgrounds for children, free strollers and wheelchairs that relieve adults of distracting stressors. I would say that more than innovating products, IKEA has innovated customers."

Minding the value-critical stakeholders has also been pivotal to IKEA's success. In particular, its tight relationships with a core of select suppliers have been at the heart of its purchasing and product development strategy. Since its first decision to source furniture from communist Poland back in 1961, IKEA has played a major role in improving the business infrastructure and manufacturing standards of its partners.[58] Professor Dan Denison notes, "New suppliers receive technical and engineering support and leased equipment to help them upgrade their performance. And the most reliable and proactive of them are given extensive responsibility for deciding when and how much to deliver, so they get access to IKEA's stock data and ordering patterns, and have to interact every day to ensure product coverage for special events such as sales promotions." Only about 1% of IKEA's 1,300 direct suppliers have this first-tier status, but the company strives to build lasting relationships with all its suppliers and takes an unusually long-term approach.

More recently, another set of value-critical stakeholders have emerged. In the 1990s, IKEA came under public pressure as journalists scrutinized the environmental, safety and child labor practices of its suppliers. Realizing the risk to the value of the brand, IKEA responded decisively. It developed a stringent supplier audit program, covering compliance, emissions, waste, chemicals, safety, child labor, work conditions, forest sourcing and other areas. In parallel, it partnered with WWF and Greenpeace on forest management and conservation, and linked with Save the Children and UNICEF. Building goodwill with these NGOs enhanced the perception of IKEA among its own employees, as well as consumers. Also, in keeping with its established approach, IKEA does not just audit suppliers and switch sources when they fall short. It works closely with suppliers to upgrade their environmental and social performance. It provides advice and sets up action plans on how to clean up their operations, and even steps in and helps suppliers to reduce environmental impact directly, through loans.

The example of IKEA shows the multifaceted challenge of creating and capturing value. Establishing a value-driven culture turns out to be a constant battle.

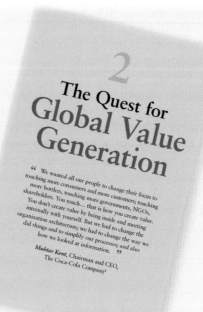

2

The Quest for Global Value Generation

" We wanted all our people to change their focus to touching more consumers and more customers; touching more bottlers, touching more governments; touching shareholders. You touch... that is how you create value. You don't create value by being inside and meeting internally with yourself. But we had to change the organization architecture; we had to change the way we did things and to simplify our processes; and also how we looked at information. "

Muhtar Kent, Chairman and CEO,
The Coca-Cola Company[1]

Where Do We Stand?

1. Who are we trying to create value for?

2. Can we provide a richer co-created experience for customers?

3. Are there taken-for-granted costs that we could pass on to others or just cut out?

4. Are we making the most of our information capabilities to improve value generation?

5. Who are our value-critical stakeholders?

6. Is our board vigilant about value destruction?

7. Are we using metrics that are inhibiting value generation?

3
The Quest for
Global Leadership Development

" In difficult times, developing people is even more important than in better times. Like most companies, we have a lot of people development programs for the middle management and top management group. But at the moment, our most important leadership program is our 'supervisory training program,' where we develop the leadership skills of our first-line managers. We have more than a thousand offices in different parts of the world. And the teams of the leaders in these small offices work with customers all the time. So the role of these leaders is truly essential. "

Matti Alahuhta, President and CEO,
KONE Corporation[1]

Xenophon: The world's first leadership guru

LESSONS FROM ANCIENT PERSIA

Leadership development was a critical issue long before the emergence of modern business. Take the case of ancient Persia, the world's first superpower. Starting off as the small kingdom of Anshan, its reserves of local talent were limited. The continuous expansion of the Persian Empire, starting with Cyrus the Great (reigned 559–530 BCE), required growing numbers of well-trained officials to administrate and govern its provinces, ultimately stretching across from Pakistan to Turkey and down from modern Azerbaijan to Saudi Arabia. The empire lasted for over two centuries until Alexander's invasion in 334 BCE.[2]

A key innovation of the ancient Persian Empire that endures today is statecraft – the need to articulate the organization's legitimate purpose and to specify the character demanded of its leaders. The Persian emperors were the first to use the ideology of ruling by the consent of the people. Cyrus's answer to the problem of leadership development was pluralism. As a ruler, his inclusionary practices were unprecedented.[3] His dictum of allowing people of different regions to follow their own faith and customs was inscribed in the Cyrus Cylinder, considered the earliest Human Rights Charter. This capacity for tolerating diversity allowed the empire to draw on and develop new talent, contributing to the resilience of the empire and its ability to withstand a series of internal and external crises.

In terms of keeping the empire together, the pivotal role was that of the satrap, who served as the ultimate representative of the emperor's civil authority in a given region.[4] Satraps were chiefly responsible for taxation and financial management, justice and public order; they also had a matrix-type authority over the military. They supervised the building of an impressive infrastructure for governing the empire, from immaculate roadways to a state-of-the-art courier system. Of course, this required paying special attention to the selection, training and socialization of satraps. Over time, the Persian satraps, drawn from ranks of the nobility across the empire, also created an intricate system of bureaucratic organization, employing the skills and knowledge of a diverse array of leaders at various levels. The emperor expected the satraps governing his far-flung provinces to be more than mere representatives, they had to make the right decisions on behalf of the empire.

The emperors' system of rule was much admired by their neighbors and foes, the ancient Greeks. Xenophon, a student of Socrates, based his treatise of leadership development on the rule of Cyrus the Great, who by then had been dead for over a century. According to Xenophon, the vitality of a state, a military unit and a family depends upon good leadership. Elements of good leadership that should be cultivated are "kindness, clemency and concern for other people, combined with strength, discipline and capacity for endurance in both a moral as well as physical sense."[5] At the same time, Xenophon was not naive about the dark arts of leadership, and recognized the need to act decisively when the leader's authority showed signs of decay.[6] As the world's first leadership guru, Xenophon had a string of illustrious disciples who studied his case example judiciously: practitioners such as Alexander the Great and Julius Caesar, and thought leaders such as Machiavelli and Peter Drucker.

The ancient Persians fashioned the prototype system for producing leaders. And the longevity and vitality of the very cosmopolitan Persian Empire was, to a large extent, a triumph of leadership development and talent management, with close parallels to the challenges faced by any high-growth international business today.

Growing better leaders

Companies have long been concerned with growing better leaders, on the understanding that leadership directly impacts corporate performance. For decades, companies have sent their outstanding executives on "leadership development" programs. Attendance was usually closely linked with succession planning for the top jobs. Other executives received "management training" or "executive education" with the aim of lifting specific performance in the current job or the next one rather than learning "for growth," bridging an identified need rather than building capacity to deal with unforeseen challenges, and developing skills rather than a mindset.

Today, leadership development has been democratized. There has been an explosion in the number of leadership programs, seminars and centers. And the debate about whether leaders are born or made has been shown to be futile, since we do not know what we are born with until we try very hard to express it.[7] Leadership development is everywhere – widely accessible and no longer exclusive.

Leadership development is everywhere – widely accessible and no longer exclusive.

Some of that is window dressing – providers of management education simply recasting themselves as providers of leadership development. Just as management once had more market appeal than "administration," so leadership sells better than management. Professor Ginka Toegel notes, "In some cases, this is little more than a rebranding exercise. There is an inflation of the word leadership, everything becomes leadership – strategic leadership, operational leadership, entrepreneurial leadership and so on – so we have to look at what lies behind the words."

Yet the swing toward leadership also reflects a fundamental shift in the challenge of preparing executives for greater responsibilities. This shift is the consequence of two converging developments.

First, it is a response to the changing nature of business. Operating in an increasingly complex global environment, companies need to respond effectively to flux in multiple locations, which requires broad-based leadership.[8] Executives have to make the right judgment calls, at the customer interface, rather than continually referring decisions upward. As Professor Martha Maznevski puts it, "The more complex and fast-moving the environment, the more we have to use what's inside people. We have to rely more on local judgment and develop that judgment. So we need leaders at all levels, people who can inspire and influence, who can see the big picture and drive change, who

The more complex and fast-moving the environment, the more we have to rely on local judgment and develop that judgment.

can learn and help others to learn and who can think about and shape the future. We can't win in the marketplace with people who are just implementing." The turbulent context erodes the conventional distinction between managers and leaders.[9]

Second, the growing demand for leadership development has been driven by our changing expectations as employees.[10] Responsibility for navigating our careers in this uncertain and unstable environment rests squarely with us.[11] Professor Maury Peiperl explains, "Where we once had employment security, we now have employability security. Talented individuals need to feel they are continually upgrading their capacities to lead teams, projects and units, to feel they are learning and building portable skills. If the company stops investing in their development, they are liable to look elsewhere."

Hence, developing leaders has become a priority in many companies. But we may feel particularly compelled to upgrade our leadership capabilities in one of two situations: when we sense a scarcity of qualified internal candidates for leadership positions; or when we sense that our business heads struggle with a particular aspect of leadership – anything from driving change to developing global perspective – that is critical to our strategy.

In the midst of unprecedented growth, people were being rushed into jobs for which they lacked the experience and the confidence.

A shortage of leaders can be a problem for fast-growing companies, notably those from the emerging economies.[12] Back in 2007, the India-based IT giant Infosys had insufficient leadership-ready executives.[13] In the midst of unprecedented growth, people were being rushed into jobs for which they lacked the experience and the confidence. That leadership crisis was exacerbated by the rapid influx into India of global IT giants, including IBM, making it harder to hang on to the most promising talents. Professor Bala Chakravarthy notes, "Infosys reacted quickly, redesigning its talent identification and development processes and expanding its existing leadership institute to create the largest corporate education facility in the world, covering 270 acres and capable of accommodating 12,000 participants at one time. It also introduced systematic mentoring, led by the founders themselves, as well as leadership workshops and innovative simulation exercises. It really stepped up its commitment to leadership development and was able to gain huge recognition in the marketplace on the strength of it."

The lack of a specific leadership capacity is more likely to manifest itself in more established companies that suddenly confront a shift in the environment. Consider the example of KONE, the Finnish lift and escalator maker. Excellent operational leadership, rooted in KONE's engineering culture, was not matched by the "people leadership" competencies of its executives. Having identified that gap, the company put in place a leadership development program with a special focus on coaching and mentoring, and sent 350 of its managing directors and senior managers to attend it. Professor Ginka Toegel elaborates, "Executives who did not work together got to practice their coaching skills by discussing each other's 360-degree feedback, with a third executive providing feedback on the process and a facilitator picking up other aspects. As part of the post-program changes, the participants were required to pair up in order to continue peer-coaching one another."

These dual preoccupations – with the quantity and quality of leaders – may have special resonance in family businesses.[14] Professor Joachim Schwass comments, "Family firms are not always good at anticipating future leadership needs. The incumbent leaders may not cast the net wide enough – privileging family members – until they face a crisis, and the development process itself often focuses more on learning about the business rather than learning about leadership. While they want their heirs to become effective leaders, the generation in power may be slow to step back and give them the space they need to grow."

Transforming our approach to leadership development can yield improved performance and alignment, while also delivering indirect benefits in terms of attracting and hanging on to up-and-coming leaders.

When setting off on such a journey, there are some things we need to think about, some things we need to do and some traps we need to avoid.

BUILDING LEADERSHIP CAPABILITY   THINK

Traditionally, our leadership development efforts focused on developing the abilities and attitudes of individuals. But over the past two decades, we have also started to think of leadership as a collective property. We therefore need to think about building leadership capability in three ways: at an individual level, at a team level and at an organizational level. To transform a culture, we have to address all three facets.

Individual perspective: Leading yourself

Companies used to assume that exposure to the latest concepts and frameworks would boost the individual leadership capacities of executives. While such investments might improve our ability to talk about leading, they have limited impact on our ability to exercise leadership.[15] As Professor Jack Wood puts it, "Virtually all business schools have classes in leadership. The professors typically lecture, discuss cases and show videos of celebrated leaders and the basic message is 'do what they do.' The problem with this approach is that it doesn't address the reality of leading.

Effective leadership development requires a safe place to explore and understand the multiple forces that motivate individual and collective behavior.

Old Perspective		New Perspective
Standardized offering	➔	Customized offering
Case method	➔	Live issues
Elite-focused	➔	Broad-based
Conceptual	➔	Experiential
Individual-focused	➔	Individual and group development
Classroom-based	➔	Blended learning
One-off intervention	➔	Ongoing journey
Learn how to learn	➔	Learn how to help others learn

Figure 1: The shift in leadership development   Source: Jack D. Wood [16]

Effective leadership development requires a safe place to explore and understand the multiple forces that motivate individual and collective behavior." There is a gulf between these two leadership development approaches: one is about absorbing content while the other focuses on co-producing learning (see **Figure 1**).

We have to learn from experience as well as acquire it. A leadership program may only be one element in the developmental edifice, but it is a cornerstone for making sense of what we have done and what we need to change going forward.[17] As Professor Stewart Black explains, "To fully leverage the job rotation and stretch assignments of individual executives, we have to provide them with opportunities to review which capabilities, mindsets and behaviors have proved effective, which need enhancing and which should be toned down or discarded."

We therefore need a space to build self-awareness and to engage in self-assessment. Self-awareness can only come from working with data that relates directly to us – our personality inventories, our multisource feedback, our personal narratives.[18] Increasingly, this data is debriefed in individual coaching sessions that have become staples of leadership development programs.[19] As Professor Robert Hooijberg remarks, "The idea is to hold up as many mirrors as possible. When used properly, these tools really open the door for leadership development. They reveal patterns of behavior that executives have perhaps been getting away with, but that represent potential derailers as those executives assume more responsibilities. We have to understand the origins and history of our workplace behavior as well as its impact on others."

Building on this enhanced appreciation of what makes us tick and our predispositions, we can then reflect on what we really want. Of course, such self-assessment also requires a clear-eyed understanding of the underlying challenges we will face as we take charge of bigger units. Professor Michael Watkins has identified seven major shifts that leaders go through as they transition from functional leadership to enterprise leadership.[20] He notes, "The main reason leaders fail in transitions is because they don't go back into a learning mode."

> *The main reason leaders fail in transitions is because they don't go back into a learning mode.*

Learning involves effort and risk. Most of us don't mind the effort, but we are less prepared to take the risk. We are inclined to stick with what we are good at.[21] Professor Maury Peiperl observes, "We often talk about playing to our strengths. But it is just as important to improve our shortcomings. Leadership development is about working on both fronts, especially allowing ourselves to experiment in our weaker areas, without having the pressure of immediate performance evaluation in our faces."

Team perspective: Exercising joint leadership

Although firms have traditionally focused on developing individual leadership talents, it has become increasingly apparent that we need to think about building the leadership capability of teams. At the turn of the millennium there was a marked shift away from the hero CEO running the corporation to the top team. We can have the best talents in the world, but if they are not functioning effectively together, they will never achieve their potential.[22] Sometimes, therefore, it makes sense for us to send a whole team to attend a leadership development program together.

Like individuals, teams expect to work on the actual issues and challenges facing them, rather than generic material. This has given rise to a new style of leadership development program – one that sits between open enrolment and customized programs – whereby intact teams work through their specific issues, then come together for plenary sessions to give each other feedback. These hybrid programs deal with the business priorities and the group dynamics in tandem.[23] Professor Bettina Büchel explains, "This approach combines learning and doing at the same time. For the leadership team, it's about changing how they look at their issues, how they think about business problems, it's opening their minds, it's changing how they interact together and how they lead their teams. We're guiding a process to help them make better decisions on their issues, not making decision recommendations."

In teams we rarely get the chance to reflect on our own dynamics and we often suppress conflict for fear that it will get out of hand or endure dysfunctional conflict for a long time. Outside the constraints and pressures of the workplace, we have a chance to develop a more honest dialogue and to explore team differences and sub-groups productively. To improve the leadership effectiveness of our team, we need a safe place to explore interpersonal tensions, taboo topics or scenarios and unspoken assumptions that may be limiting our thinking or options – what Professor George Kohlrieser calls a chance to "put the fish on the table."[24]

A key platform for leadership team development is the sharing of differences within the team. Until they are surfaced and discussed, these differences are more liable to be perceived as annoying frustrations than as real complementarities. There are several possible forms of complementary leadership including "task complementarity," "expertise complementarity," "cognitive complementarity" and "role complementarity."[25] Professor Michael Watkins notes, "Getting a better handle on our psychological fit is just as important as understanding our knowledge fit as a team. We must understand the sorts of mental models that others are bringing to the table to help us better leverage our strengths and avoid misinterpreting their words or actions. That way, different team members can take the lead on different aspects of the work without others suspecting some kind of hidden agenda."

The quality of the conversations we engage in will affect the quality of our business decisions and their execution.

To exercise effective leadership, our team also has to learn to manage its conversations better. We waste too much time talking past one another.[26] The quality of the conversations we engage in will affect the quality of our business decisions and their execution.[27] Professor Ben Bryant observes, "As a leadership team, we need to learn to identify what sort of conversation we are having and what sort of conversation we should be having. If we give free rein to multiple discussions it just creates confusion. We should regularly ask ourselves a simple question: are we trying to make sense, prioritize, make it happen or revise assumptions? Those are four entirely different discussions."

- Making sense of patterns in complex, incomplete, conflicting or ambiguous data.

- Making choices about competing opportunities and threats – and identifying critical priorities to focus resources and attention.

- Making commitments to actions aligned with agreed priorities.

- Making revisions to assumptions, priorities and commitments based on results so far.[28]

Organizational perspective: A reputation for leadership

A few companies, such as IBM, Shell and Unilever, have long held reputations for providing well-rounded leadership experiences and serving as feeder companies for their industries. But since the "war for talent" metaphor was coined in the late 1990s, many more companies have come to recognize the value of leadership development as a potential competitive differentiator.

Companies with strong leadership development reputations become talent magnets because people know they will have opportunities to learn, grow and build leadership competencies.

Companies with strong leadership development reputations become talent magnets because people know they will have opportunities to learn, grow and build leadership competencies. And thanks to rankings published in the likes of *Fortune* (Top Companies for Leaders) and *Bloomberg BusinessWeek* (Best Companies for Leadership), we have all become much more aware of which companies work hardest at grooming leaders and communicating those efforts. If people believe that a company is strong in leadership development, that is a key asset.

Developing a reputation as a great place for leaders is the essence of our "leadership brand" and, like other forms of branding, it has three basic building blocks: awareness, relevance and trust.[29] Professor Seán Meehan explains, "Building awareness, for a leadership brand, means trumpeting our innovative practices or our development spend both internally and externally, including to influencers like journalists, analysts and headhunters. Ensuring relevance is about having a value proposition that resonates with prospective and current employees – one that really prepares promising leaders for the kinds of challenges they will face, and remains relevant over time. And trust implies that we consistently deliver on the brand promise, both in terms of support systems and acting in accordance with the values."

To build up our organization's leadership capability, we also have to think critically about our leadership pipeline. It is easy to fixate on the top 200 and on external recruitment while neglecting the feeder ranks of mid-level executives in whom we have already invested, but who can slip away more or less unnoticed. We have to expand our view of talent to harness the leadership potential throughout our workforce.[30] As Professor Dan Denison puts it, "The leadership pipeline is like other supply chains. It is vulnerable to similar trends and uncertainties. We have to critically examine the shortages, the bottlenecks and the leakages. And we need to come up with innovative responses. We can't just tweak our existing HR practices and rebrand them as talent management."

Having diagnosed the weaknesses in our talent pipeline, we have to find ways to help those up-and-coming leaders to learn and develop. This requires a shift in focus from individual learning to organizational learning; from improving individual abilities to improving the capabilities of the business as a whole.[31] Professor Shlomo Ben-Hur asserts, "We have to create an organizational culture that supports learning about development, that enables it, encourages it and rewards it, that makes it an integral part of what we do day in day out."

> *We have to expand our view of talent to harness the leadership potential throughout our workforce.*

We can measure an organizational capability by its efficiency at converting inputs into outputs.[32] The same is true of leadership development. Professor Pasha Mahmood comments, "Several metrics could be used to gauge improvements in an organization's leadership capability, such as an increasing 'yield-rate' of moving people from functional or project roles to general management; fewer derailers from new leadership positions; or a reduced outflow of key leadership talent."

DO   FIX THE FOUNDATIONS

Developing leaders is expensive and difficult for companies. We must enhance personal performance as well as put in place collective processes that facilitate learning, develop behaviors, cultivate culture, allow feedback and opportunities for practice. By taking a systemic view of leadership development, we can build a hard-to-replicate source of human resource-based competitive advantage.

Of course, there are shortcuts if we do not want to invest in grooming our own leaders – by poaching from others. Yet, these shortcuts generate costs and complications of their own, demanding careful selection, attractive compensation and additional investments in onboarding and acculturation,

> *By taking a systemic view of leadership development, we can build a hard-to-replicate source of human resource-based competitive advantage.*

as well as augmenting the risks of failure.[33] Professor Preston Bottger notes, "Integrating mid-career 'stars' can be especially tricky in terms of fit. As bosses, we face the dilemma of introducing newcomers who should mesh easily with the existing culture versus profiles who may challenge us and 'add spice' to the mix. You need to think about fit with you, fit with the team and fit with the organization as a whole."

If we want to upgrade our leadership development model, we need to revisit and reintegrate four elements that many companies misunderstand: rotation, feedback, systems and commitment.

Rotate right

The most common way to prepare executives for leadership is to give them accelerated experience across different domains, by rotating them through a series of projects, functions, lines of business or geographies. Different kinds of assignments are associated with different kinds of learning and one of our biggest challenges is matching people's development needs with the right leadership challenges.[34] Professor Ben Bryant cautions, "We have to beware of burdening growing leaders with too many challenges at once, for example by combining changes in scale, business and country all at once. It can be a fine line between an assignment that stretches and one that overwhelms."

> *We do have to beware of burdening growing leaders with too many challenges at once. It can be a fine line between an assignment that stretches and one that overwhelms.*

Clearly, some companies do not have the same range of leadership-enriching assignments to offer executives. This was precisely the problem faced by a group of government-linked companies in Malaysia.[35] The six companies were all listed on the Malaysian stock exchange and seen as strategic to the country's long-term economic interests, but they all suffered from the same problem: unlike large multinationals, they could not offer their rising stars much in the way of exposure to different business environments, either in terms of industry or geography. This was a problem both for the development and retention of their best talents. The six companies responded by banding together and creating an exchange program to broaden the experience of their leaders, alert them to best practices in different industries and accelerate their development. Professor Francisco Szekely notes, "After some teething problems, relating to fear of poaching and reluctance to release talents, the scheme has been expanded. They recognized that the incoming leader brought different ideas as well as gaining new experience and adapting. But they also realized that the incoming leader had to put more faith in the existing team, which is also good for *their* development."

Because job rotations are costly, we cannot afford too many mismatches. Beyond the novelty of the responsibilities, we also have to consider the nature of the assignment. Even executives with broad exposure to multiple functions or businesses can have limited experience with different types of situation. The challenges of promotion and leading former peers are quite different from those associated with launching an activity, conducting a turnaround or realigning an organization that is heading for trouble.[36]

> *Organizations can help transitioning leaders to leverage the time prior to switching jobs by providing them with coaching support to diagnose the situation they are walking into.*

In the past, we often adopted a "sink or swim" approach to such challenges, but that has proved too wasteful a strategy. Organizations can provide more systematic support to help leaders improve their success rate in transitions. Professor Michael Watkins expands, "Organizations can help transitioning leaders to leverage the time prior to switching jobs by providing them with information, access and coaching support to diagnose the situation they are walking into, the relationships they need to build, the resources they need to secure and the expectations they need to set." Such measures can help to reduce the risk of derailment and speed up time to performance.

Intensify feedback

A key to navigating and learning from stretch assignments is regular corrective input. Paradoxically, deep self-awareness requires the help of others. To develop, leaders need feedback, however biased, cutting or irrelevant it may appear.[37] Professor John Weeks elaborates, "Leaders have to learn not just how to *give* feedback in a way that is constructive and palatable but also how to *receive* feedback and extract value even from low quality remarks. Criticism that seems wide of the mark can nevertheless say a lot about people's perceptions, attitudes or assumptions. So a critical component of leadership development is learning how to filter and process negative feedback – and companies can help to build those skills." For example, we can set up coaching networks between unrelated peers based on their joint attendance of development programs. Their reciprocal feedback will not have the same threatening and judgmental connotation as feedback from bosses, direct reports or immediate colleagues.[38]

A critical component of leadership development is learning how to filter and process negative feedback – and companies can help to build those skills.

In companies, the more feedback opportunities we can provide or encourage, the faster we can expect leaders to improve. Over the past two decades, companies have increased the opportunities for executives to receive feedback from multiple sources (including outside the organization) as well as introducing coaching and mentoring programs, often juxtaposed with other organizational development programs and formal succession plans.

But the coaching strategies are often not well thought through and in spite of the efforts made, the anticipated results do not materialize – the programs do not deliver on their promise.[39] According to Professor Jack Wood, the problem often stems from a poor understanding of the distinct roles of manager, mentor and coach, "Each is occupied with different aspects of an executive's daily job, long-term career and life. Coaching from the boss is in the service of the executive's organizational task. The role of a mentor is to help guide the protégé's corporate career choices. The pair may discuss more personal and professional development needs, but within the context of the organization. By contrast, the coach must remain independent and be free to offer impartial counsel and guidance. Good coaching skills on the part of bosses and mentors are no substitute for external coaches, who can explore sensitive personal and professional topics."

Good coaching skills on the part of bosses and mentors are no substitute for external coaches, who can explore sensitive personal and professional topics.

An interesting case of redirected leadership coaching and development is the Swedish automaker Volvo.[40] To remedy a shortage of women in leadership positions, the company initially set up a management training program for female executives and assigned them older male executives as mentors. After several years, it became clear that while the measures had helped to integrate women in networks across the organization, they were having limited impact on the retention or advancement of women leaders. In response, Volvo took several additional actions, but this time aimed at men. It introduced the "Walk the Talk" program for its most senior executives, designed to change gender attitudes and to support women leaders.

Spread over 18 months and made up of 3-day modules, the 33-day program included "homework" assignments, such as interviewing women executives and experience exchange. Participants received coaching and were required to keep a personal journal to encourage self-reflection. They were also asked to choose, as opposed to being assigned, a female mentor who was sharply different from them in background and personality. Professor Martha Maznevski reflects, "It was a multifaceted coaching effort aimed at those with the power to model and cascade new patterns of behavior, and it was backed up by a change in selection policies whereby both genders had to be interviewed for managerial positions. Changing the focus and intensity of the feedback had a discernible effect on behavior and on women's progress through the executive ranks. And Volvo became an exemplar for other companies."

Sharing personality assessments as a team can help to identify potential trouble spots and blind spots.

Besides feedback to individuals, companies can also think about feedback to leadership teams.[41] A critical aspect of leadership development is learning to work effectively with others. Professor Ginka Toegel notes, "Sharing personality assessments as a team can help to identify potential trouble spots and blind spots. Within a team, both trait clustering and trait diversity are associated with characteristic benefits and drawbacks. People can work better on teams if they have a sense of their effect on others and make specific adjustments to their style. A team that is aware of its tendencies can take specific steps to leverage its strengths or to compensate for its potential vulnerabilities." Such feedback helps individuals to become better team players and improves team dynamics.

Synchronize systems

To raise our leadership development game and have an impact on performance, our efforts have to be aligned. The first challenge is to link our leadership development approach with our strategy. In too many cases, the leadership development activities and objectives are unrelated to the drivers of the business.[42] Professor

Bettina Büchel remarks, "We often see competency models that state the desired characteristics for leaders in a particular company. That list is supposedly unique. Yet when we display it alongside a set of generic traits, executives are hard pushed to identify which list belongs to *their* company. It's vital to identify which competencies – and there may only be a few – uphold strategic differentiation and to focus hard on those."

Transforming our leadership development approach also requires us to realign our support systems: our metrics, evaluations and incentives; our selection policies and succession plans; as well as our internal and external communications. If we are serious about leadership development, it should be visible in our performance management systems. Recent studies indicate that barely 7% of organizations hold their executives accountable for developing their reports and that only a tenth hold a regular talent review with their boards.[43] Executives have to be recognized and rewarded for developing others, not just themselves. Professor Shlomo Ben-Hur comments, "At Bharti Airtel [the Indian telecom services giant], business heads are evaluated on a talent development index that considers high performer attrition and how often talent moves to another unit. And at American Express, up to a quarter of an executive's variable pay depends on success in developing talent. Beyond pay, it's really about who are the leaders we celebrate – those who deliver the numbers or those who bring people through and seed the rest of the organization with talent from their areas?"

We also need to create a support infrastructure, such as networking facilities and shared platforms – systems that promote learning and exchange.[44] A novel example is the case of Disney.[45] The company decided to publish the ratings and comments on every one of its learning programs on the intranet, encouraging attendees to go online and post their views about the relevance, utility and impact of the learning. Professor Ben-Hur notes, "It was a clever way of using technology to market its learning products and also to better serve its internal customers, effectively crowdsourcing developmental suggestions for executives."

> *Who are the leaders we celebrate? Those who deliver the numbers or those who bring people through and seed the rest of the organization with talent from their areas?*

Building leadership as an organizational capability is a long-haul effort, and one that requires regular investments. Take the case of Vanke, China's largest listed property developer.[46] When the property market was booming, Vanke was among the first Chinese companies to create its own leadership center. Each year, it brought in its top managers for leadership training and for discussions on their personal development. Professor Winter Nie expands, "Vanke's efforts were recently recognized by *Fortune* magazine, which named it as one of its top companies for leadership. The property market difficulties of the past couple of years led the company to cut investments in several areas, but significantly, not in leadership development. The top management holds a profound belief that leadership capability is the key to the company's continued growth and success." The acid test for our commitment to leadership development, and what employees notice most, is what happens when times are tough.

> *The acid test for our commitment to leadership development, and what employees notice most, is what happens when times are tough.*

To get real value out of leadership development, we have to take a joined-up approach that spans across HR systems, and also integrates IT, marketing and communication systems.[47] The return on that investment takes time to materialize, but we can nevertheless try to identify areas where it is making a measurable difference.[48] As Professor Ben-Hur puts it, "We can establish both leading and lagging metrics that are commercially relevant to our business, including engagement, intention to leave and pipeline capability levels."

The more attention we pay to leadership development outputs, the more likely it is that leaders and managers will own and actually invest time in talent management and development.

Convey commitment

The preceding recommendations of course contribute to creating a culture of leadership development and learning. But two additional factors have disproportionate symbolic impact: establishing a meeting place for development and actively involving the top team.

The venue for leadership development may be real or virtual, internal or outsourced, a program or an event, but we need a focal point that captures the essence of what we are trying to achieve and that underlines our commitment, in terms of time, energy and money.

An impressive example is the case of Nike.[49] In 2011, the sporting apparel giant overhauled its fragmented approach to learning – not just leadership development – by creating a centralized learning function called NikeU. The ambiguous name was chosen to evoke learning, but at the same time served to promote inclusiveness and aspirations; the letter U could stand for *you*, for *us*, for *unleashing* potential, for *unconventional* learning and for *unlimited* capability. NikeU developed its own intranet site, applying the language of sport and competition to learning and development, using terms like "muscle memory," development "tracks" and "The Coach's Gym Bag" to designate different tools and resources. Professor Ben-Hur elaborates, "The spirit of NikeU is very much in line with the Nike brand, dynamic, inventive and leveraging the company's sporting roots. NikeU has also created a depository of inspirational stories featuring leaders from across the organization explaining how they created change, won over a client or solved a particular business problem. It's a kind of 'learning on demand' approach." The learning brand both extends and reinforces the corporate brand.

The other unmistakable sign of our commitment to leadership development is the level and breadth of senior leadership involvement.[50] Leaders have a crucial role to play in modeling a learning orientation. Professor George Kohlrieser explains, "The most powerful organizational transformations occur when members of the leadership team get personally involved, not just showing up for the kick-off and the debrief, but actually taking part in the journey, sharing their own stories and challenges, making themselves vulnerable and open to personal change."

> *The most powerful organizational transformations occur when members of the leadership team get personally involved, not just showing up for the kick-off and the debrief.*

For example, as part of the transformation of the Indian tech company HCL Technologies, its newly promoted CEO started posting his own 360-degree feedback on the company intranet, showing his own desire to learn and improve as a leader, and prompting 2,000 executives to follow suit. Such actions have more impact than words or exhortations in changing the culture.[51] As Professor Robert Hooijberg puts it, "CEOs often claim to be committed to developing leaders, but their agendas often tell a different story. Those at the very top need to embody the transformation effort, not just as participants but also as teachers."

TALENT TRAPS   AVOID

Leadership development is to some extent an act of faith. It is based on the premise that through a judicious combination of stretch assignments, learning projects, training programs and coaching interventions, we can nurture talent. It is a slow build with no guarantee that the talent will stay or that that the competencies we set out to develop are the ones actually needed 10 years down the road. In terms of managing talent, we have to be particularly mindful of three traps.

Whistle-stop tours

Although job assignments are widely considered to be the richest form of leadership development, they often fall short of their potential.

The danger, when whisking emerging leaders through multiple assignments, is that they do not stay in place long enough to experience the full business cycle associated with the job. As a result, they fail to develop a full appreciation of either the detail or the big picture of these areas. Critically, they might never have to live with the consequences of their decisions, or get a chance to draw the necessary conclusions.[52] Professor Preston Bottger observes, "Executives have to stay in each job long enough for their failures, as well as their quick wins, to show up. When we rotate them too often, they become experts at just one thing – starting new initiatives. And there is limited incentive for them to invest in developing their people."

> *Executives have to stay in each job long enough for their failures, as well as their quick wins, to show up.*

One practice that militates against learning from experience is our tendency to transfer individuals from one assignment to the next without even a break in between. This leaves executives no time to think about the new role and which of their acquired skills and competencies will be portable.[53] Professor Maury Peiperl notes, "People are sometimes expected to handle the new job, while still handling bits of the old job. They have no time to reflect on what they've learned and they are immediately in catch-up mode on the new job."

Another contributor to this "half-baked" learning is the lack of systematic post-assignment reviews to articulate what was really learned and how it adds to the executive's experience base and mental models. Good bosses do this spontaneously, but many bosses don't, so we need a system to make sure it happens. One or more senior executives can work with the developing executive to review the choices made (or missed) and the key lessons generated from the completed assignment. Though expensive, this exercise is often the most critical aspect of the experience in terms of capturing and leveraging the learning.

One alternative to frequent rotation is to make more use of short-term work assignments. Executives stay in their jobs, but take on additional assignments outside their field of expertise or interest, as successfully practiced by pharmaceutical giant Eli Lilly.

Entitlement effects

High potential programs can signal to crucial individuals that they are particularly valued. But these programs are not easy to execute and can have unwanted side effects. By focusing on a restricted pool of talented individuals and grooming them for leadership responsibilities, we risk fostering a sense of entitlement. Anointing people early on and in a quasi-irreversible fashion can create outsized expectations, encouraging them to believe that they have automatic ascension rights. Those selected may decide to move on if they feel they are not advancing fast enough or they may become complacent and stop investing in their own learning.

By focusing on a restricted pool of talented individuals and grooming them for leadership responsibilities, we risk fostering a sense of entitlement.

Successful leadership development demands continuous learning. Having been formally designated as talent, high potentials may underestimate the self-development efforts required to maintain momentum.[54] Professor Ginka Toegel remarks, "The majority of effective leaders that we have observed or studied over the years, even 'naturals' like Richard Branson and PepsiCo's Indra Nooyi, have worked hard on themselves. Moving up the hierarchy into new roles or environments, fast trackers may be surprised to find that previous strengths – such as assertiveness or attention to detail – can unexpectedly turn into liabilities."

In addition to the risk of entitlement, talent programs can also breed a sense of frustration among those *not* selected. The problem is often rooted in our understanding of leadership and how broadly we define talent.[55] Professor Ben Bryant expands, "Some companies take an unnecessarily restrictive view of leadership talent. It's not just that they focus too closely on a minority; they also have a narrow view of who is eligible to join that pool. It can prove very divisive simply because relatively few people can even aspire to those places."

More important than the size of the talent pool are the criteria for entering or leaving it and the transparency of the process. The overriding reason that we remain discreet about who is on the list is that the process itself is difficult to justify because it is overly subjective or even unfair.

Some companies have addressed this problem by making membership of the high-potential group conditional on annual contributions that far exceed those expected of peers who are not in the high potential group.[56] Professor Preston Bottger expands, "Pepsi International came up with an interesting approach, requiring high-potentials to take on three additional projects per year. If they failed to deliver, they fell out of the program, though they could also be readmitted if they showed they could contribute at high levels, the point being that they had to continue to prove themselves worthy of responsibility in order to be recipients of rewards."

Cookie-cutter cures

We must beware of viewing talent management as the "responsibility of HR," but nor should we entrust it entirely to the business units.

It is easy to understand why we might opt to delegate talent management. Line managers are close to their people and can detect their real strengths and areas for improvement, as well as what makes them tick. This is critical for retention purposes. To keep high performers engaged, we really need to get to know what interests them, what irritates them, what keeps them here and what they want to achieve.[57] Professor Bottger observes, "The unit leader is best placed to determine what matters most to those we can't afford to lose – and to provide it. The nature of the deal is bound to differ from one person to the next."

> *We must beware of viewing talent management as the "responsibility of HR," but nor should we entrust it entirely to the business units.*

The big risk when leaving talent management exclusively to the operating managers is that they have neither the overview nor the incentives to make optimal decisions for the company or the individuals concerned. High performers are likely to be overrepresented in the talent pool at the expense of true "high potentials." And the development opportunities may be more geared to the short-term needs of the business unit than the lasting health of the organization. When we are judged on quarterly results, it takes courage to give people stretch assignments that carry a nontrivial risk of failure. And when those people surmount the challenge, the temptation is to keep them rather than making them available to other units. Of course, such sacrifices are more easily accepted when the company

> *High performers are likely to be overrepresented in the talent pool at the expense of true "high potentials."*

recognizes and rewards the development of others, and when there are strong norms of reciprocity between units – meaning that we do not ship out B players expecting stars in return.

The rationale for centralizing talent management is that these individuals represent a long-term corporate asset and must be managed accordingly. Our HR function can take a more objective and systemic view of supply and demand. It can make an aggregated assessment of the business-critical roles for the organization, the critical gaps and the lead times to prepare replacements. Moreover, if HR takes care of these people issues, then our line managers should have more time to concentrate on business issues and client interaction.

Line managers are sometimes too busy to pick up on signals of disengagement in key personnel. For that reason, one global corporation introduced "career stewards" in China to meet with rising stars, check their engagement and help them set realistic career expectations. Such measures ensure that talent does not slip through the cracks for want of attention. But centralized systems can also create problems of their own.

The risk of letting HR run everything is that it tends to let line managers off the hook for developing people. Indeed, having established sophisticated talent programs and processes, Shell itself found that it needed to redress the balance. Its head of leadership development, Paddy Coyne, commented, "There are many examples of leaders in Shell who personally develop their people, but over time it had become kind of optional. We are now shifting dramatically towards saying it is no longer optional. It's part of your day job as a leader. It will be encouraged, it will be supported, it will be measured. Your track record in developing your people will be something that determines your own career progression."[58]

> *One corporation introduced "career stewards" to meet with rising stars and ensure that talent does not slip through the cracks for want of attention.*

Developing a successful approach to talent management requires us to reconcile big picture needs with responsiveness to individual needs, to develop systems while also promoting individual accountability, and to encourage people to not only develop themselves as leaders but also to develop others.

Achieving that balance is an ongoing challenge, and one that also applies to our talent sourcing strategy.[59] As Professor Maury Peiperl puts it, "We have to plan for uncertainty, which means being flexible, and that in turn involves looking for talent in all sorts of different places around the world and creating talent pools that may be virtual. This network of virtual talent pools allows us to be agile and responsive, even proactive, when facing change and potential opportunities. But planning for uncertainty is a challenge for many HR and mobility managers, accustomed as they are to stable structures."

PAYOFF	RESETTING GENERAL ELECTRIC'S LEADERSHIP MACHINE

General Electric (GE) has long been admired for its leadership development capability. With innovative practices, disciplined processes and an annual development budget exceeding $1 billion, it produced endless waves of capable leaders, many of them courted by companies in unrelated industries. But the global financial crisis of 2008–2009 led the company to question how well it was equipping its next generation of leaders for a context of growing volatility and complexity.[60] Professor Shlomo Ben-Hur elaborates, "GE took a good look at itself and [in 2009] dispatched 35 participants from its most senior leadership development course to visit 100 organizations around the world – including Google, West Point and China's Communist Party – to gather views on how others were developing leaders.

GE despatched 35 participants from its most senior leadership development course to visit 100 organizations around the world – including Google, West Point and China's Communist Party – to gather views on how others were developing leaders.

It also invited an eclectic bunch of 'thought leaders' to stimulate reflection and debate, and after 18 months was ready to implement its new plan." GE's revamped approach to leadership development included changes to revered practices on all four fronts highlighted earlier in this chapter.

Job rotation has long been one of the pillars of GE's approach to leadership development. Its big advantage as a conglomerate is that it can offer a range of experiences – with businesses from light bulbs to jet engines to medical scanners – that few companies can match. New postings were systematically used to test the mettle of aspiring leaders. But the practice of putting promising executives through short stints in multiple units was deemed to have swung too far, with some switching jobs every two years. The revised thinking redressed the balance, placing more emphasis on deeper customer relationships and industry expertise. GE now leaves senior leaders in place for longer in order to promote accountability and to let executives see a business cycle through.

Honest feedback and regular communication were greatly emphasized under former CEO Jack Welch. He insisted that people development was a daily event, not something that happened once a year in performance reviews. Employees had to be clear on where they needed to improve and where they stood in the organization. GE developed a culture with a high tolerance for straight feedback and strong norms of internal coaching. By contrast, external coaching was mainly reserved for executives in need of remedial help. Among the changes that accompanied the revamp, Jeff Immelt launched a pilot program to bring in personal coaches for high-potential talent, thus taking a more proactive approach and recognizing the different coaching contributions of bosses and external specialists.

Systems alignment is fundamental for the company that initiated the whole Six Sigma movement. The view that "everything is process" inevitably extended to leadership development. An intense internal review process known as "Session C" ensured that leadership talent was identified and lined up for training opportunities or cross-functional moves. Leaders were judged on *what* they delivered and *how* they delivered it, and outstanding performance was rewarded with big bonuses, with special emphasis on decisiveness and positive energy, as well as the abilities to energize and execute. What became apparent was that GE was overly focused on implementation, and not enough on growth. While retaining the strong emphasis on metrics and performance, the content of the evaluation criteria had shifted. The company identified a new set of leadership traits that would be vital to creating new businesses and expanding into new markets: external focus, clear thinking, imagination and courage, inclusiveness and expertise. It is against these "growth values" that leaders are now assessed and rewarded.

Commitment to leadership development has been core to GE's strategy for decades. It was epitomized by the company's investment in Crotonville, not only as a facility but also as a brand in its own right. Crotonville developed a cutting-edge reputation as a pioneer of the "leaders teaching leaders" model as well as innovative practices and concepts such as the "work-out" program, "action learning projects" and the "teachable point of view." In spite of the mystique around Crotonville, GE was still prepared to "re-imagine" the entire set-up, and indeed to question its very existence. The thoroughness with which GE tackled the task – and the resultant

> *In spite of the mystique around Crotonville, GE was still prepared to "re-imagine" the entire set-up, and indeed to question its very existence.*

changes to the curriculum content, to the physical environment and to the learning experience – merely underlined the company's commitment to leadership development.

Of course, that commitment has been matched by the engagement of the top team, starting with the CEO. Like Jack Welch before him, Jeff Immelt considers developing people to be one of his two key responsibilities, along with driving change. Immelt reckons that he devotes one-third of his time to leadership development. As Professor Ben-Hur explains, "Immelt's leadership style is quite different from that of Welch, who tended to be more impatient and abrasive. But what they have in common is a strong willingness to experiment and challenge the status quo. They also share a similar belief in development. Both were actively engaged at Crotonville, and both found the time to discuss each of the top 600 executives each year with the head of HR."

It will take years to assess whether GE has indeed made the right choices in terms of developing a new generation of leaders. But the company has shown an impressive willingness to critique a model that did not look broken, but showed signs of not meeting future needs, and then to retool.

As shown by the case of GE, developing leaders is not a program, but a journey. The best exponents continually review their approach to try to make it more inclusive, more integrated and better aligned to the skills needed by the next generation of leaders.

3

The Quest for Global Leadership Development

" In difficult times, developing people is even more important than in better times. Like most companies, we have a lot of people development programs for the middle management and top management group. But at the moment, our most important leadership program is our 'supervisory training program,' where we develop the leadership skills of our first-line managers. We have more than a thousand offices in different parts of the world. And the teams of the leaders in these small offices work with customers all the time. So the role of these leaders is truly...

Matti Alahuhta,
KONE Chairman and CEO of KONE Corporation

Where Do We Stand?

1. Do we have a competency model that is shared across business, geographic and functional units?

2. What systems do we need to align to have a robust leadership development approach?

3. To what extent do senior managers share honest performance and behavioral feedback with one another?

4. Do we use HR, IT, marketing and communications systems to support talent management?

5. Do we have a succession plan for the top quartile of our leadership?

6. Does the top management team invest time and effort to coach the next generation of leaders?

7. To what extent do line managers own the leadership development process?

4

The Quest for
Global
Solutions

❝ In the past, the idea was to make more and
better products. Now, we do not provide a product
to customers, but a solution. In the past, selling
an item was the end of the sales process. Now,
selling an item is the *beginning* of the sales process.
Eventually, we want to turn Haier from a product
manufacturer to a service provider. ❞

Zhang Ruimin, CEO of Haier[1]

LESSONS FROM COMMODITIES

Oil is the most valuable traded commodity in the world. But what ranks second? Surprisingly, the answer is not gold or silver, but coffee.[2] Its historical spread as a beverage offers a fascinating take on the notion of "solution selling."

Introduced into Europe in the mid-17th century, coffee quickly became a popular beverage, particularly in Britain. Forty years later, there were some 2,000 coffee houses in London alone. Today, people sometimes wonder how Starbucks can charge such high prices for a drink that can be made at home or bought from another store for a fraction of the price. CEO Howard Schultz responds, "Our product is a lot more than coffee. Customers choose to come to us for three reasons: our coffee, our people and the experience in our stores."[3] It is a response that would have resonated with the 17th century coffee-house owners.

The appeal of the first coffee houses was in part due to the novelty and alleged health benefits of the drink. But the real pull lay elsewhere. Compared to the rival pubs and taverns, which were often rowdy and unpleasant, coffee houses encouraged sobriety, dialogue and deliberation. They became the venues of choice for people wishing to exchange ideas and do business. For the price of a penny, patrons gained access not just to a drink of coffee but also to the latest news, and could participate in or listen to sharp social debate.

Some coffee house owners went one better, catering for the needs of a particular clientele by providing additional services. Jonathan's coffee house issued a list of stock and commodity prices that attracted brokers and gave birth to the London Stock Exchange. Edward Lloyd provided free information on shipping in his coffee house, which later evolved into the insurance underwriters Lloyd's of London. And the great auction houses Sotheby's and Christie's grew out of coffee houses that proposed the use of salesrooms to hold auctions.

More than three centuries ago, coffee was the glue to the social networks that then spawned organizations, much like the internet does today. Coffee was really a proxy for networking. Coffee houses succeeded because they tapped into an unmet customer need (for serious exchange) and sold an experience (social, economic and intellectual stimulation), not just a rush of coffee.

Yet, making the transition from selling commodities to selling services or experiences is not easy. Even for companies that succeed, it can prove a surprisingly arduous journey. Take the classic case of IBM.[4] In the space of two decades, IBM has evolved from a seller of mainframe and personal computers to a provider of IT-related solutions, designed to help companies meet their business objectives.

The shift to selling solutions is not for the fainthearted.

Today, more than half of IBM's workforce is in the services business as opposed to selling hardware or software. But leading this transformation from products to global solutions has required some major strategic and psychological adjustments. Professor John Weeks notes, "IBM's leaders had to acquire service firms whose employees then had to be integrated into Big Blue's famously insular culture. They also had to implement painful cuts in IBM's US workforce and drive a dramatic change in mindset because the service arm could not compete if it proposed only IBM products."

The original coffee house experience

Clearly, the shift to selling solutions is not for the fainthearted. So what pushes companies across industries to embark on this journey?

The defensive goal is to decommoditize; the offensive goal is to leverage expertise more effectively.

When "solutions" provide the answer

The impetus to become a solution provider rather than just a supplier of products and services has two primal drivers: survival and growth. The defensive goal is to decommoditize; the offensive goal is to leverage expertise more effectively.

The threat of commoditization

Some companies are facing the "commoditization trap." Margins on standardized standalone products are shrinking. Cut-price rivals (or aggressive new intermediaries) with "good enough" products and services are stealing market share from premium brands.[5]

This is what happened to Australia-based Orica Mining Services.[6] The product differentiation that had fueled its growth in the commercial explosives industry began to erode. Initially, the company tried to distance itself from imitators by developing more sophisticated products for its customers, such as electronic firing systems that added precision and efficiency to the blasting process. But for many of its customers, these features were of limited appeal.

Professor Adrian Ryans explains, "At one point, Orica recognized that customers don't really want to buy explosives; what they are really buying is rock on the ground – in a quarry or a mine – that meets the customer's size specification."[7] So Orica's leaders switched strategy and started to take over the blasting activities from customers. Over time, the company developed deeper expertise in the different operating conditions of its customers around the world. It was then able to leverage that knowledge to improve the yields of its blasting solutions, creating even higher entry barriers for competitors trying to muscle in on its service business.

There were two further benefits. As customers became more reliant on Orica, they progressively lost their in-house blasting skills – indeed specialized blasting personnel were often transferred to Orica – making customers much more dependent on Orica than before. At the same time, the price of the service provided was less transparent than the standalone product, making Orica less vulnerable to price pressures. Its leaders transformed it from a fading products company into a global solution provider.

The lure of opportunity

Other companies are offering "solutions," drawn by the promise of longer-lasting and more profitable relationships with customers or access to new markets. This was the case for the French tire manufacturer Michelin.[8]

Through their own analysis and after discussion with their key clients, leaders at Michelin realized that one of the key drivers of productivity for a commercial vehicle was the condition of the tires. Tire-related issues, such as punctures and blow-outs, were the most frequent reason for a truck to break down. A truck's fuel consumption could be improved by as much as 20% by keeping tires in good condition. With these factors in mind, Michelin's leaders created an innovative business solution called Michelin Fleet Solutions.

Professor Wolfgang Ulaga comments, "Customers don't buy tires from Michelin, but rather the seamless functioning of their commercial vehicles; they buy productivity in the form of kilometers. So Michelin Fleet Services proposed an 'all-round hassle-free' service package, whereby clients delegated the management of their tire assets to Michelin for a three- to five-year period. By outsourcing tire management, logistics providers and bus operators gained peace of mind, and achieved better cost control with fewer breakdowns, lower fuel consumption, improved vehicle monitoring and reduced administrative burden. Transportation companies were able to turn tire-related costs into a variable cost."

Customers don't buy tires from Michelin, they buy productivity in the form of kilometers.

Of course, taking over the tire management process for customers meant rethinking the sales approach and realigning the organization in various ways. Michelin's leaders faced the challenge of educating the customer to reason differently: from a tangible offering (tire sales) to an intangible offering (tire productivity over its lifetime).[9] Then there was the question of internal education, because making the business case for such a solution and putting a price on it became much trickier. The transition also meant redesigning the entire supply chain and shaping new ways of working in order to deliver on that promise without alienating the traditional sales force.

It was a steep learning curve for Michelin. Within the company there is increasing realization that solution selling is a powerful way of locking in customers and increasing their switching costs. But now the competition has woken up to the idea, with Goodyear and Bridgestone beginning to experiment with selling "kilometers" as well. Yet, Michelin tires retain a genuine technological advantage that was difficult for customers to perceive or evaluate when they were just buying a tire, but which becomes clear when they are buying kilometers.

Many companies from the emerging economies were effectively born as "solution providers."

By contrast, many companies from the emerging economies were effectively born as "solution providers," picking up the labor-intensive or non-core activities of manufacturing, IT or accounting from established players. On the face of it, these outsourcing specialists have already made the transition. Yet, as their own costs rise, they are also becoming vulnerable to competition.[10] As Professor Howard Yu puts it, "The challenge for outsourcing firms is to keep moving up the value chain and to propose more complicated solutions that are harder for others to match."

When setting off on this journey, there are some things we need to think about, some things we need to do and some traps we need to avoid.

THINK   THE KILLER QUESTIONS

The question that precedes any meaningful discussion of "solution selling" is Theodore Levitt's famous provocation, "What business are you *really* in?"[11] He argued that businesses focused too much on selling products or services without reflecting on the underlying customer needs. For example, applying Levitt's logic to various companies, we could say that KONE is not in the lifts and escalators business but in the "people flow" business, Sony is not in the consumer electronics business but in the entertainment business, and Sweden's Assa Abloy is not in the locks business but in the "opening solutions" business.

Yet, deciding what business we are in is trickier than it seems. While we can all agree what a product is, defining a solution depends on how far we pull back and how abstract we want to get. For example, is Google in the information search business, the data harvesting business or, as its chairman Eric Schmidt puts it, "in the targeted advertising business"?[12] What, exactly, are customers buying from us?

So the initial question triggers a further set of questions.[13] As Professor Bettina Büchel observes, "Defining what business we are in also means establishing what businesses we are not in and which ones we should be in. We have to think about where we see ourselves in five to ten years and how big shifts could affect our business."

> *Defining what business we are in also means establishing what businesses we are not in and which ones we should be in.*

Our answers will affect the nature and pricing of our offering. They will influence what modes of expansion are most appropriate. They will guide recruitment, intelligence scanning and competitor analysis. They will shape resource allocation decisions and the type of metrics used. And they will create shared understanding that helps align tactical decision-making.

What makes a solution?

To counter commoditization and to command premium prices, we can push out in two directions.[14]

Bundling products and services into a single offer is one way we can create meaningful differentiation. The customer gets a "one-stop shop," benefiting from the speed and convenience of working with a single supplier, lower transaction costs and a more complete quality assurance for the augmented offer. For example, Home Depot added installation services to its DIY products to attract consumers looking for "do-it-for-me" solutions.[15] Of course, the value of the "bundled" whole must be well integrated to add up to more than the sum of its parts, otherwise competitors can easily disaggregate and undercut the offer.

Segmentation and customization is another way to create added value. By distinguishing more between different customer segments, we can adapt our offers around the particular, and often unmet, needs of those segments. Customers can benefit from differences in product specifications or service levels that are better suited to their requirements. For example, with its magnetic resonance imaging products, GE started targeting the specialist needs of cardiovascular, neurological and orthopedic groups.

The big challenge when trying to move into the solution business is that we need to push aggressively *on both* fronts at once. We must strive to address specific customer problems with well-integrated solutions (see **Figure 1**). We need to ask ourselves: "What is the customer headache that we can solve?"

Often, the answer implies stretching away from our core business and tapping into an underleveraged tacit competence.

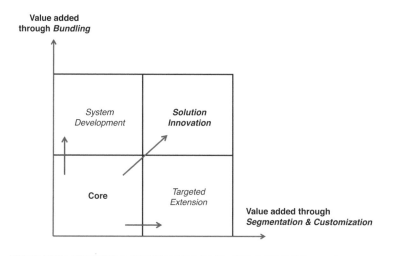

Figure 1: Moving into the solution zone   Source: Kamran Kashani[16]

Take the case of BASF, one of the world's largest producers of industrial paints.[17] In an effort to differentiate itself from cut-price competitors, it started offering start-to-finish painting solutions. Focusing on coatings for specialized applications and using its underexploited know-how in paints, it took over the paint shop operations of many large car makers, including Volkswagen and Ford. Besides technical advice and logistical support, it also supplies all the coating products specified by the customer, including those produced by competitors. The solution is tailored not only to the standard needs of the car maker but also to the specific requirements of each plant. This customized package makes a highly profitable contribution to BASF revenues.

The most common pattern is for industrial firms to augment their offering by adding services. But it is also possible for service-based companies to develop partnerships with product suppliers while also strengthening their own internal capabilities in systems integration.

> *Nestlé found a way to extract more value from ground coffee by creating a "solution" around it.*

The same framework also applies to consumer products. If we return to the example of coffee, the food giant Nestlé found a way to extract more value from ground coffee by creating a "solution" around it, but in a very different way from Starbucks.

The Nespresso business has taken a staple product and developed a system around it, by bundling it with individual-serving coffee capsules and a dedicated machine, hence pushing up on the vertical axis. At the same time, it has also moved out along the horizontal axis not only by offering a wide choice of espresso blends to suit different taste preferences but also by adding a service component. Customers who buy a machine automatically become members of the Nespresso Club, which offers free repair and return of machines as well as a replacement machine, during the time of the repair.[18]

The distribution system further reinforced this sense of exclusivity. Nespresso's leaders deliberately steered clear of mass channels like supermarkets, opting instead to create a direct link with consumers through online selling and call centers as well as through its upscale city-center boutiques. Over half of Nespresso's sales occur through word-of-mouth recommendations from existing customers who convert others. And the results have proved both spectacular and sturdy, with annual sales increasing by over 30%, even through the recession, making Nespresso the fastest growing of Nestlé's many brands.

Nespresso makes users feel special. What it really sells is an experience and a sense of community that goes beyond the product itself. Professor Kamran Kashani explains, "We tend to talk less about solutions for consumer products, but this is clearly an area where there is scope for growth. Many consumer goods companies underestimate the potential for creating systems that deliver better on customer needs and building a sense of experience into their business model."

Don't Overstretch the Brand	High Profile Failures
Your brand is what customers think you are, *NOT* what you say you are.	Kellogg's thought it sold "breakfast solutions" but could not shift its orange juice.
Beware of incoherence between a brand extension and what the brand embodies.	Bic thought it stood for "disposable convenience," but consumers shunned its perfume line.
Check that the "solution" proposed is focused and meaningful to customers.	Pen specialist Mont Blanc restyled itself as a "lifestyle" company but confused customers by selling everything from eyewear to fragrances.
Ensure the brand stretch brings value and differentiation compared to what exists.	Heinz thought it was in the "taste enhancement" business but flopped when it tried to extend its brand from ketchup to mustard.
Engage in brand building, *NOT* brand milking.	Pierre Cardin devalued the brand by lending its name to over 800 products, including toilet-seat covers.

Figure 2: Can the brand deliver on the solution   Source: Dominique Turpin[19]

Consumer goods companies often fool themselves into thinking that they are selling solutions when all they are really selling is an expanded brand proposition that does not offer *meaningful* value to the customer. (See **Figure 2** for some high-profile flops).

Defining the right solution is one challenge. But we then have to set up to deliver on it. This is where the journey becomes arduous. Only around a quarter of aspiring solution providers actually meet their targets. About the same number actually lose money, while the remainder achieve only modest returns.[20] They may generate higher revenues but their net profit margin goes down. So common is this pattern, that it even has a name: the "service paradox." [21]

> *Only around a quarter of aspiring solution providers actually meet their targets.*

DO	REWORK THE CUSTOMER INTERFACE

There is a tough learning process between deciding to deliver a solution and making it profitable. This is particularly the case for our sales people, who need to acquire new skills and perspectives.

New competencies

A product-oriented sales force is used to looking for customers whose needs match a standard offering. But delivering integrated and customized solutions requires a broader experience with more than just one product or service. It also requires a deep understanding of the customer's business processes. We now need sales people to work with customers in order to understand their problems before designing solutions.

Our sales people must understand and be able to educate buyers about the total cost of ownership and the tangible savings for customers in terms of labor, materials, energy, replacement costs and so forth. Indeed, they may face opposition to the solution from the buyers in the customer company who currently create the solutions "in-house" and hence fear for their jobs.

These can be stretching challenges for our product-oriented sales force.[22] As Professor Wolfgang Ulaga points out, "When we start selling solutions or experiences, we have to tell a different story, with different arguments tailored to different customers. We have to talk about value not features and we need to be

> *When we start selling solutions, we have to tell a different story, with different arguments tailored to different customers.*

able to talk about the client's business model. So our whole sales approach must change."

Intensive retraining and new sales tools can help to prepare our sales people for the new challenge. But the gap may be too wide for some of them and sizeable staff changes are often unavoidable (as happened at IBM).

We may need to recruit new talent from the companies we are targeting. We may also need to upgrade the caliber of the sales people since they now need to sell to decision-makers who sit two or three levels higher in the organization than the buyers of traditional standalone products. The larger the deals, the more the seller's experience and credibility play a decisive role.

The new demands have an impact on the nature and duration of the sales process. Deals take more time to conclude because of the diagnostic work upfront, which means that our sales teams must be more skilled and better coordinated.

We need to develop and reinforce these new competencies through changes to the reward system. Our performance metrics should recognize customer-focused behavior by measuring customer satisfaction, not just revenues. And our incentives must support the longer sales cycles related to larger deals. Short-term sales targets will torpedo a long-term customer focus. We need to reward sellers who nurture existing relationships, not just those who pull in new customers. We also need to recognize the team-based efforts required to develop solutions, with rewards flowing fairly to all involved, not just to the department that happens to book the revenue.

The customer relationship evolves from a sales relationship managed by a sales person, to a partnership managed by a business manager (with the sales specialist providing support).

New mindset

More generally, our sales force must adopt a new mindset, from a hunter mentality to a farmer mentality (see **Figure 3**). As solution providers, we take on responsibility not only for the performance of our products but also for the customers' business outcomes. We need to think about customers' profitability, not just our own. "Client success" means developing a long-term relationship and having "skin in the game," which has implications for the structure of the contract.

As solution providers, we accept responsibility for and associate ourselves with

As solution providers, we must ensure that our metrics reflect how the customer measures success.

The Old Ground Rules		The New Ground Rules
Pushing a menu of solutions	➜	Defining/solving customer problems
Content is king	➜	Contact is king
Cost-plus pricing	➜	Determining willingness to pay
Making the sale	➜	Boosting the relationship
Meeting quality standards	➜	Meeting customer needs
Customer support as cost	➜	Customer support as investment
Using product metrics	➜	Using customer business metrics

Figure 3: From producer to service provider   Source: Stefan Michel[23]

outcomes that are of real relevance to the customer, as opposed to internally defined quality standards. Our metrics should reflect how the *customer* measures success. For example, when BASF took over the paint shop operations of auto plants, it started charging according to the number of painted cars that passed the quality checks, as opposed to paint volumes.[24] This seems like a win-win solution.

Yet we also have to ensure that the additional expense involved in proposing and implementing a solution is offset by the additional revenues recouped over time. We have to be rigorous in aggregating the full costs of the solution as well as in assessing the *value* of the solution for the customer. Again, this calls for a mindset shift. While products are often priced on a "cost-plus" basis, our solutions should be priced according to the customer's willingness to pay.[25]

The perceived value of the solution will differ between customers. Professor John Walsh explains, "In order to price optimally, you need to understand what value the customer is getting and what costs you are taking out of their system. That's a lot harder to calculate than the value they were getting from the product." For example, when Orica takes over a mining company's blasting needs, it also reduces the labor, operational and capital costs by varying amounts. In addition to those savings, the solution may bring revenue enhancement opportunities (based, for example, on quality improvements). Making a meaningful assessment of the overall economic benefits for the customer requires deep understanding of the customer's processes and may call for the joint input of technical and operational people, not just sellers and marketers.

Customers who buy solutions do not expect a complex menu of offerings based on different permutations of products, services and service guarantees. They expect a joint effort that involves diagnosing the problem, finding a solution, innovation, implementation and long-term use.[26] In contrast to the old approach, this means that the sale does not really start until the contract is signed.

Of course, to deliver true solutions, it is not just the sales function that has to be aligned with that focus or opportunity, but the entire organization. As a solution provider, we must measure the value delivered to a client instead of counting merely the sales volume. The case of Swedish ball bearings manufacturer SKF highlights the far-reaching consequences of global solutions. Having become the leading player in its field, SKF started facing intense competition from lower-cost producers based in Asia. SKF's leaders changed the company's mindset to solution selling: SKF would shift from selling bearings to helping customers reduce or eliminate machinery downtime. The company created a computer-based solution-selling tool, Documented Solutions Program (DSP), which compared best practice data from SKF customers around the world. Following a DSP assessment, sales people could draft a customer guarantee specifying a minimum ROI from projected savings from using SKF's services. As Professor Kamran Kashani remarks, "DSP was critical to helping the sales people to go from talking about customer value to actually measuring it and delivering it. You have to document value in order to get paid for it."

The goal is no longer to clinch the deal, but to strengthen the customer relationship, increase customer loyalty and secure customer profitability. As Professor Stefan Michel puts it, "The sale becomes a catalyst for the innovation process and the implementation of the customer solution, not just a link between the product (offer) and the customer (need)."

REALIGNMENT FAILURES   AVOID

Not all companies that reposition themselves as solution providers succeed.[27] Professor Michel notes, "The effort often turns out to be unsatisfactory for one party or the other. Customers complain that they don't really receive a solution, just more complex sets of offers. And companies complain that the associated costs outweigh the additional income."

A core failing, in many cases, is underestimating the degree of change needed in the rest of the organization. Establishing the necessary sales capability and pricing levels is critical, but other barriers can prevent us from making money on solutions. Organizational inefficiencies can easily eat up the improved margins.

To deliver profitable solutions, we also have to reconfigure the internal workings of the firm for more coordinated and cooperative action. In broad terms, we must realign our organization and our culture.

Reorganization failures

A common reason for not getting the returns we expect from solutions is because we try to preserve the historical power structure while adding an integrative solution to the offers, which cuts across the traditional organizational turfs. It is difficult to create "seamless solutions" if our critical competencies remain located in silos, whether product-based, functional or geographical.

It is difficult to create "seamless solutions" if our critical competencies remain located in silos, whether product-based, functional or geographical.

All too often, we respond to complex customer needs by creating a division or adding a cross-divisional layer that integrates our diverse offerings. This structural arrangement transcends silos rather than breaking them up. As a result, it is prone to cause internal tensions. To establish credibility with customers, the solutions unit might have to offer (or even recommend) rival products, as in the case of BASF when it ran the paint lines on behalf of auto makers, and IBM when the services division had to be able to propose Microsoft and HP offerings in order to be taken seriously as a solution provider. Internal competition can lead to protectionist behavior from the existing silos and a reluctance to engage with or support sales teams that might sell something other than the firm's offerings.

Regardless of the structure we adopt, top management must find ways of leveraging back-office knowledge and resources. The front-end units develop, package and deliver the solutions, while the back-end units supply modules that can be configured in different ways. Professor Phil Rosenzweig observes, "The quality of the connections between front and back-end, even if they are organized very differently, is critical to delivering fast, value-adding and profitable solutions."

The aim is to standardize back-end processes while maintaining front-end customization.[28] We cannot create customized solutions from scratch each time. It takes too long and costs too much. Assembling pre-developed modules cuts costs and improves reliability. Our back-end units are therefore responsible for designing components that can be easily worked into different solutions.

It is not just a one-way process. Our front-end units must also pass back knowledge and validated new approaches so that these can be codified, shared and reused to upgrade existing modules. The costs of developing unique solutions can be recouped over time by reintegrating that knowledge into modules that can be replicated. The chief driver of profitable solutions is the speed with which we can convert one-off solutions into repeatable ones.

The chief driver of profitable solutions is the speed with which we can convert one-off solutions into repeatable ones.

Often, we also underestimate the extent to which we need to overhaul our supply chains. As solution providers, we need to develop or mesh two very different types of supply chains: one relating to products, the other to services.

Service supply chains are typically harder to manage than manufacturing supply chains. We have to deliver not only raw materials or finished products but also people, parts and infrastructure. The demand is less predictable and the expected speed of response is higher. Consider again the case of Orica. As a producer, its supply chain was geared to delivering enough explosives for just one day's blasting because of strict controls on the storage and handling of explosives on site. The orders were known in advance and Orica would deliver its products on the appointed day. When Orica moved into blasting *solutions*, its leaders had to transform its supply chain. Now, when a customer places an order, Orica sends a mobile manufacturing unit to mix the chemicals on site, and Orica's blasting specialists determine (with the client) the best mix for a particular blast on a particular day. The logistics of delivering a solution are hence very different, as are the necessary safety arrangements.

Cooperation failures

Even when we have reorganized the structure and operations to deliver solutions, we may fail to instill the necessary customer focus in the rest of the organization. Getting the back-end of the organization to support a solutions orientation also requires a radical shift in our culture, and many companies struggle to bridge that gap (see **Figure 4**).

We need to activate several levers in order to realign employee behaviors and mindsets around customer needs. There is little point in exhorting employees to be more collaborative and customer-focused if they are constantly running up against systems, working arrangements, incentives or competency deficiencies that constrain their actions.

A Product Culture	A Solution Culture
Siloed-thinking	Joined-up-thinking
Jargon-dominated	Common language
Centralized, bureaucratic	Flexible, responsive
Inward focus	Outward-looking
Process-driven	Market-driven
Customer orientation – make the sale	Client orientation – develop the relationship
Problem solvers	Problem finders

Figure 4: Moving to a solution culture: Mind the gap

Source: John Weeks and Jean-Louis Barsoux [29]

We may need to develop or acquire new competencies and capabilities to deliver customer-focused solutions. We will also have to replace processes and IT systems that do not support integration with knowledge-sharing processes that collect and build on client knowledge. The same goes for our HR and performance management systems. It is not just the sales force whose metrics and incentives we need to redesign. Rewards throughout the organization must support a solutions-focus and the satisfaction of front-end customers rather than endorsing individual and unit performance. Our leadership development practices need to push in the same direction. We must identify and develop leaders with a proven record of collaboration. We also need to develop leaders who have a good view of the company as an interconnected whole, which often means rotating executives through different areas and geographic regions. We send critical signals not only in the way we develop people but also with the promotion decisions we make.

> *We need to develop leaders who have a good view of the company as an interconnected whole.*

When we throw the spotlight on successful performers and reward them for their behaviors, people take note of whose achievements are celebrated – and whose achievements go unnoticed.[30] Professor Preston Bottger comments, "We have to show recognition for solutions-oriented actions, not only from the front-end 'stars' but also from the unsung heroes at the back-end."

Ultimately, cooperation can be facilitated, but it cannot be mandated. The key to promoting such a context is our top management example. Employees pay a lot of attention to what we, as leaders, say and do: The way we spend our time, the decisions we make, and the stories we tell, all serve to convey the behavior we value and expect from employees at all levels.[31]

Professor Wolfgang Ulaga warns, "A recurrent failing among companies that struggle with the move into solutions is lack of leadership commitment. We cannot take a hands-off approach. We need visible, vocal and continuous involvement from top management."

But this is trickier than it sounds. Consider the case of Xerox in the early 1990s, as it came under pressure from HP and Canon.[32] In 1993, Xerox's leaders decided to differentiate the company's offering by repositioning it as a provider of "document solutions." That meant building a sales force capable of consulting with clients about their "document needs" rather than pushing boxes. The slow progress in putting that vision into place persuaded the incoming CEO, Richard Thoman, to accelerate the pace in 1999. He reorganized the entire sales force into teams focused on the needs of specific industries. Unfortunately, he made the mistake of overhauling the structure *before* retraining the people, generating acute dissatisfaction among both staff and customers.

The fallout was such that Xerox nearly went bankrupt, costing Thoman his job (just 13 months into his tenure) and leaving the company in crisis. His successor, Anne Mulcahy pursued the strategy, but it took five years to return Xerox to profitability.

Again, the point is that switching to solutions is no guarantee of improved revenues and margins and, if badly handled, can actually precipitate a crisis.

We have highlighted some of the ways that companies get it wrong. Sometimes the solution itself is flawed (poor fit with the corporate identity/brand or insufficiently integrated and customized and therefore too easy to unbundle). At other times, the execution is to blame, with companies underestimating the necessary social and organizational changes or, in the case of Xerox, messing up the pace and sequencing.

PAYOFF	RETOOLING SOLUTIONS THE HILTI WAY

The concept of solution selling is often misappropriated for marketing purposes. It is not enough to package combinations of products and services and call them solutions. As solution providers, we must identify and fulfill a customer need. True solutions therefore impact our business model and force us to rethink the fundamentals of our organization, not just make cosmetic changes. The case of the Liechtenstein-based power tools manufacturer Hilti highlights the far-reaching consequences of a shift from products to global solutions as well as the associated benefits.[33]

> *It is not enough to package combinations of products and services and call them solutions.*

Having become the leading high-end player in its field through innovation, Hilti started facing intense price competition. Instead of haggling over prices, Hilti's leaders decided to reconceptualize the business, not selling power tools but ensuring productivity to its core customers: construction workers and their site managers. The Hilti brand is much loved by customers because of its promise of reliable performance.[34] Hilti leverages its deep expertise in the use of its tools – traditionally, close to 60% of its workforce is involved in field sales – to help customers to get the most out of their power tool investments, in other words, to reduce or eliminate tool downtime.

This change of philosophy had huge repercussions and led to the creation of "Fleet Management" in 2001, whereby Hilti now provides customers with the tools they require for a project, tracks their location and maintains and replaces them as necessary. For core customers, according to former Hilti CEO Pius Baschera, "Tool management is a pain. A construction crew's purpose is to build a house, not manage tools."[35] As one Hilti customer explained, "When I equip a new jobsite I often have a hard time finding out where my power tools are and what condition they are in. This takes hours and there is always a risk that the tools will break down just when they arrive on the new jobsite."[36] Through Fleet Management, Hilti takes that pain and risk away.

Customer interface changes driven by the top management include a massive sales force retraining program and new incentives to reward the lifetime usage of tools by a customer (instead of one-off sales transaction). The sales force is now trained to educate the customers' decision-makers about the total cost of tool ownership and to provide them with arguments to justify their investment decisions internally. Sales people have become skilled at enlightening customers about the true cost of an unavailable tool. A missing or broken power tool is typically the real reason for the huge escalation of costs caused by a hold-up on a construction site, yet it is rarely documented other than as a repair or tool-replacement.

Realignment changes include the creation of an integrated supply chain to enable solution selling,[37] as well as the development of competencies that Hilti did not previously have, such as legal contracting for the financial and operational leasing of tools. The company invested in the global rollout of Easy Fleet, a system that included a two-page contract that was as easy for a customer to sign up for as a rental car agreement. It took over five years for a 30-page leasing contract to be whittled down to two pages. This deceptively simple contract covered the contingencies that could arise from an array of services that a Hilti sales person undertook for the customer, including: producing a comprehensive inventory of each tool and each customer worldwide; repairing tools under the fleet contract for free, and billing for tools that were not part of the fleet contract; collecting the right tools at the end of the four-year contract period; and handling insurance in the case of stolen tools.

Over time, these efforts transformed Hilti into the world leader in solution selling for power tools. Fleet Management started with just 8 contracts in 2001, and ballooned to over 100,000 in 2008, and has consistently stayed above that level. This has been good news for Hilti, not just in terms of revenue, but also profit margin. Marco Meyrat, executive member of Hilti, remarks, "When I looked at the share of customers' wallets we were getting and their behavior, I saw that customers were giving us not only their tool business but also a larger share of their consumables budget (consumables can include nails for a nail gun, screws for a power drill, and so on)."[38]

Hilti's approach is best captured in its slogan, "We manage your tools, so you can manage your business." By removing the burden of ownership, the company has simplified customers' financial planning and reduced their administrative work and downtime.

4

The Quest for
Global
Solutions

" In the past, the idea was to make more and better products. Now, we do not provide a product to customers, but a solution. In the past, selling an item was the end of the sales process. In the past, selling an item is the beginning of the sales process. Now, Eventually, we want to turn Haier from a product manufacturer to a service provider. "

Zhang Ruimin, CEO of Haier[1]

Where Do We Stand?

1. Do we have a shared understanding of the "what business we are in" question?

2. In proposing a solution, what "customer headache" are we hoping to solve?

3. How will we jeopardize our existing suppliers, vendors and partners by moving to a solutions space?

4. Will the proposed solution discredit our brand value proposition?

5. What capabilities and processes are we missing in order to deliver solutions to our customers?

6. How ready is our sales force (organized, trained, credible, incentivized, equipped) to deliver solutions?

7. What cultural change do we have to undergo in order to become solution sellers?

5

The Quest for
Global Agility

" The Nestlé super tanker couldn't become faster *and* bigger. So the only way was to break it up into a very agile fleet of independent boats, with a common supply chain afterwards. The challenge is how you manage that without losing coherence and strategic direction. "

Peter Brabeck-Letmathe, Chairman, Nestlé [1]

LESSONS FROM THE SILK ROAD

The extended supply chain – spanning multiple countries, cultures and political conditions – is not just a modern phenomenon. Its origins can be traced back to the vast trading network of the first millennium, which became known as the Silk Road.

These routes stretched from China right across to the Mediterranean and down into India. Besides silk, traders transported an array of precious stones and metals, glassware, spices and medicinal plants, as well as ideas, religious beliefs and technologies.

The merchants who dominated this trade were not Chinese, Indian, Turkish or Persian. They were Sogdians, a now forgotten people originating from the region of modern-day Uzbekistan. Sogdia was not a strong military or political power, but rather a conglomerate of city states, the biggest being Samarkand. So how did its people come to exert such influence over early international trade? What characteristics enabled that?

Sogdia had an unusual heritage. Its lack of centralization made it vulnerable to attack and it had come under the rule of various neighboring powers, including the Persians, the Greeks and the Kushan Empire. As a result of their exposure to different peoples, the Sogdians had developed what one historian described as a "resilient adaptability."[2] Sogdians typically grew up multilingual and were noted for their tolerance of different religious beliefs.

Whereas other societies trained and conditioned their young males for combat, the Sogdians focused instead on education and trade. The seventh century Buddhist pilgrim Xuanzang noted that boys were taught to read and write from the age of five and were later taught commercial skills. By the age of 15, many had left home to join the ranks of itinerant merchants doing business in neighboring states.

Over time, Sogdians settled in trading towns along the Silk Road, forming a diaspora that was well integrated with host communities. In some cities, the Sogdians set up temples and these served a secondary function as venues for trade facilitation: the exchange of money and bonds and writing of promissory notes.

So, while other traders traveled back and forth over small distances, some Sogdian merchants were able to travel the length of the Silk Road or extensive portions of it. Sogdian settlers provided them with vital lodging and supplies as well as serving as guarantors and liaisons with local society and authorities. In the process, Sogdian became the lingua franca along the Silk Road.[3]

Sogdian letters dating from the early fourth century reveal the existence of a well-organized communication system linking Sogdian communities throughout Central Asia with Sogdians back home. They also contain details of important events and conditions in China, which helped the traders to mitigate risks. Although the Sogdians were never politically united and never possessed their own military force, they built a commercial empire that dominated Eurasian trade during the first millennium, and especially between the fifth and the eighth centuries. For this modest population to control such a huge trading network for so long required various forms of agility. The Sogdians would certainly have understood the issues of supply chain flexibility and lead time that continue to preoccupy leaders today. They also showed cultural agility in their capacity to adapt to different

The Sogdians: Cultivating agile trade

societies. And they were strategically adept in realizing that domination was not their game, but that they could achieve power instead through transaction.

Uncertainty rules

Uncertainty has always existed in business. But previous generations of executives typically believed it stemmed mostly from the moves of known competitors or from technological innovation. Strategy scholars developed models that framed major changes as occasional exceptions – "disruptions," "jolts" or "punctuations" – to a relatively stable norm.

Although that may still hold true in a few sectors, the reality for many of us is that change itself has become the norm. We have to contend with shifting consumption patterns and expectations, the emergence of new and non-traditional competitors, regulatory upheavals, informed and unforgiving stakeholders, and fluctuations in energy, commodity, exchange and interest rates. The interaction of these factors puts more pressure on companies to alter their mode of responsiveness to change.

> *A neat definition of organizational agility is the firm's capacity to evolve without having to change traumatically.*

Whereas scholars used to talk about firms becoming more adaptable, they now talk about them becoming more agile. It is a subtle distinction, but adaptability implies a one-time adjustment to a newly transformed environment, whereas agility conveys a sense of constant vigilance and a capacity for rapid reconfiguration in the face of novel situations, whether threats or opportunities.[4] As Professor Albrecht Enders puts it, "A neat definition of organizational agility is the firm's capacity to evolve without having to change traumatically."

The need to become more nimble was brought into sharp focus by the convergence of three forces – globalization, deregulation and digitization – which exposed companies to unknown and remote competitors, game-changing technologies and sudden shifts in market conditions.[5]

The impact was most visible in the high-tech sector which served as a strategic arena for studying fast-paced change.[6] In this volatile environment, the key to survival was not efficiency but the ability to locate the constantly changing sources of advantage, as evidenced by the disappearance of once leading players including Digital Equipment, Wang, Atari and Compaq in laptops.

Core competencies, it became clear, have a nasty habit of turning into core rigidities.[7] Success encourages us to do more of the same, but better. We invest resources in structuring functions, subsidiaries and business units to deliver particular outputs in a consistent way. But as we accumulate know-how and hone our signature skills to enhance profits, we also develop inertia. We grow attached to past investments, social structures and routines, as well as certain cognitive styles, behaviors and decision templates. The interlocking system becomes difficult to modify.

And it is not just the internal factors that are to blame. Reflecting on why agility is such a challenge for multinational corporations, Professor Winter Nie comments, "Firms in developed economies face an agility handicap. They are stable and well balanced. When you reach that stable stage, you sacrifice agility. Being accountable to multiple intertwined stakeholders makes them slow moving. Companies from transition economies have fewer forces governing their actions, so agility is their chief weapon. When you have nothing, your only advantage is the ability to move fast."

When you have nothing, your only advantage is the ability to move fast.

The very strengths, balance and focus that drive our success can also blunt our reflexes when the environment changes. It is not just that we become too slow moving, we may not even realize that change is needed. This is the familiar curse of success. The answer is not to abandon the pursuit of efficiency, but rather to find a way of capturing both efficiency and agility.[8] Professor Michael Wade notes, "We have to learn to be agile in areas that are dynamic or that require local adaptation, and we need to be efficient in areas that are more stable and less differentiated. We sometimes use the term ambidexterity to capture that dual need."

Agility as an antidote

Agility has become a major preoccupation for many firms and resonates strongly with executives. A recent survey of international senior executives showed that organizational agility was the priority that impacted more executive jobs than any other transformation initiative.[9] Agility was seen as a key differentiator in many businesses and a critical factor for business success.

So who needs agility? Professor Bala Chakravarthy reflects, "It's a function of the industry space. The companies most in need of agility are those facing rapid, complex and interdependent changes, like those in the tablet sector. Apple comes up with something, then Samsung comes up with something else, and it keeps going back and forth. If you're not agile, you're dead. But in industries that are less turbulent, some players can differentiate themselves by being more agile than the competition, like Zara and Amazon did in their respective sectors."

In other words, increased agility may be a way to stay in the game or to stay ahead of the pack. It can even be both at once, as in the case of former state-owned monopolies that suddenly find themselves exposed to fast-moving competitors. Take the case of Deutsche Telekom.[10] DT had long been one of the dominant players in Europe, but its share price collapsed in just a few years – as did its grip over its home market – and its share of new broadband customers in Germany fell to below 10%. The huge advantage conferred by its fixed-line network and brand name was fast being eroded by the mobile operators. Professor Shlomo Ben-Hur comments, "To halt the slide, DT launched a sweeping transformation effort in 2006. The goal of that effort was to make the fixed division more like DT's smaller and more agile mobile arm, and the starting point was the massive injection of senior management talent from the mobile operation into the mainstream business." In the space of a few years, the company regained a dominant position in its domestic market and its prospects looked much healthier.[11]

Organizational agility is an ever-growing concern as companies in developed markets come under increasing threat from faster, cheaper and sometimes more innovative competitors from transition economies.

When setting off on this journey, there are some things we need to think about, some things we need to do and some traps we need to avoid.

THINK   **ANGLES ON AGILITY**

Organizational agility is a concept with strong intuitive appeal, but it is also very hard to pin down and clearly signifies different things to different people. Sometimes it refers to high level strategic moves, at other times to culture, capabilities, organizational forms, supply chains, IT infrastructure or HR practices. There is the type of incremental agility associated with flexible operations or processes and playing the game better than our competitors, and there is the type of radical agility more often associated with strategy and changing the game altogether.

So while there is a consensus that agility is valuable, there is considerably less clarity on what that means and how it can be achieved. Professor Phil Rosenzweig proposes that organizational agility revolves around three core features, "We are agile if we are able to sense changes and, having sensed them, we have a repertoire of responses and can act in a timely way. So it's about sensing, versatility and speed."

We are agile if we are able to sense changes and, having sensed them, we have a repertoire of responses and can act in a timely way.

We can use that lens to show how different companies have emphasized different facets of agility to achieve competitive advantage. Journeys in pursuit of organizational agility do not just start from different places, they head off in different directions.

It is therefore critical for organizations setting out on this journey to clarify, "What sort of agility are we targeting?" As Professor Rosenzweig notes, "The big question is, where in the organization, in terms of functions, levels or activities, will agility be a real differentiator? Which parts of our organization need to become agile – and how do we do that – and where is it less important?"

The challenge of gaining organizational agility makes more sense if we consider it from three distinct organizational vantage points: strategic agility, supply chain agility and cultural agility.

Strategic agility: Fast big moves

The emergence of strategic agility as a business imperative relates to the increasing speed of change in many industries. As Professor Carlos Cordón puts it, "The concept of lasting competitive advantage is a thing of the past. The new reality is temporary advantage. The only way to achieve consistent success is to keep seizing that temporary advantage."

The new reality is temporary advantage. The only way to achieve consistent success is to keep seizing that temporary advantage.

A striking example is Apple, which has transformed itself from a personal computer company to a consumer electronics and mobile pioneer. The company has succeeded in transforming its core business without losing momentum.

The fundamental challenge in achieving such agility is the trade-off between commitment and flexibility.[12] Indeed, strategic agility is something of an oxymoron. As Professor Bettina Büchel points out, "Being strategic implies making big choices that are difficult to reverse quickly. And clearly that sets up a potential contradiction between the need for agility to cope with external change pressures and the need to commit to resource investments."

We need to find ways to overcome that dilemma. Take the realm of organizational design. Paradoxically, the challenge is to create structure without having to create structure. And a striking shift over the last two decades has been the way that companies have embraced more open organizational designs – outsourcing work, collaborating with unlikely partners and creating virtual entities in order to capitalize on market opportunities without making irreversible commitments.[13]

Grabbing such opportunities often boils down to the speed of decision-making inside the firm, and that relies on the top management team and its aptitude to make or respond effectively to game-changing moves.

The key challenges involved in pursuing such agility hinge on the top team's ability to stay informed, to ready itself for fleeting opportunities, to challenge one another and engage in robust discussion, and yet to act decisively when the moment arises. As leaders, we need to find a balance between openness and focus.

Openness

To prepare the organization for big shifts, we need people on the top team with different perspectives. We need people who are tuned in to the environmental signals as well as people who have great internal connections, people with the kind of networks and understanding that make them reliable assessors of what is going on inside and outside.

We also need people with a range of talents. One key to developing super-flexible strategies is to build up a diversity of styles, perspectives and skills in the top team. As human beings we all have limits in terms of the range of situations we can master. So it is critical to include people on the top team who can manage different pieces of the business according to the special needs of those activities. As competitive realities evolve, leaders can decide to pull a certain management team or leader out of the wings and into center stage when the group faces a challenge that resembles one they have been dealing with.[14] As Professor Paul Strebel puts it, "It is a matter of having a range of management talent that is suited to different contexts and whose competencies can be leveraged when the organization faces change. Change may be constant, but it is not always the same. Different contexts require different types of change and change leadership."

Change may be constant, but it is not always the same. Different contexts require different types of change and change leadership.

Focus

Although diversity is critical for sensing strategic threats or opportunities and developing novel responses, it is not conducive to agreement. When agility is our goal, we need to be able to achieve swift alignment, and the more diverse we are, the harder that is.

Professor James Henderson observes, "Ultimately, strategy is about commitment. So there has to be a time when we stop the debate and sign up. If you remain flexible all the time, rivals who are more committed are going to kill you."

The art of balancing openness and focus is well illustrated by the example of Medtronic, the global medical technology firm, whose spectacular growth has been fueled by continuous renewal.[15] Medtronic has repeatedly targeted new patient groups with new appliances. This has been made possible by the careful attention of successive leaders to maintaining a balance between the business and research dimensions by including medical doctors and research fellows on the top team.

> *If you remain flexible all the time, rivals who are more committed are going to kill you.*

The company has learned to blend organic growth, acquisitions and alliances but has also struck a balance between top-down and bottom-up strategic planning by alternating perspectives each year. Successive leaders have also managed to reconcile the established businesses with the new businesses, instilling a strong understanding of how they need each other. The head of the pacemaker division, Medtronic's core business, has fully understood the need for his division to "take care of the family" and to provide the cash so that the "aggressive younger siblings" can take the necessary risks to push for growth in new directions.[16]

Top team composition and dynamics are therefore critical to the sensing, assessment and fast decision-making capabilities that drive strategic agility.

Supply chain agility: Responding to shifting demand

In the 1990s, companies like Dell and Zara showed that supply chain agility could become a core differentiator and indeed the very backbone of their business models. Suddenly, we saw chief supply chain officers finding a place at the top table and CEOs keen to learn more about supply chains.

Supply chain agility is about the firm's ability to adjust to shifts in global consumer requirements for its offerings. The pursuit of such agility raises questions about where and when to be flexible. What activities should be outsourced, what functions should be centralized and where should they be located, what benefits can be reaped from integrating with suppliers and customers, what tools can help, and what risks does this expose us to? Again, it is critical to understand the kind of agility we are aiming for. We have to match the level of agility to the nature of the demand and the type of offering.[17]

Although developing supply chain agility clearly has a strategic impact, it is not the same thing as "strategic agility." Professor Carlos Cordón makes the point forcefully, "Some people refer to the fashion chain Zara as an example of strategic agility. This is misleading. Zara is extremely agile from an operational perspective, but everything is aligned to the model of delivering fast fashion. Zara's *strategy* has not changed."

> *Zara is extremely agile from an operational perspective, but its strategy has not changed.*

In 2008, Zara (owned by Inditex) overtook Gap as the world's largest clothing retailer. The aspect of Zara's supply chain agility that draws the most attention is its amazing time to market – just two weeks from design to store shelf – and its ability to refresh its collection continuously. This not only encourages consumers to visit stores much more regularly but also reduces risk, saving on inventory and avoiding heavy discounting at the end-of-season sales.

This agility is built on the tight vertical integration of design, just-in-time production, delivery and sales. Yet, operational flexibility can be wasteful without reliable market intelligence. What often gets overlooked is the retailer's sensing ability, its capacity to detect trends as they emerge. This is not only based on the aggregation of point-of-sale information but also relies heavily on the individual store managers. Every day, they check which new designs are available and place their orders. They are also canvassed by the 350 designers at head office for insights into customer appetites and desires, and thus help shape designs.

Design teams then translate the insights into patterns, and the decision about which designs get produced is made in conjunction with sales people. These decisions take less than an hour, compared, say, to Benetton where designs are subject to lengthy reviews and approval by committees. Careful filtering is understandable when we are placing much bigger bets. The Zara model downplays the trendsetting aspect of fashion and relies on rapidly establishing the actual demand pattern. If Zara gets it wrong, it can readjust and target another trend for the following week.

Although Zara's supply chain agility is outstanding, it is by no means the only route to agility. Zara's supply chain has a high level of vertical integration, with its own stores, factories, designers and even a controlling interest in a dyestuffs producer.

In the same industry, but at the other end of the spectrum, we find Li & Fung, which acts more like a broker. Like Zara, it boasts delivery times as short as two weeks on some orders. Yet, the Hong-Kong based group does not invest in design, production, transportation or outlets. Rather, it acts as an intermediary between big retail stores and a network of 15,000 small subcontractors (including designers) around the world.

It compresses delivery times by getting different suppliers to work concurrently on a single batch, so a single garment is likely to have several manufacturers. For each batch, the company designs a unique value chain, depending on spare capacity, costs and exchange rates, but also to prevent shrewd retailers from replicating the supply chain for themselves.

To reach that level of agility requires exceptional IT and logistics capabilities. For Li & Fung, the key challenge has to do with orchestrating the network, which is largely based in Asia. Its goal is not to own the assets, but to control them. Without owning a single factory, Li & Fung is arguably the largest manufacturer in the world. As Professor Bill Fischer puts it, "Li & Fung will forever be the middleman, but it is being in the very middle of the knowledge chain of the industries they serve that ensures their value."[18]

In this role of intermediary between multiple manufacturers and multiple customers, Li & Fung harks back to the trading empire of the Sogdians (who also controlled access to the market without actually producing most of the goods they sold), and revives both the links and the spirit of the old Silk Road.

Supply chain agility can thus take different forms depending on whether it relates to a standalone firm or to the way a firm is embedded in the wider supply network.[19] But in between these extremes – of high and low

Supply chain agility can take different forms depending on whether we want to be an integrator or a broker.

vertical integration – multiple permutations are possible. Again there is no universal best answer. Even in the pursuit of supply chain agility, it depends on whether we want to be an integrator or a broker.

Cultural agility: People who can improvise

The human side of agility is not about big moves, but about responsiveness on the front lines and in everyday interactions

An agile culture is one in which people are switched on and flexible in their thinking and exchanges with customers and colleagues.

among employees. It is about building up individual and collective capability to handle emergencies, solve problems creatively, deal with uncertainty, learn new ways, and make incremental improvements. It depends to a great extent on the quality of individual conversations.

An agile culture is one in which people are switched on and flexible in their thinking and exchanges with customers and colleagues. Frontline improvisation is especially important in high-touch service businesses, such as airlines and retailers.

If we want employees at all levels to be responsive, to take initiatives and come up with novel solutions, then we need to provide them with the technology and HR systems to support such behaviors. The systems and processes need to be aligned, but deciding which agility enablers matter most depends on the challenge faced. Where we put our emphasis determines the type of agility we get.

HR enablers

If we want to create or revive a culture of agility, we need to think about our selection, promotion and performance management practices.

Take the case of Zappos, the world's largest seller of shoes online.[20] Its obsession with delivering outstanding customer service is clearly supported in its hiring and socialization processes. It has an unusual recruitment process involving two interviews, one to assess fit with the job and another to assess cultural fit with the company. All successful recruits go through the same five-week training course, including two weeks on the phones in a call-center and one week working in the warehouse. At the end of induction, everyone is offered $2,000 to quit as a test of commitment.[21]

In addition, realizing that the number one contact is the call center, Zappos treats it as an investment rather than a cost. Because it pays close attention to recruitment and training, the company is able to give staff more autonomy in their jobs. Call-center employees are empowered to take the necessary action to make customers happy and are urged to do what seems appropriate to rectify their problems without constant managerial approval. In addition, to encourage responsiveness, employees have no scripts or call-time metrics. Customer service calls lasting up to an hour are treated as a marketing expense, since happy customers will tell their friends.

Of course, these performance management practices would be pointless without other policies and systems that reinforce the customer service obsession – like its free-call number, free shipping and returns, 365-day return policy and 24/7 availability – but the key differentiator is frontline agility.

At Zappos, HR practices take the lead role in defining cultural agility, but this is not the only route to customer responsiveness.

Technology enablers

IT applications and infrastructure clearly support frontline decision-making and responsiveness. For example, customer relationship management (CRM) systems deliver comprehensive details about customers and their past interactions with the firm, allowing people on the front lines to make informed decisions and to adapt to the changing needs of customers.

But information capabilities can also play a key role in *driving* customer responsiveness. Take the example of Scotland-based Aggreko, the world leader in the rental of temporary power generators. In 2005 it started using a new customer satisfaction metric, known as net promoter score (NPS), based on the simple question, "How likely are you to recommend this company/brand to a friend or colleague?"[22]

NPS focused all attention on customer interactions and changed the internal conversations at Aggreko, putting the voice of the customer back into the day-to-day running of the business. Instances of customer failure suddenly became visible to everyone – with all employees having online access to all the company's NPS data. Early warning signals allowed staff to be more proactive in addressing potential problem situations.

The NPS scores did not in themselves improve the customer experience but they highlighted the areas that needed attention and motivated managers to investigate disappointing results. They also improved line of sight for top management, which received monthly updates of the NPS status of the far-flung local operations.

The results were spectacular. By the end of 2010, Aggreko's North America operation had the highest NPS score of all the surveyed B2B companies, and ranked ahead of several paragons of customer service, including Amex, Southwest Airlines and Fedex.[23]

In a totally different way from Zappos, the Aggreko example shows how good systems can help to shape internal conversations and customer responsiveness, progressively becoming part of the cultural fabric. Professor Don Marchand points out that

> *Good systems can help to shape internal conversations and customer responsiveness, progressively becoming part of the cultural fabric.*

what distinguishes agile companies is the use they make of such tools, "What really differentiates organizations is their ability to create an environment in the company for people to express, share and use their knowledge between colleagues, across functions and geographical entities. You have to work at creating that kind of flow of knowledge and ideas, and you have to promote it as a company, from the leadership down. Ideas and information move so fast that we have to develop an operating culture and a style of management that is going to take advantage of the potential for human intelligence to be magnified across the world."

DO   CONSOLIDATE AGILITY

As we have seen, organizational agility looks quite different depending on whether it relates to strategic, supply chain or cultural agility. Yet certain practices apply across the board. Consider the following four complementary ways of enabling agility.

Develop sensing tools

Information about external change is not absorbed by osmosis – it has to be caught. Which means we need the right people, with the right tools, fishing in the right places. For example, as Puma shifted its emphasis from serving athletes to catering for "people who like the sporting look," it had to develop new sensing capabilities. It started to employ brand scouts around the world to monitor and report back on the latest street fashions. The "lifestyle group," which started out as an experiment, flipped the direction of the entire company, with Puma morphing into a fashion brand, so successfully, in fact, that it wound up as part of the French luxury giant PPR, alongside exclusive brands such as Gucci and Yves Saint Laurent.

Social media are also rich potential sources of information for individuals and companies with the right sensors. Individuals can stay abreast of leading-edge developments in their fields by following the right experts on Twitter. And companies can create specialized units to mine social media for customer insights that are both rich and unmediated.[24]

Toyota set up such a team as part of its crisis management response during the "sudden-acceleration" recall. The team monitored and addressed false rumors on Facebook and elsewhere, and identified online fans whose comments could be recycled (with permission) through its own channels to put the quality issues into perspective.[25]

To respond quickly and effectively, we need methods to track what is going wrong, to transmit and amplify distressing information and ensure that it gets to those who need to act on it.

Multiply the options

To develop appropriate responses, we need to be able to draw on an array of alternative organizational capabilities.[26] Professor Paul Strebel remarks, "The key is to have people in the organization exploring new realities and developing capabilities that can be deployed when growth opportunities open up." Developing individuals and teams with diverse perspectives and experiences is key to generating a wider repertoire of responses to challenges – agility through diversity. Rotation between different areas and assignments gets executives used to dealing with the unexpected, forcing them to frame and resolve novel problems.

Proposing multiple options not only enriches the discussion, it also diffuses conflict, preventing teams from polarizing around just two possibilities. With different opinions flying around, we feel less inhibited about criticizing the preferred option. What often stops us from expressing a nagging concern is the fact that no one else has spoken up or voiced a contradictory opinion of any kind.[27]

Have a clean fight

In organizations, we have grown accustomed to working virtually, occasionally getting together for review or realignment purposes. But when big change or responsiveness are needed, these routines often fall short of the mark.[28] According to Professor Bill Fischer, "In fast-paced, high-stakes situations, we need to make work a contact sport." Agile responses demand intense, face-to-face confrontation of views. These don't just happen. We have to create an environment where people can come together quickly and efficiently to make vital

In fast-paced, high-stakes situations, we need to make work a contact sport.

decisions and design processes that allow for frank exchanges. To make these discussions productive, we have to modify the rules of engagement. We have to agree to suspend hierarchical concerns and to create a psychologically safe environment where, without fear of recrimination, we can "put the fish on the table."[29]

For example, in 2005 Microsoft gathered together its top 15 executives to discuss the threats posed by a new breed of rivals, notably Google. Significantly, Bill Gates agreed not to attend so as not to inhibit the discussion, and the retreat was not led by CEO Steve Ballmer, but by Ray Ozzie, a revered industry figure, who had joined Microsoft only two months earlier.[30] Ozzie's fresh perspective and critical eye helped the entire team revisit the company's failure to capitalize on internet technologies, some of which it had developed, and to see the growing competitive advantage of businesses based on online services. The team emerged with its own "burning platform" to fundamentally change how it did everything.[31] A few months later, this gave birth to the major transformation effort needed to shift Microsoft's entire product line toward the internet.

More generally, we need to identify people who can deal well with conflict, because uncertainty always generates disagreement among those who are looking at it.

Prototype fast

We sometimes come up with new insights or ideas, but fail to follow through fast enough. We want more complete information before placing a big bet on an uncertain outcome. We feel intimidated by the level of resources required and the risk of failure. "Quick prototyping" is a way past this problem.[32] It

Quick prototyping is vital for firms that want to turn breakthrough thinking into commercial responses.

enables the transition from thinking to productive action without committing major resources in an irreversible way. It generates knowledge and feedback that allow us to focus on unresolved questions and to refine the approach.[33] Though mostly associated with products and services, prototyping applies equally to processes. This is a vital reflex for firms that want to turn breakthrough thinking into commercial responses.

When envisaging major initiatives, firms also conduct field tests. Several factors contribute to the fast roll-out of a successful pilot project, but the overriding one is the choice of a credible pilot location. Research conducted by Professor Bettina Büchel suggests that it is a case of "horses for courses."[34] For example, KONE the Finnish elevator and escalator company, which has a strong record of converting pilots into full-blown initiatives, uses the US for piloting sales processes but Finland for operations projects. And

Tetra Pak, the international packaging company of Swedish origin, pilots finance projects in Europe and operations projects in Brazil or Mexico. The keys to subsequent adoption are the perceived expertise, status and representativeness of the pilot location.

AGILITY ASSASSINS   AVOID

As discussed earlier, organizational agility is founded on sensing external information, then interpreting it and delivering sharp responses (both swift and smart). Of course, that chain of activities is only as strong as its weakest link. So we have to avoid pitfalls on all three fronts.

Scanning failures

Problems start when we fail to collect available information, which may be caused by an absence of monitoring or inattention to particular classes of information, perhaps because we lack a clear set of priorities when scanning. Do frontline employees know what type of signals to look out for and track?

Misplaced or overly narrow attention is a problem that afflicts individuals, companies and even whole industries. Barnes & Noble was caught flat-footed by an unexpected entrant, Amazon.com, and the entire music industry was blindsided by Napster. Selective

Blind Spot on...	The Right Questions
Trends	What are the relevant global movements in terms of demographics, regulation and consumer markets?
Customers	Listen to customer feedback. Which needs are being met and which aren't? Which needs are mis-perceived?
Benchmarking	Which adjacent sectors provide relevant examples of best practice for different parts of the value chain?
Category extension	How do consumers define what they want? Are you missing opportunities to extend the business?
Capabilities	How can you leverage your base capabilities in new ways? Could they be offered as a service?
Technology	What upcoming technologies might be incorporated into new products or services?

Figure 1: Sources of strategic intelligence   Source: Bettina Büchel[36]

attention can also lead to missed opportunities. For example, Kodak, General Electric and IBM all turned down the opportunity to build the original copy machine that later became Xerox.

Professor Büchel talks about "organizational blind spots," in which important information either goes unnoticed or gets discounted as transient and insignificant. The traps include misjudging industry boundaries, failing to identify emerging competition, falling out of touch with customers, over-emphasizing competitors' visible competence, and allowing corporate taboos or lack of foresight to limit their frame of reference. Any one of these mistakes will prevent us from integrating the right information into our thinking or taking advantage of available opportunities.[35] (See **Figure 1.**)

A lack of agility is often based on a failure to devote the necessary resources to collecting information. It is hard to become conscious of our own blind spots. Yet there is no shortage of information for those with the courage to look. Entire websites and forums are devoted to the complaints of disillusioned users or employees. These can be useful sources of insight into our own rigidities and vulnerabilities.

Sensemaking failures

Sometimes, the information is available but we fail to join the dots into a coherent pattern. The clues do not add up to an actionable insight, meaning that the individual or organization is unprepared when the relevant threat or opportunity presents itself. Professor Michael Watkins calls these "predictable surprises."[37]

At an individual level or team level, we may not have the tools to aggregate the information or the time to reflect on it and make sense of it. At an organizational level, two communication flow problems may be to blame: one is the failure to combine insights that are dispersed across separate silos; the other is the failure to transmit relevant information upward (especially when it is negative).

It is rare for companies to be completely unaware of a potential threat or opportunity. Often there are pockets of individuals scattered through the organization – people working in sales, after-sales/complaints, technology or finance areas, people working in distant markets – who notice critical trends or indices, but lack the opportunity or incentives to make their insights known. Those with the necessary insights may not have the status or the voice needed to get the attention of the decision-makers. Or else their strong recommendations get diluted as they rise through

the organization. The net result is that those who
have to formulate a response are missing vital
parts of the picture.

*Those with the necessary
insights may not have the
status or the voice needed
to get the attention of the
decision-makers.*

Thus, the top team should go out of its way
to solicit, encourage, listen to and reward the
people who speak up. If we want to make
an example of someone, it should not be the
messenger but the people who knew and did not speak up.

Responsiveness failures

Individually or collectively, we may perceive the potential threat
or opportunity, but fail to act on what we know.

We may discount the threat or opportunity, overestimate the
time we have to respond or simply lack the resolve to act on it.
Professor Howard Yu illustrates the point, "Polaroid mastered
digital technology as far back as 1987. But it was unable to
realign its activities to succeed with a technology that required
a different organizational set-up, and ultimately went bust.
Kodak also failed to make the transition, in spite of getting a
digital product out, because it could not bear to cannibalize its
own existing business." By contrast, Fujifilm, which faced the
same problem, looked for ways to apply its capabilities in new
markets – including cosmetics and medical-imaging equipment –
and managed to bounce back.

Lack of will is one reason for lack of responsiveness; arrogance
is another. Longstanding success tends to foster a dominance
mindset or a sense of invulnerability. This was the case at
Deutsche Telekom and IBM until new CEOs came in. We may
also have a top team that is in denial or that frames the visible
threat as an irrelevance. A case in point is Nokia. In the early
days of the iPhone, Nokia executives constantly dismissed it as
a toy. Of all the mobile companies that were caught flat-footed,
Nokia was perhaps the slowest to respond. This was ironic for
a company that came to prominence as a result of sensitivity to
market demand, successfully anticipating both the potential for
mobile phones and their emotional pull as branded goods. It also
illustrates the danger of hubris in established firms.

Different types of companies are liable to be more vulnerable
to particular failures. For example, there is evidence that family-
influenced companies recognize discontinuous technologies later
than their non-family influenced counterparts.[38] By contrast, they
often implement decisions more quickly and with more stamina.
Professor Denise Kenyon-Rouvinez explains, "The concentration

of capital and voting rights in family businesses means that once they make a decision, they can move much faster than corporations because the interests of owners and managers are more closely aligned."

Similarly, companies led by CEOs with more narcissistic personalities are more likely to take bold and unconventional actions – and to demonstrate the more radical agility mentioned earlier – for example, by investing in new technology considered novel and unproven.[39] But, as Professor Albrecht Enders warns, "It turns out that narcissism might occasionally be an asset for leaders. The problem is that their conduct tends to lead to extreme outcomes, sometimes beneficial, sometimes catastrophic. There is often a fine line between self-confidence and hubris."

PAYOFF	REBUILDING LEGO

Organizational agility comes in many guises and they are not necessarily complementary. We therefore have to figure out which type of agility makes most sense to our situation. Consider the Danish toymaker LEGO.

In 2004 the family-owned group lost money for the fourth time in six years and edged toward bankruptcy. Many of its innovation efforts – theme parks, Clikits craft sets (marketed to girls), an action figure called Galidor supported by a television show – were struggling for profitability.[40] Its problems were partly due to diversifying into too many new activities. At the same time, its focus on creativity, innovation and superior quality had created a proliferation of stock-keeping units (12,500 in 100 colors) and of suppliers (over 11,000). Overall, it lacked focus and was sinking under the weight of its own complexity.[41]

Jørgen Vig Knudstorp, a former McKinsey consultant who had joined the company in 2001 as director of strategic development, was named CEO and tasked with developing a rescue plan. The thrust of the resulting plan was a move "back to the brick."

Strategically, this meant refocusing the group on its core business, selling off the LEGO theme parks for some $500 million and scrapping other distracting LEGO "lifestyle" offerings, such as watches, clothing and dolls.

Operationally, the key priority was to improve the supply chain. In 2005, through a series of collaborations between different functions in the company, LEGO executives re-examined every aspect of product development, sourcing, manufacturing and logistics process. They cut the color assortment in half, slashed stock-keeping units to 6,500, and outsourced logistics and production. Through discussions with its major clients, LEGO executives also realized that customers did not need daily or next-day deliveries, but were content with weekly deliveries. In both its product range and its delivery performance, LEGO had in fact sacrificed agility by trying to be too responsive.

LEGO had in fact sacrificed agility by trying to be too responsive.

As a result of the changes implemented, on-time delivery surged from 62% in 2005 to 92% in 2008, and clients started advising their other suppliers to benchmark LEGO for customer service and supply chain excellence.[42] As Professor Carlos Cordón puts it, "LEGO suddenly became more agile because it was allowed to be agile – the outcome of reducing the complexity."

Culturally, Knudstorp's objective was to "create an organization that doesn't rely on me to make decisions."[43] The company needed empowered managers, so he pushed decisions as far down the hierarchy as possible and stopped participating in weekly sales-management and capacity-allocation choices. He also moved leaders within the company and altered organizational structures and ways of working. He changed the incentive systems so that a larger proportion of managers' bonuses, including his own, were based on customer satisfaction surveys of retailers, parents and children.

Knudstorp's efforts to model and promote faster, more informal and collaborative exchanges (both internal and external) are reflected in his blog. Although time-consuming, the blog gives employees a sense of his thoughts and feelings about key issues, what he is learning from his wide network of global business and academic contacts, as well as from his meetings with adult LEGO enthusiasts. It not only gives him the chance to reach out to LEGO employees in far-flung locations but also serves as a channel for upward feedback: "I have people sending me three or four pages of ideas of how we should organize differently, how we should think about things. It's an incredible tool."[44]

The transformation to a much more fluid, collaborative and responsive culture is palpable. Knudstorp was very articulate about removing people or things that hinder collaboration and information sharing, and then following through on those pledges. And the results speak for themselves: between 2005 and 2011 – in spite of the economic crisis – sales grew by over 150% while profitability increased more than five-fold.

The underlying message is that delivering increased agility is sometimes about reducing activities and customer options. LEGO's earlier efforts to reach for greater organizational agility through strategic agility and customer responsiveness were misplaced. It overreached, trying to be all things to all comers – and fell short on both fronts. When it refocused its efforts and resources on supply chain agility and cultural agility, its sales took off again.

Sometimes strategic agility is not about dramatic moves into new areas, but about shifting between different types of incremental agility and prioritizing different aspects of organizational agility at different times.

5

The Quest for
Global
Agility

" The Nestlé super tanker couldn't become faster *and* bigger. So the only way was to break it up into a very agile fleet of independent boats, with a common supply chain afterwards. The challenge is how you manage that without losing coherence and strategic direction. "

Peter Brabeck-Letmathe, Chairman, Nestlé [1]

Where Do We Stand?

1. Is our priority strategic, operational or cultural agility?

2. Can we create distinctive advantage in our business by being more agile?

3. Which parts of the organization need to be more agile and in what way?

4. What tends to slow down our decision-making?

5. What mechanisms do we use to try to detect patterns and trends that could threaten our business?

6. What measures do we take to capitalize on new opportunities using pilots and experiments?

7. Can we identify blind spots that have proved costly for us in the past?

6

The Quest for Global Co-innovation

" The future of competitiveness is no longer about one company against another; it's much more about one network against another network. The company that is able to form and establish the best network with the best partners will be the winner in the future. "

Barbara Kux, Member of Board of Directors of Total and Henkel [1]

LESSONS FROM CLOCKMAKERS

Before the 18th century, the biggest barrier to international trade and exploration was the lack of a reliable method for navigating the seas. In particular, ships had no accurate way of determining longitude. Every ocean voyage was a journey into the unknown and orientation errors caused the loss of numerous merchant ships. The human and economic advantages of solving the "longitude problem" were clear.

Several European nations, starting with Spain in 1567, offered prize money for a solution. Spain augmented the incentive in 1598 and the Netherlands put up an even bigger reward in 1636. Britain followed suit in 1714 in the wake of a spectacular maritime tragedy caused by a miscalculation of longitude.

The British scheme proposed a sliding scale of awards for solutions to increase accuracy, starting at £10,000 for a method accurate to within 60 nautical miles (111 km) and double that for precision to within 30 nautical miles (56 km). The initiative was open to the public and the British government created a committee called the Board of Longitude, which included scientists and instrument makers, to assess the proposed solutions. The board controlled not only the prize money but also discretionary funds to support promising efforts. It was authorized to make advances of up to £2,000, worth around $300,000 today, for experimental work.

Mathematics and astronomy were widely assumed to hold the keys to the problem, but the winning solution came from neither community. It was proposed by John Harrison, a carpenter and self-taught watchmaker.[2]

Existing pendulum clocks were too easily disrupted by movement, as well as changes of humidity and temperature, to be of any use on ships. So Harrison came up with a marine chronometer that could keep accurate time at sea and hence allow navigators to determine longitude from the hour difference. Harrison received the bulk of the prize money from the board for his invention, while other contributors received smaller rewards for refinements to his clock.

This event perhaps marks the first successful example of crowdsourcing and highlights one of its key precepts – that innovation and creativity can come from anywhere. The prize focused attention and talent on a critical challenge and unleashed diverse initiatives.

As Professor Bill Fischer observes, "To stay ahead in today's world, astute companies need to understand that the more ideas you can work with, the better. In fact, taking this to the next logical step, the more minds you can engage in the hunt for new ideas, the better."[3]

Harrison's invention not only enabled the development of safe and rapid shipping routes, it also paved the way for the rapid expansion of the watchmaking industry. Both developments fundamentally altered the way business was conducted.

The mother of co-innovation

In spite of this early success story, the idea of opening up innovation to multiple contributors was not really taken up by business. In 1936 Toyota held a contest to redesign its corporate

Crowdsourcing comes of age: The Board of Longitude at work

logo and chose the winning entry from 27,000 contributions, but this was a rare example and was tangential to the core offering.

Most companies preferred to keep serious invention in-house, where they could control and protect it. In fact, it was very much the preserve of a select band of employees such as engineers, designers, researchers and scientists, whose responsibility it was to generate and test new ideas, often in a separate location. AT&T's Bell Labs and Xerox's PARC are prime examples. The chief concern was building more effective filters to avoid pursuing ideas that would not yield commercial returns.

Today, much of that has changed. We talk about innovation as the "responsibility of the entire organization." Indeed, innovation efforts are no longer confined to the boundaries of the corporation. We are increasingly reliant on suppliers, vendors, lead users, consumers, partner organizations, university labs and independent inventors for new ideas and insights.[4] At a recent conference for chief innovation officers, discussions of effective innovation solutions consistently revolved around some type of collaborative arrangement.[5]

This apparent U-turn is the natural culmination of two trends. It has its roots in the move to open up new product development to functions other than R&D.[6] IMD President Dominique Turpin notes, "As new product design evolved into a more inclusive process, it became logical to start including close value chain partners, notably component suppliers, particularly in Japan."

Co-innovation also grew out of the movement toward more outsourcing. This started with support services and manufacturing, but as companies got used to boundaries becoming more porous it was only a matter of time before they also started outsourcing elements of innovation.

Of course, two external drivers accelerated this process, pushing co-innovation to center stage. The first is the imperative of speed. Shifting industry boundaries mean that change is happening faster and is coming at us from all directions. As Professor Bill Fischer explains, "The clock-speed of industrial change is accelerating to such an extent that it has become obvious 'we can't do it all by ourselves,' or 'we can't do it fast enough if we rely only on ourselves.'" We increasingly have to link up with external partners to create new technologies and offerings. In some sectors, such as the commercial aircraft and biotechnology industries, closed innovation is no longer an option.

The second driver is the explosion of connectivity. Advances in information and communication technologies (ICT) have created both an awareness of distant ideas and a low-cost means of accessing them.[7] Firms can and must cast their nets wider to capture the knowledge they need to develop new offerings. Professor Michael Wade observes, "Individuals, organizations, institutions and communities are all networked and interdependent, creating all sorts of new possibilities for joint innovation on a much larger scale. Online tools are helping to unleash the full power of collaborative innovation."

The bottom line is that it is becoming harder to innovate alone. Faced with the challenge of generating continuous innovation, more and more companies are reviewing their traditional models and embracing a more open approach to innovation. It is a general movement, but for some of us, improving our ability to link up with innovation partners is a business imperative.

Craving co-innovation

We are especially likely to feel the need to upgrade our co-innovation capabilities in two generic situations: when we lack ideas or when we lack resources.

Lack of ideas

Many traditional companies have resources and power but lack the flow of new ideas or responsiveness to maintain their standing in the industry. The challenge is to revive innovation productivity.

The most celebrated case is P&G.[8] When A.G. Lafley took over as CEO in June 2000, the consumer products giant was struggling with its innovation portfolio and pipeline. Lafley saw that the company's own labs would have difficulty delivering the volume of continuous innovation needed to support ambitious growth targets. He also realized that the company's core strength lay in collecting, prototyping and developing "fragile ideas," whether these came from inside or not.

Lafley initiated a program called "Connect and Develop." At the time, less than 15% of P&G's new product initiatives involved an outside partner, mostly members of P&G's existing supply chain. The objective was to get to a point where half of the company's new products had at least one outside partner.

This was a huge challenge to P&G's proud tradition of internal innovation. It called for unprecedented levels of collaboration with organizations, science communities and individuals around the world.[9] For example, P&G started running big innovation fairs over two or three days in search of innovation partners. But in order to receive, employees first had to learn to give and to reveal concepts or technologies in need of partners. The company posted these needs on its PGConnectDevelop.com website, where people could submit their ideas. And it hooked up with a number of brokerage firms specializing in open innovation. Over time, P&G built up an ecosystem of new sources of innovation and learned to tap into them.

By the time Lafley retired in 2009, P&G's sales had more than doubled and over 50% of the new products brought to market included at least one component from an external partner. Its stable of billion-dollar brands had grown from 10 to 22, while brands with sales between $500 million and $1 billion had increased fivefold. P&G's stock had more than doubled.

> *The biggest challenge in this turnaround was shifting the mindset from "only invented in P&G" to "proudly found elsewhere."*

Although it was a great success, this co-innovation capability took several years to embed. Professor Cyril Bouquet notes, "Several P&G managers have conceded that the biggest challenge in this turnaround was shifting the mindset from 'only invented in P&G' to 'proudly found elsewhere.'"

Lack of resources

Smaller firms, especially entrepreneurial ones, might have the ideas but lack the resources to develop or commercialize these ideas alone. A good example is Babynov, a small French supplier specializing in infant foods.[10] Having come up with a prototype for Ambient Ready Food (AMR) products, Babynov approached the Dutch firm Numico, a much bigger player in the industry. The product was well matched to a concept that Numico's top team had once envisaged. After refining the ingenious packaging concept, the two parties quickly worked out a deal.

Unfortunately, the implementation of co-innovation almost proved to be beyond them. Neither party realized the extent to which they would have to learn new ways. There were several communication breakdowns, caused in large part by the absence of project owners in both companies. For example, Numico failed to communicate its demand forecasts to Babynov. In addition, when the first shipments arrived, there was abnormal spillage owing to ill-fitting lids and incorrect stacking on the pallets. Such setbacks, and the finger-pointing that accompanied them, highlighted the absence of boundary spanners, shared language and trust across both companies and nearly sank the partnership.

Realizing the strategic importance of this new product category for both firms, Numico's incoming supply chain director took charge of getting the relationship back on track. He stressed that a contract was only as good as the will behind it and that both firms had to try to resist falling back into sterile zero-sum thinking. Ultimately, sales soared despite the declining birthrate, persuading the French powerhouse Danone to acquire Numico for 22 times Numico's earnings.[11]

Both the P&G and the Babynov/Numico cases underline the difficulty of developing organizing principles to nurture and support joint innovation. When embarking on such a journey, we should not underestimate the effort required. How much we struggle depends largely on our culture. Professor Bettina Büchel points out, "Some companies have a secretive culture that makes it difficult to innovate with others and can even hinder collaborative behaviors *within* different parts of the organization, like sharing ideas." These fences are visible in all sorts of systems, policies and practices , as highlighted in **Figure 1.**

Potential Barriers	How High Are Our Fences?
Company access	How many process steps do people need to go through before physically entering our building?
Secrecy agreements	Must people sign non-disclosure agreements before we give out any information? Do we often check requests with our lawyers?
IT systems	How flexible is our IT infrastructure? Can we easily communicate with other companies?
Social media	How open are we to social media and external input?
Conference policies	How much can we share with others when we attend conferences?
Internal silos	Are cross-functional teams standard features in our organization?

Figure 1: Open to co-innovation   *Source: Adapted from Bettina Büchel*

When setting off on this journey, there are some things we need to think about, some things we need to do and some traps we need to avoid.

COLLABORATE TO CREATE   THINK

Paradoxically, the people involved in innovation are not always the most amenable to change. This is a problem because the rules for winning at co-innovation are somewhat different from those associated with traditional closed innovation (see **Figure 2**).[12] As Professor Stuart Read puts it, "Successful co-innovators understand that it is no longer about hiring the smartest research talent and doing it all yourself, but rather about orchestrating the contributions of various innovation partners, whether individuals or firms."

The Old Ground Rules		The New Ground Rules
Secretive and isolated	→	Open and networked
New ideas come from inside	→	New ideas can come from anywhere
Recruit the best R&D talent	→	Connect with the best source of ideas
Reflection-driven	→	Interaction-driven
Research facilities matter	→	Research platforms matter
Control the IP	→	Leverage the IP
Grab all the pie	→	Create a bigger pie

Figure 2: Reinventing innovation   Source: Stuart Read and David Robertson [13]

> *Open-source innovation and crowdsourcing have attracted a lot of attention recently, but these are but two strands of the co-innovation spectrum.*

To make that transition we have to alter our mindset in three fundamental ways.

Think spectrum

To leverage the innovative contributions of outsiders, we first need to develop a more nuanced view of co-innovation. Open-source innovation and crowdsourcing have attracted a lot of attention recently, but these are just two strands of the co-innovation spectrum.

Co-innovation actually covers a wide spectrum of alternatives (see **Figure 3**). At one extreme, we have inclusive innovation. This applies to people from our own organization who may be located in remote outposts and were never previously invited to contribute to the innovation process. IBM, for example, used its corporate intranet to launch a 72-hour "Innovation Jam" to solicit ideas and new business opportunities from 150,000 IBM employees.[14]

A little further along the spectrum, we can engage the value chain partners, starting with the longstanding suppliers and vendors. For example, many innovations in the auto industry,

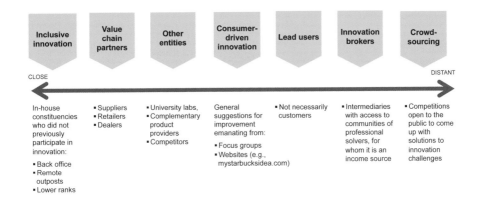

Figure 3: The co-innovation spectrum   *Source: Adapted from Bill Fischer*

such as airbags and stabilization systems, were proposed by suppliers and developed jointly with the car manufacturers.

Next, there are entities with which we have weaker ties, including university research labs, complementary product manufacturers and even competitors. Then, we have insights developed from close interaction with consumers through focus groups or by eliciting consumer suggestions via social technology. Examples include Del Monte, which uses a private community to understand the desires of pet owners, as well as Starbucks and Dell, whose customers can contribute ideas directly through dedicated websites (mystarbucksidea.com and Dell's ideastorm.com).

One step beyond, there are the "lead users," who may not even be our customers but who are struggling with problems that our customers *will* face and can point the way forward for our innovation efforts.[15] For example, Medtronic relies heavily on individual physicians for working prototypes of new products or concrete suggestions for improvements on existing products.[16] The big challenge is to find and engage with those lead users so we can build on their efforts to address unmet needs.

At the far end of the co-innovation continuum, we come to innovation brokers and crowdsourcing. Here we make the innovation challenge public and elicit ideas either indirectly – through innovation brokers, such as Innocentive,[17] with connections to networks of specialists – or directly from communities or individual contributors.

Given this expanding spectrum of potential partners, we have to make choices as to where we want to focus. The answer may be "all of the above," as in the case of P&G.[18] But

How wide do we want to open the aperture in order to come up with something that's really different for our industry?

few companies have the resources to pursue joint innovation on all fronts. So we first need to consider where to direct our efforts. As Professor Stefan Michel puts it, "The key questions are: What resources can we gain or exchange through co-innovation, who has access to those resources and why does it make sense to innovate with them? It's also a matter of how wide do we want to open the aperture in order to come up with something that's really different for our industry."

Think frugal

Co-innovation is partly a response to the relentless squeeze on innovation budgets and time frames. For companies that have traditionally boasted well-funded research departments, making that adjustment is not easy. Those of us on the receiving end not only have to do more with less but we also have to do it quicker and with outsiders. This cocktail of constraints can drain our energy and hinder our co-innovation efforts. But with a different mindset it can also act as a stimulus to creativity.[19]

In developing markets, severe budget constraints on customers force companies to rethink products or services from scratch and to seek out like-minded value chain partners. Business groups are key sources of innovation in emerging market economies.[20]

Because the customers are frugal, the companies innovating have to be frugal too.

Professor Pasha Mahmood observes, "Because the customers are frugal, the companies that are innovating have to be frugal too. Collaborative innovation is often a necessity because the entrepreneurs lack access to customers, suppliers, scientists and developers, and they can't get funds from venture capitalists at key stages of development."

It would be easy to be disheartened by these constraints, but "frugal innovators" learn to work with them and indeed leverage them. Undaunted by scarcity, frugal innovators rely on partners to achieve quick commercialization and to deliver products that "do the job" at a low price. Frugal innovation is about delivering 80% of the value for 20% of the cost. Some larger companies in the emerging markets have also embraced this ethos.

A high-profile example is the Nano car, launched by Tata Motors in 2008 and selling for just $2,500.[21] The key to delivering this low-cost innovation was multiple collaborative partnerships with suppliers. Around 80% of the component design and manufacturing was outsourced, with supplier involvement starting at the conception phase. Tata Motors put in place an early vendor integration program to capture innovative ideas for lowering design and manufacturing costs by leveraging, exchanging and sharing knowledge within the network.[22]

The leading suppliers were given considerable latitude to design components as they saw fit – allowing Tata to pass on some of the risk and the R&D costs to the suppliers – and they came up with several innovative features to save space and weight, simplify the manufacturing process and reduce components. Professor Bala Chakravarthy notes, "Sales of the Nano turned out to be disappointing, but the real benefit for Tata Motors has been the radical new approach to innovation, including the 34 global patents for the vehicle's platform."

Frugal innovation can serve as an inspiration for the co-innovation efforts of companies in advanced markets. Professor Howard Yu remarks, "Leaders of mature companies must think more like frugal innovators, in terms of reconfiguring existing technologies in new ways, leveraging their full range of contacts, embracing suppliers as innovation partners not just executors, and reframing limitations as opportunities. Frugal innovation is helping companies in emerging markets to come to grips with collaborative innovation at an accelerated rate."

Think win-win

Closed innovation is based on a "winner-takes-all" mentality – the notion that if we get an innovation to market first we will win, and that we must control our IP so that rivals do not profit from our ideas. Breaking out of that mindset requires two important changes.

First, we have to accept that others will play a major role in the success or failure of our innovation effort.[23] Professor Bill Fischer reflects, "The big challenge, of course, is trust – giving up absolute control over end results and trusting others to contribute their best to a group effort. Participating chief innovation officers, in fact, have spoken of 'fear' when it comes to sharing idea leadership with their value-chain partners."

This reluctance was largely responsible for the collapse of MySpace, once the darling of internet users and Wall Street. Whereas Facebook focused on creating a sturdy platform to allow outsiders to develop new applications, MySpace relied on itself. Its co-founder and former CEO Chris DeWolfe conceded, "We tried to create every feature in the world and said, 'OK, we can do it, why should we let a third party do it?' We should have picked five to ten key features that we totally focused on and let other people innovate on everything else."[24]

The issue of risk is not to be taken lightly, but at some point we have to take that risk if we want the joint benefits.[25] Professor Fischer adds, "Are we putting our intellectual property at risk? I think we are. But I think we can do it judiciously. And I think the risk question we have to ask is: How much do I have to put up in order to be able to get full value out of the collaboration I'm looking for?"

The second aspect of win-win is of course to make sure that innovation partners feel they are also getting their fair share of the rewards. As Professor Margaret Cording points out, "We have to make absolutely sure that both parties are getting something out of it, and that people feel it's fair. Because I will be more likely to 'steal' from you if I think you are taking advantage of me."

Fairness is a critical component of successful co-innovation, and it has three facets. First, we must make sure that the parties receive compensation in line with their efforts, which is termed distributive justice. Second, we have to take care that the process for making decisions is mutually acceptable (procedural justice). And third, we have to ensure an appropriate level of respect and information exchange between the parties (interactional justice). Or, taking the negative view, we have to be confident that penalties are proportional to the breaches, that there are clear and consistent rules for resolving disagreements and that people who are not collaborative will be removed from the interface.

Professor Ginka Toegel observes, "Because co-innovation partners lack information on each other's trustworthiness and the size of the prospective cake, fairness perceptions can have a big influence on their commitment, knowledge sharing and cooperation." The tensions between Babynov and Numico, mentioned earlier, illustrate the problem.

Beyond developing a more flexible, resourceful and collaborative mindset, joint innovation also requires us to *act* differently.

DO   SET UP FOR SUCCESS

To build sound innovation partnerships, regardless of the type of collaboration, we need to change our practices along all four domains of the co-innovation chain – requirement clarity, response intensity, receptive capacity and relationship quality (see **Figure 4**).

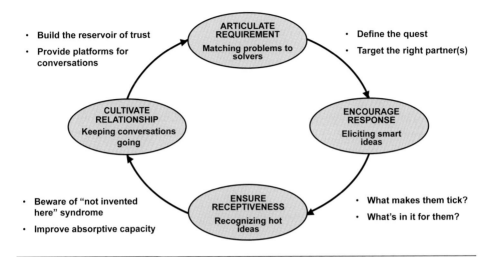

Figure 4: The co-innovation chain   Source: Jean-Louis Barsoux and Anand Narasimhan

Articulate the requirement

The first challenge of joint innovation is defining the quest. What is the innovation challenge we face? Is the problem clear-cut? Can it be divided into small well-defined chunks that contributors can work on independently?

We have to structure the problem so that multiple innovations are easily recombined with the rest of the puzzle. According to Professor Stuart Read, "The way the initial environment is configured and how we set up risk is critical. If we take big risks, then failure is a disaster. If we take risks according to what we and our innovation partners can afford to lose, then failure can be co-transformed into learning and ultimately into valuable innovation."

We must therefore spend time and effort defining the problem upfront and breaking it down so that we ask the right questions in the right ways.[26] Articulating innovation challenges in ways that generate innovative and pertinent answers is a competence, and we need to identify and reward people who can act as "problem facilitators," helping the organization to ask the right questions and manage the process. As Professor Ben Bryant notes, "The way we frame the problem determines what kind of answers we get. Rather than just posing a broad innovation challenge, it's better to come up with a specific 'what if' question that would have real business impact if it were resolved."

Besides defining our quest, we also have to decide who is best placed to assist us in finding an answer. Depending on whether it is an open or a closed problem, we are likely to come to very different conclusions about who can tackle it. Partners who are part of our existing value chain may be the preferred option when tackling more open-ended challenges that are company- or situation-specific. Longstanding suppliers or vendors know what we do and have good channels of communication with us. Often, the challenge with these contributors is to break out of our established patterns of thinking.[27] Professor Martha Maznevski cautions, "When we co-innovate with our suppliers or customers, we may be working with people who are too much like us, for example researchers with the same training and industrial background as ours or the same people we've always talked to. So they may have difficulty thinking outside the box. Or else, we may need to give them permission to show us their 'weirdest' ideas."

> *When we co-innovate with our suppliers or customers, we may be working with people who are too much like us.*

By contrast, tapping into an external community often makes sense when trying to solve a narrow technological problem. For example, Mammut, a Swiss manufacturer of alpine sportswear, had a problem with conventional zippers, which let in air and were therefore never fully sealed. They wanted to find a zipper that was water resistant, but that could also be opened very easily. It was a closed innovation challenge, so they put it out to a crowdsourcing agency where experts could propose solutions. The winning proposal drew inspiration from the plastic sealing mechanism on freezer bags.

When the innovation challenge is more open-ended, identifying the right group of contributors is not always straightforward. Do we want to focus on experts and people screened for their creative skills or do we opt for a more open approach as in the "longitude model," based on the assumption that creativity can come from anywhere.

Consider the example of Emporia Telecom, an Austrian company aiming to design a mobile phone for people over 75 years of age. The company targeted three different groups for ideas and concepts: industrial designers, students and senior citizens. The suggestions received from the first two groups were mostly infirmity-related – big digits, simplified menus, high-contrast displays, extra-loud speakers, hearing aid-compatibility and an emergency button. Professor Michael Wade comments, "The senior citizens' suggestions were quite different. It turns out that they are still very active and the last thing they want is to carry around something that looks like a brick with huge numbers. They wanted cool things, interactive features. They even suggested a 'dating' button." The example shows the power of going to our target customers rather than just relying on received wisdom.

Encourage a response

To find the right incentives to motivate different parties, we must first try to understand what makes them tick. And we must be clear on "What's in it for them?"

With partner firms, this means determining how the benefits generated by the collaboration will be distributed between the parties. In particular, it means figuring out who owns the intellectual property (IP) and how to carve up the pie when appropriating value from it. The problem is that when two partners are bringing together unique skill sets, defining what constitutes an equitable risk–benefit ratio can be tricky.[28]

At the same time, different categories of partners have different expectations.[29] In business-to-business contexts, for example, customers typically do not expect a share of the IP. Professor Stefan Michel remarks, "When we go into a joint development with a supplier, they will fight for the IP, whereas the client often does not care. If a client comes up with a good idea and one year later we make a trillion with it, the client may not be bothered, but a supplier would expect a share of the returns."

As companies have increasingly profited from customer suggestions, the question of property rights and rewards is becoming more salient.

Historically, distributors, vendors and dealers had few opportunities to contribute to innovation, so incentives mattered less. But as companies are increasingly profiting from customer suggestions, the question of property rights and rewards is becoming more salient.

When targeting communities or individual idea submitters on the open market, the IP is unlikely to be up for grabs, but we still need to find the right ways of rewarding contributors for their time and efforts.

The motivations of outsiders who engage in open innovation, through communities or open markets, are surprisingly varied. Financial incentives may be paramount in some instances, but other participants can be inspired to co-innovate by incentives like peer recognition or external visibility. High-profile companies often use the association with their brands as part of the payoff. For example, LEGO taps into the innovative ideas of adult enthusiasts and some new products are even labeled "created by LEGO fans."[30] Similarly, Amazon identifies top reviewers and ranks them against one another to encourage their participation. The most valued reviewers, known as Vine Voices, can also order pre-released copies of books free of charge. The German software group SAP allows volunteers to provide solutions to customer inquiries; many of the problem solvers are ambitious consultants from emerging markets aiming to establish their reputations with SAP customers.

The point is not that money is unimportant, but that its role is often overestimated. Clued-in companies focus as much on the social and personal drivers of discretionary effort as the material drivers.[31] And whatever we do with regard to monetary incentives, we should never fail to reward idea practitioners with attention.

Ensure receptiveness

Recognizing and integrating good ideas from outside is harder than it seems. Professor Bill Fischer remembers talking to people at Sharp, a company that manufactures pagers, "One executive recalled that when the pagers got old, the customers would hand them on to their kids. The kids would take them to class, and that is essentially where chat and texting started." According to the executive, the company never took this trend seriously because they were "just kids." "Looking back, we could have become a key player in the texting industry, but we just didn't get it. We didn't realize we were witnessing the future."

A significant part of the problem is the familiar "not invented here" syndrome. But the root of our resistance to external ideas is often misdiagnosed.[32] According to Professor Martha Maznevski, "People talk about the not invented here syndrome as if it is strictly a motivational issue – people being too proud – but it is also a cognitive issue. There's a real skill involved in seeing 'How this could apply here.' It is quite a cognitively complex thing to do."

> *There's a real skill involved in seeing "How this could apply here." It is quite a cognitively complex thing to do.*

Assimilating knowledge from outside is tough, especially if we are not used to it or set up for it.[33] Trying to develop a co-innovation strategy without attending to the culture is pointless. Professor John Weeks remarks, "In organizations where people have long been praised and rewarded for inventing things, it's quite destabilizing when we suddenly start to value people who know where to go to solve that kind of problem rather than how to solve it themselves."

This is a profound cultural change, so CEOs have to be willing to stand behind it and to hold their reports accountable for holding their teams accountable. This is why A.G. Lafley at P&G made it clear that 50% of innovation would come from outside and that you were either on the bus or not.[34] We need C-suite buy-in to the open innovation agenda, and people throughout the organization must feel authorized to look outside for help on innovation challenges. We have to develop the habit of looking out for ideas and insights whenever we attend trade shows or conventions and to share our findings in a constructive way when we return.

We should not underestimate the level of internal reorganization needed to support the joint exploration and exploitation of unique opportunities.[35] Performance management systems and training programs can also help us to assimilate ideas. We can encourage employees to be more alert, open-minded and practiced in applying external knowledge or insights. Professor Margaret Cording comments, "Through training and incentives, we can help our scientists and researchers to change the way they usually go about things, which is very individualistic, and to develop more team-oriented, trust-based approaches. We have to both trust and be trustworthy."

It's quite destabilizing when we suddenly start to value people who know where to go to solve that kind of problem rather than how to solve it themselves.

We can further improve our company's ability to interpret and incorporate good ideas by assigning the right executives as boundary spanners, individuals who can create linkages that integrate and coordinate across organizational boundaries.[36] Professor Maznevski adds, "The people we need in those liaison roles have to be able to translate incoming and outgoing knowledge between the partners. But they also need to be curious and capable of listening to the other party's point of view. They often have to be able to exert influence without authority, so it's a pretty unusual set of capabilities." Such people have to be developed and celebrated.

Cultivate the relationship

As we interact more and more with parties we know less well, trust inevitably becomes an issue, particularly in high-stakes projects. Formal requirements are no substitute for frequent, high-bandwidth communications, which are critical for resolving unanticipated problems.[37] Professor Stuart Read points out, "In a context of co-innovation, surprises – both good and bad – are inevitable. The challenge is how to embrace them, how to transform them with your partners into value that might be greater than you imagined when you started."

Based On	The Partner Is Perceived to....
Credibility	Be consistent, "keep promises" (provide "advance warning") and not "let us down."
Fairness	Take responsibility for problems, distribute benefits fairly and adopt a long-term view regarding the relationship.
Loyalty	Stand by us in times of crisis or market pressure, give us the benefit of the doubt when there is some kind of shortfall.
Realism	Avoid unilateral demands, understand our capabilities and constraints and not set impossibly high standards.
Shared Value	Have similar views of appropriate and inappropriate behavior and be prepared to make concessions to find compatible ways of working together.

Figure 5: Comfort level between co-innovators   Source: Based on Kim Hald, Carlos Cordón
and Thomas Vollmann [38]

Our response to surprises depends very much on the quality of our relationship with external parties. How do we expect the relationship to evolve, how dependent are we and what level of comfort do we perceive? (See **Figure 5**.)

Bad dynamics between co-innovation partners often take root early on. After that, a lot of time and energy can be spent trying to salvage the situation, often to little avail. We therefore need to invest in the relationship upfront to create a positive momentum.[39] Professor Carlos Cordón remarks, "To influence partner attraction, we can do things like make relationship-specific investments that show commitment, adapt our ways of working to show goodwill or increase information exchange to help coordination and prevent misunderstandings." Such actions build up a reservoir of trust between the partners.

Co-innovation does not just happen. We have to appoint someone to be responsible for making it happen. Professor Margaret Cording observes, "Co-innovation is about collaborating for the creation of new knowledge. And although we talk about collaboration between organizations, it really occurs at a person-to-person level. So what really matters is the ability of those individuals to trust one another."

Although we talk about collaboration between organizations, it really occurs at a person-to-person level.

The project owners on both sides of the relationship must work diligently to form a relationship that can bear long-term pressure and scrutiny. We need to get to know our counterparts, to keep the lines of communication open and to remain in tune with how they view the association. We also need to agree on a process for handling future issues and bringing them up for discussion before they escalate.[40]

We have to construct environments that enable bits of information to find each other, where people can contribute, regardless of whether they are employees, users, partners, suppliers or virtual communities. We must therefore provide the communication platforms needed to engage and maintain conversations, and to develop a shared language.[41] Professor Bill Fischer notes, "When I think about innovation, I think about conversations. If you want to be a manager in an innovative setting, think about conversational engineering: Who's involved, when are they involved, what's the context?"

We also have to remember that co-innovation is a two-way process, and that our feedback can either fuel or deter continued participation and commitment. Of course as the relationship strengthens, we can expect more of a two-way exchange and a better chance of our partners proposing their best ideas. As Professor Stuart Read puts it, "Give people the opening to co-innovate *with* you. Not *for* you. Not to implement your vision. But with you in a way that encourages them to commit themselves to the process, to bring the means they have available into the equation, and to let them co-shape what the outcome looks like with you."

CO-INNOVATION CHOKERS   AVOID

Co-innovation is hard work. Professor Margaret Cording remarks, "There is little point launching into it, with all its attendant risks and hassles, unless it's going to create a unique capability that the customer values, that competitors can't copy and that guarantees us a fair return."

But even when our co-innovation efforts make strategic sense, they are often hampered by excesses on three fronts.

Overreliance on tight contracts

With intellectual property at stake and a lot of uncertainty surrounding respective efforts and likely rewards, we can expect contract design to loom large in co-innovation discussions. It may be tempting to try to specify the mutual obligations and penalties in great detail. But our efforts to avert opportunistic behavior through complex contractual conditions and sanctions can become a major hindrance to achieving stronger partnerships.[42] Professor Bettina Büchel recalls a partnership between two small manufacturing firms, "The insistence on formalizing and itemizing multiple contingencies in a 128-page document led to suspicion and rigidity between the parties. They were constantly in monitoring and policing mode."

The contract and the accompanying negotiations set the tone for the relationship and indicate whether we expect it to be productive or difficult. To avert later problems, we must think carefully about what to put in and what to leave out, as well as the granularity of the contract. Also, the framing should be positive, setting out the gains rather than focusing exclusively on compliance and penalties.

> *To avert later problems, we must think carefully about what to put in and what to leave out of the contract, as well as its granularity.*

In short, if we expect our partners to act opportunistically or not pull their weight, and we put lots of effort into control and monitoring, we may actually drive the dysfunctional behavior that we seek to avert.[43] Professor Carlos Cordón notes, "We have seen the consequences of being too tough and too professional and basically providing just exactly what is in the contract, and neither party being willing to go the extra mile."

Rather than spelling out in minute detail what is expected, a more fruitful approach may be to specify what is off limits. It is typically easier to agree on what kind of information will not be shared. Once that is clear, we are able to request information and pursue value creation opportunities that fall within the framework.

We can also use the contract to promote coordination by including conditions that encourage communication and information sharing on a regular basis, to help us plan and align our joint activities.[44] Professor James Henderson observes, "We are much more likely to resolve disputes with supply chain partners when we have a contract that focuses on *coordination* mechanisms rather than on *control* mechanisms."

> *We are much more likely to resolve disputes with supply chain partners when we have a contract that focuses on coordination mechanisms rather than control mechanisms.*

At the same time, our contract cannot remain static. The document has to evolve with our joint thinking. For example, in a partnership between Ericsson and HP – to develop a new telecom management platform targeted at telecom operators – the two lead managers met every six months to check the relevance of their formal agreement.[45]

Overinterpreting ambiguous signals

The relationship between innovation partners is often fragile. Successful co-innovation depends on their joint ability and willingness to come up with answers to questions that were not foreseeable at the outset. This is difficult to achieve and maintain.

The partners may have serious misgivings about the unintended transfer of capabilities. As a result, the levels of mutual vigilance may be high from the outset. According to Professor John Weeks, "There is evidence that in social transactions, the human mind is extremely alert to indications of cheating. So co-innovation partners may be oversensitive to potential or perceived breaches of trust."

In social transactions, the human mind is extremely alert to indications of cheating.

Where trust is low, deviations from expectations, whether behavioral or in terms of outcomes, may take on disproportionate significance. These are liable to generate anxieties and misunderstandings, all the more so if there is also a cross-cultural dimension to the partnership.[46] Simple organizational dissimilarities may be enough to trigger mutual doubts. As Professor Martha Maznevski observes, "Culturally different approaches to work are reflected in everything from scheduling to decision-making protocols to etiquette, and are easily mistaken for attempts to frustrate or take advantage of the partner."

If one partner starts to doubt the commitment, goodwill or competence of the other party, various actions may ensue. Typically, monitoring and controls will be stiffened. Contractual agreements may resurface and full reporting requirements may be enforced, while tolerance for unplanned variances diminishes. Unfortunately, such actions often undermine the relationship, indicating a lack of trust and commitment, and encouraging the other party to respond in kind. Once we have the makings of a vicious circle, the partnership can quickly unravel.[47]

We therefore have to be very careful not to overintentionalize the actions of our innovation partners, which means letting them explain and giving them the benefit of the doubt rather than jumping to conclusions. As Professor Carlos Cordón puts it, "Continually attacking and reducing misalignment is a critical part of the co-innovation process."[48]

Also, while we are often highly sensitive to the shortfalls of others, we are often less demanding of ourselves. Our partners do not like shortfalls or unexpected requests any more than we do, so advanced warning and appropriate explanations are key to dampening the effect of such surprises.

Managers should constantly monitor their own behavior toward the partner and bear in mind that sins of omission are likely to be interpreted as sins of commission.

Overlooking internal R&D

With all the talk about open innovation and harnessing the ideas that lie beyond our walls, it is easy to neglect the R&D talent within the firm. But developing that talent is critical on two counts. First, because external innovation is not always better, or indeed cheaper. Take the experience of the Diagnostics Division of Roche, the Swiss pharmaceuticals giant.[49] In 2009 it identified six technology challenges that needed solving and decided to put an experiment into place. The challenges were simultaneously opened up to the internal R&D community *and* to the external technology community through two leading innovation brokers. The internal response rate was very low, but one of the proposals was so inspired that it paid for the entire experiment. Externally, the $1,500 prize money helped to generate ten times more responses (than internally) and again one worthwhile solution emerged. The difference is that two years later the company was still working through the details of the licensing agreement with the external solution provider.

External innovation is not always better, or indeed cheaper.

Roche's experience is only one example, but it provides a useful reminder that open innovation is not a panacea.[50] Professor Cyril Bouquet observes, "The benefits of open innovation, in terms of providing a company with access to a vastly greater pool of ideas, are obvious. But the licensing and transaction costs can also be high. The smart approach is to use the tools of open innovation selectively."

The second reason not to neglect internal R&D talent is that we rely on those people both to manage external innovation partners and to sift through external contributions. Professor Ralf Boscheck points out, "When we outsource innovation, it does not mean that we can walk away from it. We have to maintain some level of *defensive* R&D to be able to assess the quality of insight of others in any type of venture. We have to remember the 'co' in co-innovation."

We have to remember the "co" in co-innovation.

The danger we face if we fail to retain our R&D talent is a progressive hollowing-out of the company. For example, HP initially outsourced low-value segments of its PC operation (such as motherboards) to the Taiwan-based firm ASUSTeK, but ended up giving away even the design of the computer.[51] Now, ASUSTeK can – and does – supply an equivalent computer directly to retailers, such as Best Buy and Amazon, at a lower price.

Professor Howard Yu notes, "If a firm opted exclusively for open innovation, then it would probably have enormous difficulty even asking the right questions. Open innovation works when our questions can be effectively codified. To do that, our marketing and product development people must talk to our R&D people, who can translate the needs into technical language in order to post them to the relevant external communities."

ACCELERATED INNOVATION AT PORSCHE   PAYOFF

Porsche makes some of the most technologically advanced cars in the world. Yet, maintaining that edge is not easy against giants like BMW and Mercedes-Benz, which produce around 10 times more cars and have R&D facilities to match. So Porsche has to resort to other means of competing, relying heavily on a wide spectrum of innovation partners.

These co-innovation efforts range from award-winning customer–supplier breakthroughs on the Porsche 911 Turbo to crowdsourcing initiatives designed to pique the creative interest of talented designers. Entrants were asked to "design an object smaller than a living room and bigger than a purse, which references three design elements taken from Porsche 911s of the past or present. (But not a car!)" The prize on offer was a one-year lease on a new Porsche 911 or a cash-equivalent of $20,000. But Porsche's commitment to co-innovation is best illustrated by the strong university alliances it has established and which have been responsible for key R&D advances.[52] A striking example is its revolutionary ceramic brake system, adapted from aerospace applications, with help from academic institutions. Porsche beat its better resourced rivals in spite of starting later on the project and having few internal experts in lightweight and composite materials.

The company finances academic research in key domains, setting up research initiatives that are run exclusively for Porsche. It also brings masters' students into its R&D facility on paid internships. Each year, 600 students are asked to work on well-defined tasks in R&D alongside Porsche's 2,000 staff engineers for up to six months. While focusing on basic R&D, the students experience the full cycle of innovation, right through to commercialization. They collaborate on production techniques that combine the latest research from their universities with the practical know-how of suppliers, and even help Porsche to identify new suppliers for the technologies they develop.

Porsche's approach illustrates all four elements of the co-innovation chain.

Requirement clarity comes from identifying the right individuals and institutions to tackle the right challenges. Porsche's few material researchers are not focused on internal exploratory research but rather on global networking and technology intelligence to identify and combine the leading sources of know-how in this domain. Similarly, incoming students are deployed in some of the most challenging and value-adding areas, even when these involve sensitive information.

Response intensity stems from having a clear understanding of the motivations they are tapping into. Universities and interns receive financial support, but Porsche also plays heavily on its brand appeal. Of the 2,000 intern applications from all over the world, Porsche picks students who love the product or industry, putting creativity and passion ahead of high grades. For about one in ten of the interns, there is the added motivation of landing a full-time job at Porsche.

Receptive capacity is boosted in several ways. There is a high absorptive potential, with more than half of Porsche's 2,000 engineers belonging to different expert networks. Project leaders are fully authorized to leverage external resources for innovation purposes. There is also a strong focus on communication, with students being encouraged to make regular presentations of their findings to other parts of the company so that the research is quickly diffused and integrated. And behaviorally, the engineers at Porsche show consideration for their young university counterparts and value what comes out of the research network.

Relationship quality is visible at several levels. Porsche maintains strong relations with the universities that undertake much of the research and supply it with interns. It also goes out of its way to treat interns like employees, not only integrating them into development projects but also inviting them to after-work events and providing them with detailed performance feedback. Moreover, those who do not land full-time jobs are invited to become part of an active alumni network. Used by project teams for strategic technology intelligence, the alumni meet up several times a year and provide advice on research and technology, while also enjoying early test-drives of the company's latest models.

Porsche's co-innovation model, particularly its distinctive academic alliances, have been central to its success. But its openness to co-innovation has not all been one-way. It also works inside-out. Core technologies are licensed to other car manufacturers, including Peugeot and Hyundai, and over half of Porsche's total engineering time is sold to other companies. Professor Benoît Leleux observes, "Co-innovation is also about leveraging the intellectual property developed in-house that is never used and is surplus to requirements. It can either be licensed or sold off, otherwise the company is leaving money on the table."

As the Porsche case illustrates, successful co-innovation is not an additional form of outsourcing, but a coherent program, developed over many years.

Co-innovation is also about leveraging the intellectual property developed in-house that is never used and is surplus to requirements.

6

The Quest for
Global
Co-innovation

" The future of competitiveness is no longer
about one company against another; it's much
more about one network against another
network. The company that is able to form
and establish the best network with the best
partners will be the winner in the future. "

Barbara Kux, Member of Board of Directors
of Total and Henkel [1]

Where Do We Stand?

1. What's our innovation bottleneck?

2. What networks should we develop in order to access new ideas more rapidly?

3. How ready are we to open up and disclose information to outsiders in order to acquire new know-how?

4. What points of the co-innovation spectrum are we not addressing?

5. How do we improve receptiveness to new ideas in our organization?

6. What are the threats to our internal R&D in an open innovation ecosystem?

7. What systems and processes are we lacking to support fruitful exchange with innovation partners?

7

The Quest for
Global
Sustainability

" I see business as a force for change.
Companies have to define their role in society.
And because they attract the best talent and have
great people and have access to resources, they
also should discharge a larger responsibility. "

Nandan Nilekani, Former Co-Chairman,
Infosys Technologies [1]

Sowing the seeds of sustainability: A Mayan maize god

LESSONS FROM THE EVOLUTION OF MAIZE

A greater weight of maize is produced annually than any other grain. Maize as we know it today is a human invention. The plant never existed naturally in the wild. It only exists because humans cultivated and developed it. It has played a central role in the population growth and trade of the Americas, and offers a fascinating lens on the complex relationship between sustainability and human invention.

Modern genetic testing recently traced back the origins of maize some 9,000 years to a wild grass called teosinte.[2] Its initial domestication is attributed to the people of the Central Balsas River Valley in southern Mexico. Over thousands of years, they systematically collected and cultivated the plants best suited for human consumption, transforming a plant with many inconvenient, unwanted features into a high-yielding, easily harvested food crop.

The plant proved very responsive to hybridization and adaptable to a wide range of environments. From Mexico, maize spread north and south through much of the Americas. In the process, the region developed a trade network based on surplus and varieties of maize crops. As reflected in the deities of the Mayas, Incas and Aztecs, maize growing took a central place in their cultures.[3]

Over time, the indigenous Americans found ways of making maize the central element in their diet without contracting the deficiency diseases that were later to ravage populations on other continents. They learned that soaking the maize in alkaline water liberated key nutrients and prevented the often fatal disease pellagra. This practice, combined with the ease of cultivating maize, its high nutritional value and great storability, provided more reliable sources of food and enabled rapid population growth where it had not previously been possible. The indigenous Americans also learned to use all parts of the maize – the husks were braided and woven to make sleeping mats, baskets and moccasins, while the cobs could be used for fuel.[4]

Centuries later, maize became the basic crop in the long-continuing American frontier experience. Initially, it was directly tied to human nutrition, but in the fast-expanding, railroad-building, industrializing United States, it also became a key element in the production of meat and dairy products (as well as Bourbon whiskey). By the end of the 19th century, maize constituted the backbone of American agriculture, transforming the landscape as farmers cleared large areas for the crop and paving the way for the concept of agribusiness.

In the 20th century, manufacturers found further uses for maize and it came to influence trade in new ways. For example, as a cheap alternative to imported cane sugar, corn syrup became a ubiquitous ingredient in many US-made processed and mass-produced foods and soft drinks. Corn oil, with its high smoke point, became a valuable source of frying oil, as well as a key ingredient in industrial products such as paints, adhesives, inks, explosives, insecticides and biofuel.

What humans have done with maize encapsulates our complex relationship with sustainability. The evolution of maize is a testament to several millennia of human endeavor to improve its yield, resistance and other qualities, and to find new uses for it. But it also highlights that some things we do in the interests of development can turn out to have unintended consequences for sustainability.

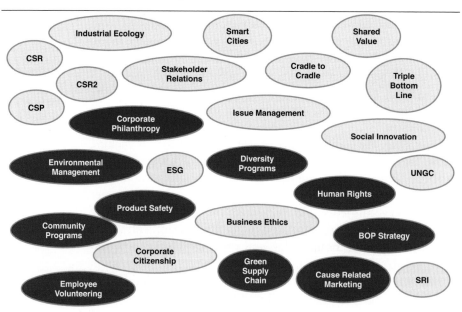

Figure 1: The sustainability swamp   *Source: Daina Mazutis, IMD presentation*

A multitude of sins

Sustainability can be a confusing topic for executives. The terminology can be a barrier in itself.

Sustainability can be a confusing topic for executives. They are faced with a barrage of terms – including corporate citizenship, industrial ecology, corporate accountability, sustainable development, corporate social responsibility, corporate social performance and ESG (environmental, social and governance) – which are often ill-defined. Even proponents of responsible business practices cannot seem to make their minds up. The United Nations Global Compact produces a report in collaboration with CEOs across the world every three years. The questions in 2007 were about ESG, yet the same questions in 2010 fell under the heading of sustainability. The UNGC annual reports themselves are couched in terms of responsible citizenship. The terminology can be a barrier in itself.[5]

Professor Daina Mazutis studied this jumble of terms (see **Figure 1**) and concluded, "I found two dozen different terms that are conceptually very similar. They have different emphases, but fundamentally they are about the same thing, and even scholars use these terms fairly interchangeably. They all represent a discourse around business's relationship to society. For now, sustainability provides a useful umbrella term."

Another source of confusion is that the key sustainability concerns vary dramatically by industry.[6] Professor Ralf Boscheck remarks, "In pharmaceuticals, the main concern is the demand for affordable medicines in the developing world. By contrast, in energy it is primarily about the environmental impact of drilling and of fossil fuels on global warming. In food companies, sustainable agriculture and obesity are key concerns. And in the apparel industry, it is mostly about the labor and environmental practices in the supply chain. So sustainability means very different things in different sectors, which complicates discussions with stakeholders, especially the regulators, who are often generalists."

Sustainability means different things in different sectors, which complicates discussions with the regulators, who are often generalists.

Sustainability reaches the C-suite

Sustainability has moved onto corporate radar screens for two main reasons: resource concerns and accountability pressures.

Dwindling natural resources have become a concern across industries and continents, especially with the explosion in demand from emerging countries. We can no longer just rely on having the best products at the best prices for the right customers. A natural resource crunch upstream in the value chain could wreak havoc on a company, or even a whole industry.[7] Take the example of the Swiss company Barry Callebaut, the world's largest business-to-business chocolate maker. In the words of its chairman, Andreas Jacobs, "Cocoa grows in very difficult countries – politically, socially, economically difficult – and so we have to make sure that cocoa is going to be around... The sustainability of cocoa, in terms of getting cocoa in five years, in ten years and in twenty years, is the thing that keeps *me* awake at night."[8]

Corporations are subject to mounting external pressure from multiple constituencies to act more responsibly. Their environmental and social impact has come under increasing scrutiny from regulators, consumers, media, ethical investors and, of course, NGOs[9] Professor Michael Yaziji observes, "Before, you could worry about your investors, suppliers and customers and kind of shut out the rest of the world, but that's no longer the case. Today, every stakeholder can get a voice, and that is what is pushing firms to go beyond mere compliance."

Today, every stakeholder can get a voice, and that is pushing firms to go beyond mere compliance.

Classic examples include Shell's experience with its Brent Spar platform[10] and Monsanto's with genetically modified organisms,[11] both targeted by Greenpeace. More recently, the spate of suicides at Foxconn drew media attention, damaging the reputation not only of the Taiwanese manufacturer but also of Apple, as one of its big customers.[12] The rise of social media, combined with ever-increasing information transparency, means that stakeholders are much better informed about firms' operations. They can track products all the way back to source and broadcast questionable practices to the entire world.

A key development in bringing sustainability to executive attention was the notion of the "triple bottom line" first coined by John Elkington in 1994.[13] This term resonated with the business community.[14] As Professor Ralf Seifert points out, "It converted sustainability-speak into a language that executives at least understood. The triple bottom line equated the traditional financial performance of the corporation with its social and economic performance, suggesting that the company needed to attend to three Ps – profit, people and planet – not just one, when making decisions."

This helped to open up a fresh perspective on sustainability, which we had previously understood to mean a company's capacity to endure and to increase its earnings steadily. Now, we increasingly recognize that sustainability in the old sense is closely bound up with its newer meaning – that our companies will not survive in the long term unless we also accept our wider social responsibility.

Who cares?

Although many companies are keen to transform their sustainability credentials and performance, far fewer firms regard it as the top priority. Among companies that do take it seriously, we can broadly distinguish between those that are reacting to external pressure and those that are taking a more proactive stance.

External pressure was the main reason that sustainability came onto the strategic agenda of the UK-based retailer Tesco.[15] By the end of 2005, it had achieved such a hold over UK retailing that it had become a growing target for attacks from a wide range of pressure groups. These included farmers, small businesses and environmental campaigners who decided to join forces to form the Tescopoly alliance in order to highlight the environmental and social impact of the chain. Tesco responded vigorously with ten pledges designed to establish the company as a "good neighbor." The main plank was a £100 million investment in solar and wind technologies to halve non-renewable energy consumption in its stores within five years. It converted its entire fleet of 2,000 distribution lorries to biodiesel and introduced battery-powered delivery vans, as well as shifting significant volumes of product from road to purpose-built "green" trains. It also introduced biodegradable carrier bags and new counters in stores for regional products, as well as more promotions for healthier foods. And it promised to consult local communities more about new outlets and to redesign convenience store fronts to fit their surroundings. Previously an industry laggard on sustainability issues, Tesco was featured as one of *Fortune*'s ten "green giants" in 2007.

Other companies take a more proactive stance, embarking on sustainability efforts long before the imperative arises. The driving force is often a CEO who recognizes the importance of sustainability and wants to integrate sustainability into the entire organization. A case in point is the example of Martha Wille, managing director of the Bolivian pasta business Coronilla.[16] Taking over the family firm at a point of financial crisis, she became convinced that the only way to rebound was to pursue a

Tesco achieved such a hold over UK retailing that it became a growing target for attacks from a wide range of pressure groups.

sustainability-oriented strategy. Her view was that the workforce would only commit to the painful measures ahead if the company had a social purpose. The company transformed itself from a traditional wheat pasta producer to an exporter of specialized gluten-free pastas and snacks made from Andean grains. It established Fair Trade relations directly with Andean farming communities to procure raw materials, and it set up a positive discrimination policy to favor the hiring of women and disabled people in the workforce. The radical change program paid off and Wille later handed over the family business to her son.

This kind of proactive, CEO-inspired approach to sustainability is perhaps more likely to occur and to gain traction in a founder- or family-controlled firm.[17] Professor Joachim Schwass explains, "A general feature of family businesses is that they tend to have a broader definition of what's needed to be successful and sustainable in business. Implicitly, it's always been about sustainability – of the family and the business that feeds the family, and of the community that feeds the business. As CEO, you know you'll be judged on what you leave for the next generation. That's very different from being evaluated by the analysts at the end of each quarter."

Action is what matters. What starts off as rhetoric gets the discussion going and builds internal and external pressure to walk the talk.

We too often get caught up in discussions about the intentions behind a sustainability strategy. Are we doing this because it's the right thing to do or because we are worried about our corporate image, impending regulations or changing customer trends? In reality, a complex set of motivations are likely to be involved and untangling them serves little practical purpose.[18] Professor Francisco Szekely remarks, "People spend too much time asking what the true motivation is here. But that's not very important. Action is what matters. What starts off as rhetoric gets the discussion going and builds internal and external pressure to walk the talk."

When setting off on this journey, there are some things we need to think about, some things we need to do and some traps we need to avoid.

THINK   EXPAND THE VALUE HORIZON

In many companies, we have to shift from a compliance perspective of "doing things right" to a sustainability mindset of "doing the right things." To do this, we have to broaden our thinking on three fronts: in terms of purpose, systems and opportunities.

Redefine the purpose

Pursuing sustainability as a strategy not only requires us to change how we do business but also forces us to rethink why we do business. It has profound implications for our understanding of success and the need for growth, as well as the time horizons we adopt, our view of stakeholders, our partnerships, our business models and our understanding of value creation and capture.[19]

As Professor Carlos Braga puts it, "Traditionally, firms were built to optimize the benefits to shareholders, to internalize the revenues and externalize the costs. Now there is increasing regulatory pressure on companies to assess societal costs – like pollution and health damage – and to assume their responsibilities. So that forces companies to look hard at the impact of the goods and services they produce and to critically re-examine their role in society."

There is increasing pressure on companies to assess the impact of the goods and services they produce and to critically re-examine their role in society.

Taking sustainability seriously impacts what we stand for and what opportunities or behaviors we will encourage, tolerate or rule out. Consider the case of the Swiss pharma giant Novartis.[20] The company's longstanding commitment to eradicating poverty-related diseases in developing countries required it to learn to work with NGOs and government institutes to run programs, as well as extending its research program to conduct pro bono work on these diseases. It then emerged that even when drugs were made available free of charge – which was the case for malaria pills in selected countries – they often failed to reach remote patients in time.

Recognizing that this was essentially a problem that could be solved with better information management, the CIO of Novartis, Jim Barrington, asked for early retirement in order to work on it. This tested the boundaries of Novartis's commitment to social responsibility, but the company agreed to sponsor Barrington and a colleague to work on it full-time, and 17 selected employees to work on the project when needed. Roll Back Malaria, an arm of the World Health Organization, with experience of dealing with public health authorities, was selected as the lead sponsor of the project. The company also accepted Barrington's request to transfer ownership of the project from Novartis to the World Health Organization in order to increase its neutrality when asking other partners, such as IBM and Vodafone, to contribute. A simple mobile phone based solution was found, which allowed rural health facilities to provide weekly updates on stock levels.[21] As Professor Don Marchand explains, "The 'SMS for Life' pilot program was so successful that it was extended to multiple countries and multiple products, not just malaria drugs. Novartis received several awards for the initiative, and now the company is even considering how the model could be applied to the private distribution of drugs in emerging markets."

It is significant that the first reaction was not "how do we monetize this?" but how do we solve this information problem? This pushed the company to think beyond its core business of producing and selling drugs. And yet the solution that emerged may transform the business model across emerging markets.

A shared sense of "why we exist" helps companies to adapt and thrive in periods of economic and social change.[22] If companies commit only to making the most money for shareholders, it is not a terribly inspiring corporate purpose for employees.[23] According to Professor John Weeks, "In a context in which attracting top talent is increasingly difficult, the company's approach to the environment, ethics, transparency and so on can attract or deter applicants. Beyond salary and career prospects, many are assessing whether they would be proud to work for the company, and happy to tell their friends. People who have a choice worry about the public image of the company."

In a context in which attracting top talent is increasingly difficult, the company's approach to the environment, ethics and transparency can attract or deter applicants.

Take a systemic view

Many companies still have a view of business systems that does not stretch much beyond the traditional value chain. But the world is increasingly complex and interdependent, so we have to try to develop a more systemic view. Of course, this means considering impacts across the life cycle of our products and services and minimizing waste. But beyond that, we also have to integrate new parties into our strategic thinking.[24]

Take the case of Vestergaard Frandsen (VF), a Danish-born disease control company, now based in Switzerland.[25] The company came up with an ingenious gadget, known as the LifeStraw, to purify water as it is sucked up through a small filtration tube. The reusable invention had huge potential health benefits in developing countries, where drinking unsafe water remains a leading cause of infant mortality. However, since this needy population was also too poor to afford the device, VF hit upon the idea of distributing it to millions of people free of charge using carbon credit financing. Leveraging the fact that LifeStraws eliminated the need to burn wood to boil water, the company was able to sell the reduced emissions to buyers wishing to offset their own carbon footprint.

This inevitably raised the issue of measurement and satisfying independent auditors that the reduction in emissions was real. In response, VF partnered with another company to develop a smartphone informed database; smartphones were issued to 4,000 health educators, enabling them to take photos and gather basic information on each of the households visited. The resulting dataset was more comprehensive than the national census and provided the platform for the external auditors to verify the information submitted.

Professor Salvatore Cantale explains, "The real innovation was in the business model, including the partnerships created with local governments and NGOs. The revenue stream does not come from selling products, but from selling the carbon certificates. Obviously, this creates some ambiguity around who are the customers, the partners and the clients."

Such complexities will only increase as more companies adopt the logic of the circular economy.[26] The underlying principle is to build industrial systems where the waste products of one industry become the critical input for another industry. As Professor Michael Yaziji puts it, "In some cases, it can be quite confusing because you're being paid by a firm to take their trash, which you are then using as fuel or raw material. We're used to seeing up and down the vertical chain, and suddenly we need to think much more horizontally because circular economies are going to cut across multiple industries. And that's not being driven by ethical concerns but by economics."

Recognize the opportunities

Companies have long approached sustainability from a risk perspective.[27] Professor Didier Cossin comments, "Risk was the reason that sustainability first made its way onto corporate agendas. In the 1980s and 1990s, as companies became much more global, their control over distant operations left them much more vulnerable, raising the risk profile of their activities and the potential repercussions for their reputation and brand."

Sustainability is to some extent tainted by that heritage. We need to let go of this rather negative vision of sustainability that concentrates mainly on what could go wrong.[28] Professor Francisco Szekely observes, "By framing sustainability as a challenge, it sounds unappealing, very much a constraint, linked to compliance and minimizing risk. We must reframe it as an additional source of competitive advantage and be more open to the possibilities that it offers."

Social entrepreneurs find some unmet need that was thought to be of zero business interest and address it in a way that is self-sustained.

The mindset of looking for opportunities in sustainability is best embodied by social entrepreneurs. Their approach is to find some unmet need that was thought to be of zero business interest and address it in a way that is self-sustained. A good example is that of Grameen Bank.[29] It is difficult to imagine a less promising client base than people living in the slums of Bangladesh. Yet, Muhammad Yunus, a Bangladeshi economist and banker, saw the need of these people for microfinance in order to escape the poverty trap. On the basis of small loans, without collateral or legal contracts, Yunus ended up not only creating an empire but also earning the Nobel Peace Prize for spurring economic growth in poor communities. Today, the bank boasts 2,600 branches (including some in the US) and default rates as low as 1%. Professor Stefan Michel notes, "The crux of Grameen's success is that 97% of its loans go to women, who turn out to be more reliable borrowers than men, and that the loans are not made to individuals but to groups."

Another unlikely example is the case of TerraCycle, a company built on waste.[30] Its founder, Tom Szaky, started out by recycling products previously destined for the waste stream. The company first fed organic waste to millions of worms, which consumed and processed it, and then used old soda bottles to distribute the resulting fertilizer. Building on that success, the company then expanded into upcycling – making products from waste that is difficult to recycle and would otherwise have been sent to landfills – and selling these consumer products, such as pencil cases and backpacks, through major retailers. Today, the company collects more than 50 different waste streams in 20 countries.

These two company examples endorse the power of sustainability to point the way to new offerings and new customers. Some markets turn out to be "hidden" right in front of us.[31] What might start out as an attempt to meet stricter regulations can create unexpected value. Under the right cultural conditions, constraints can spur invention, resulting in product or productivity breakthroughs or the identification of underserved markets.[32] Professor Szekely comments, "The word sustainability has two parts – sustain and ability – so it is the ability to sustain. We have to think about what we want to do, but we also have to build up our ability to do it."

EMBED SUSTAINABILITY   DO

We can easily get carried away discussing the "why" and the "what" of sustainability, while neglecting the "how." Implementing a sustainability strategy requires particular attention to four facets: leadership commitment, stakeholder engagement, performance metrics and employee involvement.

Lead responsibly

Responsible leadership can seem like a tautology, but there have been sufficient examples of irresponsible leadership in recent years to justify that prefix.[33] It encompasses taking the long-term view, taking into account the wider impact of decisions and taking an interest in the well-being of the collective.

To a greater extent than for other transformation efforts, the journey toward sustainability is closely bound up with leadership.[34] As Professor Szekely puts it, "Sustainability means transforming the way we do business. It is a leadership issue because it is against the status quo. We need to redefine the ongoing business models and to transform organizations into something different."

To pursue such a strategy, our leaders must "make happen what otherwise would not happen."[35] Professor Ben Bryant remarks, "Responsible leadership is actually about how we exercise power. Human beings have a natural predisposition, once they get into positions of power, to use more than is beneficial for society. So when you assume authority, you have to choose what sort of organization you want and what sort of society you want."

To embed sustainability in an organization, top management has to be visibly committed to the change. Consider the case of Stef Kranendijk, CEO of Desso, a Dutch carpet tile manufacturer.[36] Inspired by the cradle-to-cradle concept (based on endless recycling), he invited one of its originators to speak to Desso's top management. Kranendijk was convinced that Desso could differentiate itself on its sustainability practices, as its US rival Interface had done. He also understood that adopting a cradle-to-cradle strategy would imply a transformation of the entire business model (see **Figure 2**).

Dimension	Old Perspective		New Perspective
Target market	Industrial contractors	→	Architects, interior designers
Value proposition	Price-focused	→	Design-focused (health and sustainability benefits)
Key activity	Manufacturing	→	R&D, customer service
Key competence	Undifferentiated	→	Co-design with suppliers/customers
Key partners	None	→	Suppliers, architects/interior designers, certification body
Customer relationships	Transactional	→	Ongoing – old products picked up and replaced

Figure 2: Desso transforms its business model   Source: Michael Yaziji[37]

Staking his legacy on this strategy, Kranendijk boldly announced a goal of zero environmental footprint by 2020, meaning that all the raw materials used in the company's products would be free of toxic chemicals and designed for easy disassembly and recycling.

His ideas met relatively little resistance from the top management team or indeed the board. He held regular sessions with staff and with shareholders to convince them that this strategy had the potential to raise Desso from a low-margin, competition-on-price player to a premium-priced competition-on-differentiation one. But it was a much tougher sell with the suppliers. Professor Michael Yaziji observes, "The new strategy depended on convincing the suppliers to invest in R&D to develop new products for which there was an uncertain demand. It also meant shifting from a transactional type of relationship to one based on co-design. It was grinding work for Kranendijk to personally persuade enough of the suppliers to make the required investments."

It is in these crunch situations that the authenticity of the leader's commitment really comes under intense scrutiny.[38] As Professor Daina Mazutis puts it, "Making a public announcement is the easy part. The real test comes when the CEO has to drive sustainability through the organization and work externally to persuade other stakeholders that the strategy makes sense."

The real test comes when the CEO has to drive sustainability through the organization and persuade other stakeholders that the strategy makes sense.

Engage stakeholders

When we announce our commitment to sustainability, it will trigger different stakeholder reactions. Some constituencies, such as suppliers, shareholders and analysts, may resist any move that lacks a robust business case, and those we might expect to welcome the news, such as community and environmental groups, may doubt the authenticity of our commitment and actually increase their scrutiny of our activities.

Some form of stakeholder mapping will help us identify and prioritize our actions in relation to core and fringe constituencies. That exercise applies to our company as a whole as well as to the individual divisions, business units and plants. We need to know who the stakeholders are and what they care about, and we need to decide how we manage the individual relationships.

Forging links may be particularly tricky when we approach two traditional foes of business, NGOs and regulators. NGOs have long been regarded as thorns in the side of business.[39] But as we struggle with our sustainability issues, they can actually become valuable partners.[40] According to Professor Michael Yaziji, "NGOs offer hard-to-acquire perspectives, competences and resources including legitimacy with other stakeholders, specialized knowledge, access to local expertise, and sourcing and distribution systems. These can be especially valuable in emerging economies."

NGOs have long been regarded as thorns in the side of business but they can actually become valuable partners.

Take the case of Unilever's Lipton tea brand.[41] The company's decision to differentiate itself by guaranteeing that the brand was 100% environmentally and socially sustainable had far-reaching implications, as Professor Ralf Seifert notes, "Making a public commitment back in 2007 to eventually source all Lipton tea from a sustainable supply base was a big leap forward for Unilever, especially as its leaders realized that for this transformation to be credible, similar efforts would be expected from them in other product categories."

For its tea business, Unilever needed third-party sustainability certification of the plantations. Potential partners were assessed for consumer recognition, capacity, experience of working with local organizations to train employees, and ability to recruit and train teams of regional auditors. Unilever finally joined forces with the Rainforest Alliance, a US-based NGO set up to conserve biodiversity and ensure sustainable livelihoods. This partnership worked well in the large established tea estates of Kenya, but in other contexts it was necessary to find additional local partners to work with thousands of loosely organized farmers unaccustomed to applying best practice in agriculture.[42]

Sustainability issues also loom increasingly large on the agendas of regulatory agencies. More frequent interaction could allow the company to "educate" the regulator and to influence the regulatory agenda or to anticipate emerging legislation. Of course, this plays into the hands of dominant firms.[43] Professor Ralf Boscheck notes, "Across more and more sectors we see regulators consulting with companies to define the regulatory frameworks. That creates a problem because some companies are big and can afford to have their own regulatory team while others just have to follow the new standards – so this distorts competition."

You need to apply a customer focus to all stakeholders.

Smaller companies can nevertheless boost their influence by partnering with NGOs, many of which are well connected to like-minded legislators and able to pass on concerns.[44] More generally, we need to nurture our relationships with stakeholders. As Professor Yaziji puts it, "You need a positive net present value with each of your stakeholders. That is something firms already know from dealing with customers. It's a matter of repurposing standardized tools and methods to apply a customer focus to all stakeholders."

Use critical measures

Developing new metrics is vital in helping decision-makers set goals, benchmark and compare alternatives (changing suppliers, raw materials or technologies) from a sustainability perspective.[45] Professor Francisco Szekely points out, "Internally, sustainability metrics allow us to assess progress and celebrate success. They help to keep people focused and energized. And externally, reporting enables stakeholders to judge our performance and make informed decisions on how and to what extent they want to interact with our company."

Recognizing that if we can't measure it, we can't manage it, we need to find ways of gauging sustainability-related costs and benefits for different processes within the organization. Consider the case of Puma.[46] Despite operating in a sector at high risk for human-rights abuses, Puma became one of the first global brands to put a monetary value on its environmental impact. In 2011, the sport-lifestyle company issued its first environmental profit and loss account (EP&L), detailing the true costs of its products on greenhouse gas emissions, water use, land use, air pollution and waste.

Collecting and validating the figures was a complex undertaking, requiring assistance from PwC and Trucost, an environmental research company, to develop the methodology. But the report pulled no punches, estimating the environmental damage caused by Puma and its suppliers in 2010 at €145 million ($196 million). Dr Aileen Ionescu-Somers, director of IMD's Global Center for Sustainability Leadership Learning Platform, notes, "Puma really pushed the boat out and was unflinching in assessing the full life cycle of its products. This kind of honest self-assessment is what creates a culture of sustainability. Only once you have the information can you really change the way you do business and keep refining your efforts." For example, a key finding was that a mere €8 million of the total came from Puma's core operations, such as offices, warehouses, stores and logistics, while Puma's supply chain accounted for the remaining €137 million.

These findings underline the need to tackle sustainability not just at the firm level but more comprehensively along the whole supply chain.[47] Supply chain environmental management (SCEM) is emerging as the new frontier in corporate sustainability initiatives. Professor Ralf Seifert comments, "Gaining visibility over your supply base can bring unexpected benefits. For example, Nespresso can now map all of the coffee plantations in Colombia and knows the yields, the qualities, the investments and so on. As it becomes a more constrained market, that's a big competitive advantage."

Supply chain environmental management (SCEM) is emerging as the new frontier in corporate sustainability initiatives.

Most organizations focus on lagging indicators to manage their environmental impacts and neglect leading indicators.[48] Lagging indicators record the effects of prior actions, whereas leading indicators are presumed to be predictors of future performance. For example, energy use is a lagging metric, while our investment in energy conservation represents a leading indicator. It is therefore important to develop a mix of lead and lag indicators. Professor Szekely also insists, "You need to measure

> *Without robust data, we can easily waste resources on projects or misguided investments.*

things that make a difference, not frivolous things. It is important to focus on those aspects of the business that have the greatest real or potential impact on the environment and the organization. Without robust data, we can easily waste resources on projects or misguided investments because we can't properly evaluate the potential payoff of particular sustainability initiatives."

Developing the baseline data is one thing, but we then need to organize the information in a way that best supports decision-making relating to sustainability.[49]

Develop momentum

Having so far emphasized the top-down aspects of a sustainability strategy, we also have to consider how to create widespread participation. Embedding sustainability in the organization is a broad implementation challenge, but two interrelated challenges deserve special attention: we need to organize ourselves to manage the effort; and we need to mobilize employees to innovate and to look for ways to reduce waste, costs and impacts.

While we aim to make sustainability a part of everyone's job, the reality is that we probably need someone to shepherd the effort, at least in the initial stages. Sometimes the CEO plays the role of champion, but we can also choose to create a position, such as chief sustainability officer, to keep sustainability high on the agenda and to facilitate discussions between parties who have different objectives and different views of the organization.

> *Naming a "sustainability champion" can encourage other senior executives to feel that someone else is taking responsibility.*

This role brings its own challenges.[50] Professor Daina Mazutis remarks, "The big danger is that naming a 'sustainability champion' can encourage other senior executives to feel that someone else is taking responsibility for the issue on behalf of the company, so they do not need to."

Moreover, that coordination role is often one of influence without authority.[51] Professor Cyril Bouquet notes, "Such roles involve a lot of collaborating, coaxing and convincing. So it's critical that we select someone with the necessary experience, expertise and clout to be effective, as well as being a direct line to the CEO."

Consider the case of the Irish electric utility, Electricity Supply Board (ESB).[52] In 2008 its CEO Padraig McManus announced that he would make ESB the world's first carbon-neutral electric utility. To drive that initiative, he appointed the former director of human resources, John Campion, as sustainability director. Critically, Campion's appointment was for one year, a clear signal of the intention to turn over responsibility to the management team after that. So one option when creating the CSO role is to clearly frame the job as temporary and to emphasize the importance of integrating sustainability into the organizational decisions and processes.

One option, when creating the CSO role is to clearly frame the job as temporary.

One of Campion's first actions was to speak to all employees via webcast and invite people from all over the company to get involved in the sustainability initiatives and to share their knowledge. His "call to arms" elicited an enthusiastic response. Those who responded became ESB's sustainability champions – around 150 of them – and Campion organized workshops to bring the champions together.

Since sustainability is about "the whole system," we need cross-functional task forces to work on issues and processes that cut across organizational boundaries, and we may need to include external stakeholders.[53] As Professor Michael Yaziji sees it, "We have to get the system into the room – whether its NGOs, unions, governments or communities – sustainable solutions generally demand an interdisciplinary multi-stakeholder approach."

Of course, once we elicit widespread input, we need to ensure that the systems are in place to manage employees' ideas and contributions. We can too easily get ahead of ourselves, training employees on sustainability and generating excitement without having a system in place for vetting and implementing their ideas, and thus risk losing that hard-won momentum.

We can start small with pilot projects and experiments, and build up our competence.[54] Professor Ralf Seifert comments, "Companies need to create opportunities to get their feet wet and learn, because otherwise they will never find out how easy or difficult it is to tackle sustainability or what they might stand to gain in terms of better deals, higher quality, better visibility over their supply base, maybe marketing benefits. It's just too important to be ignored and it will come back to haunt us if we don't develop a competence in it."

Ultimately, corporate sustainability can prove a valuable tool for exploring ways to drive out costs, innovate, galvanize employees, attract talent, deepen ties with

Corporate sustainability can prove a valuable tool to drive out costs, innovate, galvanize employees, attract talent, deepen ties with partners and reach new customers.

partners and reach new customers. The key question is no longer whether sustainability pays, but how it pays.[55] Professor Mazutis explains, "Many firms dabble in sustainability. Taking a strategic approach with an overarching vision has been shown to have a greater impact on financial performance than adopting a jumble of initiatives."

However, integrating sustainability thinking and practice into our organization requires us to sidestep some traps.

AVOID   CARELESS WAYS

Three failings can hold back or derail our sustainability strategy at various stages of its development – unawareness of changes on the fringes of our industry, poor implementation based on misaligned incentives, and backlash based on exaggerated declarations.

Neglecting emerging economies

As established players in our industry, we might try to benchmark the sustainability efforts of our close competitors but we are unlikely to pay much attention to developments in the emerging economies, which are tainted by their poor records on issues such as pollution, health and safety and resource depletion.

The game-changing innovations in sustainability are likely to come from the emerging economies.

Our preconception is that sustainability advances emanate from the industrialized countries before flowing to the emerging economies. But in more and more cases the current is being reversed.[56] Professor Francisco Szekely elaborates, "The game-changing innovations in sustainability are likely to come from the emerging economies. China, for example, is confronted with tremendous challenges in terms of environmental impacts and has incorporated sustainability objectives into its five-year plan. In fact, China now has higher emission standards for cars than the US. Such measures are likely to drive sustainable innovation in companies."

Also, in many emerging economies, corporations are gaining accelerated experience with sustainability issues by getting involved in public–private partnerships on infrastructure projects. For example, in the Philippines, the family-controlled business conglomerate Ayala Corporation took on the challenge of improving Metro Manila's water distribution, finding creative solutions to engage the slum communities to contribute and enable them to pay for the water distribution services.[57] The group's commitment to the triple bottom line won plaudits from Finance Asia, which ranked it as the best-managed company in the Philippines, as well as best for corporate social responsibility.[58]

Beyond feeling the environmental effects and resource constraints more keenly, the developing world often provides a better "incubating" environment for sustainability practices. Emerging economies are less likely to have entrenched infrastructure or legacy systems in place. In the developed world, new technologies can rarely match the performance standards of existing technologies.

The developing world often provides a better "incubating" environment for sustainability practices.

But in certain parts of India, China and Africa, the existing infrastructure is so weak that the performance hurdle is way down. Professor Howard Yu cites the case of renewable energies: "The alternative energy source is immediately comparable or even superior to the existing solution. Once local demand takes off, the provider can continue to innovate and plow money back into R&D to improve the technology, and that is a much more sustainable approach economically than having the government keep pumping tax money into certain technologies in the hope that they will catch up."

As a result, these rapidly growing economies are spawning their own sustainability champions. A good example is the privately held Broad Group in China. Founded in 1988 by Zhang Yue, the company uses the waste heat from buildings to power its non-electric air conditioning units. This technology avoids the use of ozone-depleting refrigerants used in electric cooling, and although it consumes less energy overall, the up-front costs made it a hard sell. Significantly, the initial demand came from areas with unstable electricity systems, but with improved technology, exports have spread into developed markets and large installations such as international airports.

Later, in the wake of the disastrous 2008 earthquake in Sichuan province, the company turned its attention to constructing safer, less environmentally impactful buildings. Professor Daina Mazutis observes, "Using prefabricated components assembled on site, the company has managed to slash the volume of construction materials used and the associated waste. Its buildings have double the energy efficiency and can withstand magnitude 9 earthquakes. Just recently, it

For Western firms operating in the BRIC countries, a commitment to sustainability can help secure local talent.

managed to build a 30-story skyscraper in only 15 days. It has really raised the sustainability bar in the construction sector and caught the big players off guard."

A few Western firms have recognized that fast-growing economies are often more receptive to sustainable innovation and are using their reach advantage to experiment overseas. For example, McDonald's has started fueling its delivery trucks with recycled cooking oil from its own vats, but it does so in the United Arab Emirates, not in the US. Professor Yu notes, "As a multinational company, you can look to countries like China, where the government is eager to embrace alternative energy. And this is why GE's center of excellence for wind turbines, clean coal, nuclear power stations and solar panels is located in Shanghai."

For Western firms operating in the BRIC countries, a commitment to sustainability can also be an important differentiator with regard to securing local talent. Companies report that the best talents in China are making their choices based on sustainability criteria.[59]

Obstructive incentives

As in any transformation journey, it is important to realign the performance management systems. Our existing incentive structures are generally counterproductive for sustainability in two respects. First, they reward and thus perpetuate short-term oriented behaviors, whereas addressing sustainability issues typically requires a long-term outlook. Second, they encourage us to focus on division or unit performance as opposed to corporate-wide performance, and this undermines the cross-boundary collaboration and systemic thinking needed for sustainability breakthroughs.[60]

According to a major cross-industry research project, an absence of incentives for managers to change behaviors is a key internal obstacle to implementing sustainability strategies.[61] This can be the case when making sustainability the responsibility of one department. Dr Aileen Ionescu-Somers explains, "Misaligned incentives may not stop you from pursuing various sustainability initiatives – maybe based on voluntary efforts – but they will limit the real integration of sustainability into the business strategy. Executives outside the CSR function must also be evaluated and rewarded on sustainability results."

As a rule, the more seriously we take sustainability, the more employees will have it in their objectives. Take the case of Brazil's Natura Cosméticos, a manufacturer of personal care products.[62]

The direct-selling company has built its reputation on its commitment to sustainability: working with rural communities to develop ways to extract raw materials in sustainable ways; working with its suppliers to produce sustainable packaging, including a new "green" plastic derived from sugar cane; and working to reduce its own greenhouse gas emissions and water consumption. In 2001 it was the first company in Latin America to adopt the standards of the United Nations' global reporting initiative, producing an integrated report based on its environmental and social performance, as well as its financial results. In accordance with this commitment to the triple bottom line, all three categories impact the managers' performance ratings and bonuses.

Beyond their motivational impact, such changes to the evaluation and reward systems guide our attention and signal the true importance of sustainability to the organization.[63] Professor John Weeks observes, "As far as many employees are concerned, until we get paid for sustainability, we won't believe that the organization is taking it seriously. Having said that, sustainability can be difficult to monitor or measure, so if we can't do those things in a way that is transparent and comprehensible, we may trigger unwanted gaming behaviors or frustrations. Plus, as soon as we start to measure, we also simplify. That's good insofar as it provides clarity and focus, but the downside is that we could miss other ways of creating value through sustainability."

As far as many employees are concerned, until we get paid for sustainability, we won't believe that the organization is taking it seriously.

Some companies have done an outstanding job of building sustainability into their employee evaluation and compensation processes. One of the keys to Tesco's impressive surge on sustainability, mentioned earlier in the chapter, is that it drilled this new commitment into the performance management system with the same rigor and consistency that it had previously applied to its customer focus.[64] In particular, Tesco added a fifth pillar to its balanced scorecard (Steering Wheel), putting its "community" goals on a par with its four existing business drivers, which means that it also contributes to evaluations and bonuses (see **Figure 3**).

Of course, there are other incentives besides monetary rewards. Symbolic awards, recognition and praise may actually speak more to employees than evaluations and bonus payouts.[65] As Professor George Kohlrieser puts it, "Sustainability is deeply bound up with people's values and identities, which transcend

Figure 3: Tesco's steering wheel   Source: Tesco Corporate Responsibility Report, 2011

their organizational roles. One of the risks of attaching big rewards to pursuits that people already value is that it can crowd out their intrinsic motivation. So we have to tread carefully and balance the incentives."

Reckless claims

In terms of sustainability, probably the biggest mistake we can make is to broadcast our intentions without following up. This discredits the value of our ongoing initiatives and lays us open to accusations of "greenwashing."[66] Dr Aileen Ionescu-Somers elaborates, "Whenever we leverage sustainability as part of our competitive positioning or value proposition, we set ourselves up for greater scrutiny and a potential backlash."

> *Whenever we leverage sustainability as part of our competitive positioning or value proposition, we set ourselves up for greater scrutiny.*

A classic example is BP.[67] In 2000, under CEO John Browne, the company took a pioneering stance on climate change and further differentiated itself from rivals by investing in renewable energy and claiming that its initials stood for "Beyond Petroleum." These moves generated positive press, but also drew more attention to its actions.[68] In December 2009, with Tony Hayward now in charge, BP received a "Bad Company Award" from a global consumer body for talking up its commitment to alternative energy but quietly pulling out of major renewable projects.[69] Four months later, BP felt the full weight of public outrage in the wake of the largest offshore oil spill in US history, leading to the ousting of the CEO.[70] Professor Didier Cossin observes, "BP's deeds simply did not match the rhetoric. Its board failed to name a CEO with a strong commitment to the sustainability strategy or to change its own composition itn accordance with that strategy. Even more telling than the catastrophe itself was BP's response, which betrayed its lack of genuine concern for the environment."

People are not easily fooled and are increasingly willing and able to point out gaps between the firm's stated values and its practices.

Many companies have tried to surf the wave of sustainability, adopting slogans along the lines "doing well by doing good."[71] But people are not easily fooled – and consumers, NGOs and former (or disgruntled) employees are increasingly willing and able to point out gaps between the firm's stated values and its practices.[72] Professor Michael Yaziji adds: "Charges of hypocrisy have been leveled at companies partnering with humanitarian NGOs or signing up to the UN Global Compact. This is sometimes called 'bluewashing' in reference to the UN's blue logo. It's when companies spin the communication about their social commitment."

Of course, the larger the organization and the better-known the brand, the more vulnerable it is to such allegations.[73] But even smaller companies can find their efforts drawing unexpected flak. Take the case of the fashion house Noir Illuminati II.[74] Its Danish founder Peter Ingwersen decided to position the brand as socially responsible luxury clothing, using only Fair Trade and organic textiles. It also made contributions to essential medicines and healthcare for the Ugandan cotton workers. Reviewers of the London and New York Fashion Weeks gushed about Ingwersen's trailblazing efforts in the fashion world. But some readers' comments on the same websites condemned the strategy as "greenwash" – trying to make conspicuous consumption acceptable – while others, amid growing concerns about anorexia, attacked the company's choice of skinny models.

Professor Benoît Leleux notes, "The problem highlighted by Noir for companies that take the sustainability route is that they expose themselves to finger-pointing on other CSR issues, especially if they are just targeting the low-hanging fruit. A single discrepancy can damage the whole value."

Clearly, deciding whether or how much to promote our sustainability efforts is tricky. We may elect to stay low profile until we have significant results to report or even to keep our accomplishments for internal consumption only. For example, a large-scale survey of ecolabeling practices shows that over a third of adopters choose not to display their ecolabels on their products.[75] Professor Ralf Seifert comments, "Some companies hold themselves and their suppliers to the standards needed to obtain certification, but do not use it for branding purposes. Increasingly, ecolabels are just part of the price of doing business, rather than significant differentiators."

> *Increasingly, ecolabels are just part of the price of doing business, rather than significant differentiators.*

PAYOFF   TNT REDISTRIBUTES ITS EFFORTS

Consider TNT's journey.[76] It started in November 2001, when Peter Bakker was promoted to CEO of the logistics group, the product of a Dutch–Australian merger. One of the first big decisions Bakker faced was whether to sponsor the Dutch Open Golf Tournament. While good for visibility, Bakker reckoned that the event did little to enhance employee pride or indeed the company's reputation.

Professor Robert Hooijberg observes, "TNT decided instead to invest its expertise and solutions into helping the World Food Program (WFP) fight world hunger. There was enough food, but it was not getting to the people most in need: it was a classic logistics challenge. The partnership between TNT and WFP was also a good cultural match – both very much action-oriented – which is not the case for all NGOs."

> *TNT showed itself capable of setting up a food aid supply chain to victims of natural disasters much faster than any NGO or government could manage.*

TNT employees participated in specialist assignments to improve aid delivery through transport optimization and fleet and warehouse management, as well as responding to international emergencies. TNT showed itself capable of setting up a food aid supply chain to victims of natural disasters much faster than any NGO or government could manage. Beyond those special assignments, TNT's global staff participated in awareness campaigns against hunger, such as Walk the World, to engage more people in support of the cause.

Over half of TNT's 160,000 employees participated in some way, forging new links between disparate divisions and raising employee engagement. TNT's external profile also benefited as it climbed to the top of the Dow Jones Sustainability Index for its sector. Bakker commented, "[Our] service is as good as the motivation of the employees. As CEO, you can talk until you are blue in the face, but the day-to-day interface with customers is done by the mailmen, the mailwomen, the parcel-delivery van drivers. So anything we can do to drive up their pride, to make them a little more motivated for TNT, will help them put in that extra effort for the customer."[77]

While building on the company's core capabilities, this initiative was still at the philanthropic end of the sustainability spectrum rather than contributing directly to strategy. In 2008, Bakker announced an ambitious new program, designed to reduce the group's global carbon footprint and titled "Planet Me." While the previous initiative had focused on TNT's core capabilities, the new initiative targeted the other side of the ledger. As Bakker put it, "As a transport company, we produce only one thing... Our core business is to emit CO_2. That's all we do."[78]

> *As a transport company, we produce only one thing – CO_2.*

This tough self-appraisal spurred TNT's goal to become the world's first zero-emission delivery firm. Implementation of the program illustrated all four sustainability recommendations.

Responsible leadership for a transport company has to include a commitment to minimize its impact on the environment. To underscore the business case for this program, Bakker raised the possibility that TNT could soon run into regulatory problems if it did not reduce its carbon footprint and might not even be allowed to deliver in certain areas like inner cities. As he put it, "Planet Me has nothing to do with 'being nice for the world'; basically, it is going to determine our license to operate." But the program went beyond corporate objectives, setting out to inspire employees to reduce CO_2 levels in their private lives.

Significantly, TNT also maintained its partnership with the WFP and its commitment to ending hunger, signaling that this was no passing fad.

Engaging stakeholders this time round was not so much concerned with convincing investors of the strategic value of the program, which had been an issue for the WFP partnership. To slash CO_2 emissions, electric vehicles (EV) were the most promising technology. The problem was that their high price did not encourage large-scale purchasing. So TNT persuaded 30 Dutch businesses from a broad cross-section of industries to place a collective order for 3,000 electric vehicles. It added up to a commercial investment of €150 million, with TNT making the largest purchase of 600 vehicles. As Bakker explained, "This consortium is an effort to stimulate the kind of change we want to see in the EV market. If we can reduce the barriers for electrifying fleets and make them more financially attractive to business, that result will benefit not only consortium partners but will help to create more demand for sustainable transport solutions."[79]

Critical metrics were developed to track separate KPIs for air transport, road transport and buildings. TNT's "CO_2 Index" provided the platform for setting emission reduction objectives and translating those into measurable actions throughout the organization; highlighting the strategies that were paying dividends, as well as tying the group's CO_2 performance to the top team's bonus objectives. Symbolically, TNT published its CSR report on the same day as its financial results. As Bakker put it, "We think that's important because the vision behind it is that we're growing into a world where CSR is demanding the same discipline inside your companies and gets the same attention from some of your stakeholders as the financials do."[80]

If you get sustainability thinking right, it changes the energy in the organization, including the type of discussion you have with customers.

Developing momentum was essentially a matter of tapping into the same energy and pride that had characterized the partnership with the WFP. One of the initiatives organized by TNT was the annual "Drive Me" challenge, involving teams from TNT offices worldwide competing to be the most fuel efficient. Special technology fed information back in real-time to allow the drivers to adjust their driving behaviors in order to lessen emissions and fuel consumption. Other initiatives to raise awareness and spread best practices ran alongside the efforts to create a community through websites and programs to encourage staff to bring up their ideas. Bakker reflected, "When the person at the top says try something, of course it is easier to get buy-in. But very early on I figured out that this was not sustainable. So I brought in a wide group of managers covering 85% of the workforce into the discussions. What I discovered was that if you get sustainability thinking right, it changes the energy in the organization, including the type of discussion you have with customers. And you realize that for staff it's more than just having financial incentives."[81]

With its own sustainability efforts bearing fruit – and drawing recognition – TNT was able to turn its attention to helping suppliers and subcontractors develop models to estimate emissions and meet their goals too.

Epilogue

After a decade as CEO of TNT, Bakker is now President and CEO of the World Business Council for Sustainable Development. This CEO-led global coalition of some 200 companies provides a platform for companies to share experiences and best practices on sustainable development issues and advocates for their implementation, working with governments, as well as non-governmental and intergovernmental organizations. Bakker took on that role with a firm conviction, "If you apply the skill, the organization, the alertness of businesses to some of the world's problems, you get whole new solutions, and certainly much more speed in the delivery of them."[82]

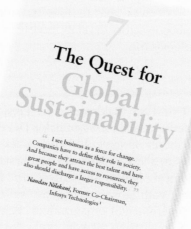

7

The Quest for Global Sustainability

" I see business as a force for change.
Companies have to define their role in society.
And because they attract the best talent and have
great people and have access to resources, they
also should discharge a larger responsibility. "

Nandan Nilekani, Former Co-Chairman,
Infosys Technologies [1]

Where Do We Stand?

1. How important is sustainability to our strategic thinking?

2. What is the key sustainability concern in our industry, business or operation?

3. Which new parties should we integrate into our thinking and engage in order to become more sustainable?

4. What are the potential costs of pursuing sustainability?

5. How should we measure and communicate our progress toward sustainability?

6. How will we mobilize the entire organization to participate in the effort to become more sustainable?

7. What sustainability innovations can we adopt from the emerging economies?

Conclusion: Learning from Transformation Journeys

" I try to have clear goals for myself as well as the company. But I also try to enjoy the journey towards the goal. **"**

Igor Allinckx, CEO, Sekisui Alveo AG[1]

LESSONS FROM CHINA'S SECOND ACT

China was once the world's leading innovator. Until the early 15th century, China had been the dominant force in scientific discovery and technological advancement for over a thousand years.[2] In addition to the fine silks and ceramic products produced by Ming Dynasty artisans and traded across vast areas, China had given birth to wood-block printing, paper money, canal lock gates, chain suspension bridges and gunpowder.

With 600 years of sailing experience, it had also become the leading naval power.[3] The Chinese boasted key maritime inventions long before the West, notably magnetized compasses and watertight bulkhead compartments, enabling Chinese ships to cover massive distances. The ships also featured on-board vegetable patches, where soybeans were cultivated in tubes as sources of protein and vitamin C to ward off scurvy.[4]

The best known of China's naval explorers was Admiral Zheng He, who made seven major voyages in the early decades of the 15th century.[5] Zheng He traveled to more than 30 countries with a fleet of over 300 ships (junks) and 28,000 sailors. He sailed down the South China Sea, into the Java Sea, up the Bay of Bengal, down across the Indian Ocean, up the Arabian Sea, then into the Red Sea, and even around the Cape of Good Hope 76 years before Vasco da Gama did.[6]

But the admiral's exploits turned out to be the end point rather than the starting point for China's domination of the seas and mercantile expansion. Soon after Zheng He's final expedition, the Ming court adopted a policy of isolationism, banning overseas travel, shutting down the shipyards and destroying the ocean-going ships, as well as the records of Zheng He's travels. Later they even prohibited trade with foreign nations and people.[7]

This isolationist stance lasted centuries, during which time China lost its lead in science, technology and innovation, as European powers took over exploration of the seas, world trade and launched their own scientific and industrial revolutions. Instead of being a shaper of globalization, China became an observer, some might even say a victim, of it.[8]

Essentially, China did not recover until its leaders chose to engage with the world again under Deng Xiaoping in 1978. By this stage, following the disastrous experiments carried out under the regime of Mao Zedong, China was on the verge of economic collapse. Professor Winter Nie explains, "Having understood that retrenchment was no longer a viable option, China's rulers executed a 180-degree turn, choosing to engage with the world and to learn from it, through trade and collaboration, inward foreign investment and technology transfer. Initially, China became a 'factory for the world' but very quickly, Chinese multinationals started to establish themselves in knowledge and technology-intensive businesses."

China also learned from the vibrant examples of Hong Kong and Taiwan, which had benefited from the exodus of Chinese business leaders and foreign investors following the Communist victory in 1949 and the purges that followed.[9] According to Professor Jean-Pierre Lehmann, "The demonstration effect of Hong Kong and Taiwan, both of which were able to grow spectacularly through open trade policies, had a significant

When China dwarfed Europe: Zheng He's flagship towers over Columbus's Santa Maria (to scale)

impact on the thinking of the Chinese reformers in the late 1980s. These economies served as models or even 'pilot schemes' for what reform could achieve."

The case of China represents a remarkable example of the possibilities of large-scale transformation. It also highlights the importance of journeys of exchange as enablers of innovation and progress. When China stopped trading, it lost its appetite for change and the flow of ingenuity stopped.

Metaphors matter

The journey as a metaphor for *personal* change has a long history stretching back to the Mesopotamian *Epic of Gilgamesh* 4,000 years ago, *The Odyssey, Sinbad the Sailor, Don Quixote, Gulliver's Travels, Heart of Darkness, The Lord of the Rings*, right up to *Star Wars*. The journeys undertaken by the protagonists enabled them to grow and to gain new insight and understanding of themselves and the world around them.

Increasingly, the journey frame has also become a feature of the way we talk about organizational change. The journey metaphor likens the corporation to a traveler. Corporate strategies are often expressed in terms of maps, destinations, milestones, paths, barriers and setbacks. Professor Ben Bryant comments, "Metaphors play a vital role in helping us to project ourselves into the future. They help us to picture the challenge and engage our emotions. They play a key mobilizing role by bringing a shared collective understanding to a situation that is confusing and poorly understood. They help us communicate the nature of the initiative, the possibilities for action, and they make the challenge feel manageable."

Metaphors play a key mobilizing role by bringing a shared collective understanding to a situation that is confusing and poorly understood.

This is powerfully illustrated by the case of the UK-based insurer Prudential.[10] The journey metaphor was central to the transformation of its UK and European business from a siloed operation with an outdated business model into an integrated and customer-responsive organization. To persuade employees that the sacrifices would be worthwhile, CEO Mark Wood spoke to them about the "1,000-day journey," giving a strong time-bound element to the effort and underlining the fact that *every day counts*. He gave an additional twist to the metaphor by projecting into the future, with the transformation already completed, and relating what it would feel like looking back. The story was evocative of positive experiences and joint action.

As one executive commented, "It captured the fact that most people in an organization this size have much greater empathy with the customer than they have with the organization. They're not turned on by financial results or rates of return. But they're really interested in how they can personally provide a good service to the customers to make them feel good about themselves. That's what the story really nailed." The story contained the goal, the path for getting there and how one would feel at the end of the journey. It gave people a "big picture" understanding of what needed to be done.

The journey metaphor and the notion of a quest have been adopted as a theme throughout the book because they are persuasive and facilitate communication. But the means of transport is also important. Unlike plane, train or bus journeys, which all evoke the idea of one driver and many passengers, transformation efforts are collaborative ventures requiring strong relationships and open communication.

The most compelling image is therefore that of galleons or junks setting forth on expeditions into a world only partially known. Such voyages share key characteristics with the context and dynamics of corporate transformation efforts. Even though the skipper and crew embark on the voyage with a planned route, the map does not indicate the conditions and perils they may encounter from various quarters. Careful preparation, ample supplies and an experienced crew provide only limited security. Unsure of the challenges they will confront, the crew members need to constantly review and adapt the strategy to the changing conditions. Unified action is critical and they all have to play their usual role and even improvise when needed. The seagoing voyage also captures some of the sense of adventure and the rewards for getting it right, including the transformational impact of the journey on the crew and eventually on the globe itself.

The journey metaphor also helps us to reflect on some of the overarching lessons learned from the preceding chapters.

JOURNEY LESSONS

The central premise of this book is that leaders change corporations by embarking on transformational journeys. Some quests are forced and some are chosen. Sometimes we are pioneers and sometimes we are following well-charted routes. Some journeys hold out the promise of rapid rewards, while in other cases the payoff is distant and diffuse. Before agreeing to set off on an arduous and possibly perilous quest, we would want to know at least four things: why we must move now, where we are heading, how to get there and whether the journey will be worthwhile.

Why we must move now

As discussed in each chapter, our reasons for embarking on a journey may differ greatly, but in all cases we need to be clear on our starting position. What is our current reality and what tells us that it is unsustainable? This is more complex than it sounds, not so much because we lack the data, but because we are reluctant to discuss it openly.

To make an honest appraisal, we must look at our organization from the outside-in, taking the perspective of external stakeholders, such as suppliers, dealers and customers, both those we like and those we do not. Given half the chance, they would gladly let us know where our company is falling short, provided there are no sanctions. Often, people *within* the organization – especially those on the front lines – know very well what the outside world thinks of us. But raising those issues in public is difficult and may be seen as disloyal. We generally prefer to focus on our strengths and to convince ourselves that our weaknesses occur in areas of limited interest.[11]

> *We generally prefer to focus on our strengths and to convince ourselves that our weaknesses occur in areas of limited interest.*

The first step in a transformation process is therefore to face reality and to establish a joint perception of that reality. How clear and pressing are the forces driving our quest, and how ready are the people who will be most involved in or affected by the change? Looking at the change curve (see **Figure 1**), we can broadly distinguish between changes that are anticipatory, reactive and critical.[12]

The further we move along the change curve from anticipatory change to crisis change, the easier it is to justify change, in that we can all see the need for it. The problem is that we no longer have the same time, resources or options available. In parallel, the cost of change also rises since it may involve workforce reductions and selling off valuable assets cheaply, with potential repercussions on the reputation of the firm in the eyes of customers, suppliers and society. With anticipatory change, the main problem is internal resistance since nothing is visibly broken – plus there is the risk of misreading the dim signals and pursuing the wrong transformation. Starting too soon can be just as damaging as starting too late.[14]

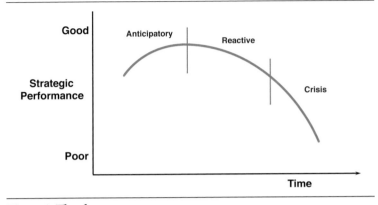

Figure 1: The change curve   Source: Mary Crossan, Michael Rouse, Joseph Fry and Peter Killing[13]

According to Professor Peter Killing, "The problem is that we all have different opinions on where we are on the curve. The top team may think it has the best view, but their view can be biased because they don't see what is happening further down in the organization; they don't feel the resistance or the pressures that are experienced in different businesses or regions. In fact, we delude ourselves by looking for a single point. To understand the change challenges that we face as a company, we have to appreciate that different parts of the business face different pressures and opportunities for responding."

Without a common understanding of the long-term trends impacting our industry and our current weaknesses, we may hold vastly different views on where the problems lie and what kind of response is needed. It is important to establish why we must move, and why now is the best time to start.

Where we are heading

A recurring theme in the quests is that the very same words – agility, value, sustainability and global – can mean totally different things to different parties. This can be a source of richness and strength if the differences are discussed, but it can lead to confusion and conflict if they are not surfaced.

Transformational change requires a clear idea of where we want to go. So as a leadership team we must build a shared ambition of the future path along which the company will move.[15] Professor James Henderson points out, "There are no right or wrong answers. Therefore, making these choices *together* is a fundamental task of leadership teams. They have to reason in terms of 'what *must* we do?' rather than 'what *can* we do?' –

which obviously means stepping out of their comfort zone."

Agreeing among ourselves is one thing. Communicating the message is another. If the resulting direction and destination are hazy, collective motivation to move forward will quickly flag. This seems too obvious to state. Yet as leaders we often overestimate how clearly we have communicated the direction and destination. We also forget to allow for the fact that we have been privy to these strategic discussions for months and that employees also need to be given time to make the same mental journey.

This puts the onus on us as leaders to assess whether people across the organization are able to see the destination or target clearly.[16] Professor Stewart Black explains, "If the desired future state is clear enough, people should be able to describe it and to speculate about its likely implications. They should be able to translate it into concrete behaviors for the situations they confront."

How we get there

If we hope to get people to move on a quest, we need a credible plan. While each of the transformation journeys prioritizes different actions, an underlying commonality is the need for realignment. According to Marina Gorbis, executive director at the Institute for the Future, "You need to look at every aspect of your organization and ask yourself a question: If you were starting this today, with today's set of technologies, with today's set of knowledge, would you organize it the way you have it organized right now?"[17]

If you were starting this business today, with today's set of technologies, with today's set of knowledge, would you organize it the way you have it organized right now?

A lot has been written about implementing corporate transformations. We have *process* models that tell us the appropriate sequence of actions to build momentum, starting with a sense of urgency, and we have *content* models that emphasize the multi-faceted nature of corporate change and the need to integrate our efforts as we redesign the reporting lines, systems and processes.

Unfortunately, there is still a significant gap between what we recognize as good practice and what we actually do. For example, one of the fundamentals of transformation is the need to realign rewards with the new goal. Yet IMD surveys of international senior executives show that performance evaluation objectives and compensation are only tied to ongoing transformation efforts in 55% of cases. This ranges from a low of 30%, for executives involved in a journey to co-innovation, to a high of 83% for those pursuing greater agility. Without claiming that incentives guarantee commitment or even superior effort, we do know that sticking with the old reward system hinders progress, if only for signaling reasons.

Another fallacy is our tendency to think that if we change things, then people will follow.[18] As Professor Black points out, "The reality is that organizations change only as much or as fast as individuals change. We have to start by changing the mental maps that have guided our actions in the past. We have to move from the individual-out, rather than the organization-in."

Our role is to create the set of conditions that support the people in the front line, that allow them to know more, care more and contribute more.[19] Professor Dan Denison observes, "Successful transformation efforts result not only in productivity improvements but also in behavioral and attitudinal changes. One way of determining the extent of change is to conduct organizational culture surveys to track progress as the transformation unfolds."

Transformation journeys cannot be mapped out entirely in advance. As leaders, we must steer a course between order and disorder at the same time, leaving room for experimentation and divergent views, while simultaneously providing boundaries and key ideas so that the energy can be channeled. Like navigators at the helm of a vessel, we have to harness the opposing forces of the changing winds and currents just to maintain a particular course.

It will be worth it

Beyond knowing where we're heading and how we plan to get there, we also have to *believe* in where we're heading. Transformations require us to undergo large amounts of stress and to make significant sacrifices. Before signing up, we therefore want some reassurance that the benefits of the journey will exceed the costs, some sense of the time and effort we will need to invest before we see the fruits. Put another way, why should we stay the course?

Even if our company's existence hangs in the balance, our big concern is not whether the company will survive, but what it will look like afterwards. Survival in itself is an uninspiring goal.

Even if our company's existence hangs in the balance, survival in itself is an uninspiring goal.

As employees, we want to feel a sense of excitement about the future.[20] As Professor Paul Strebel puts it, "People are energized by the opportunity to grow personally and to be part of a larger winning purpose that extends beyond the immediate value of their services in the marketplace."

The defining characteristic of organizations is precisely their capacity to allow ordinary people to do extraordinary things, and as leaders we must build on that. Besides increasing the future "gain," leaders can also reduce the immediate "pain." To take change on board willingly, people need a secure base from which to operate in order to feel trust and safety, and this relies in large part on the quality of leadership throughout the organization.[21] Professor George Kohlrieser comments, "In the midst of upheaval, leaders need to provide a sense of protection and stability. When leaders fulfill their role as secure bases, followers feel safe enough to stop focusing on the dangers and to start seeking the benefits sooner than employees without secure bases."

A lifelong journey

Large organizations have traditionally been built for stability, not only in their structures and processes but also in their strategies. The holy grail of strategy is to establish a permanent competitive advantage. From that perspective, corporate change has tended to be viewed as a necessary evil, often requiring a crisis to stir us into action. Periods of change have long been regarded as intrusions, punctuating the normal equilibrium. Professor Maury Peiperl notes, "Corporate transformation is too often regarded as an intervention, a parenthesis to business as usual, to be launched then discontinued once the desired outcomes have been achieved."

Such "start-stop" models of transformation are out of sync with the realities of an environment characterized by turbulence and incessant change. We now operate in a much more fluid and dynamic environment, requiring us to morph endlessly from one shape to the next. Changes come thick and fast, sometimes driven by external events or by initiatives in different parts of the organization. Our ability to absorb change is severely tested by the need to implement overlapping changes. Such a context requires us, as leaders and change agents, to rethink our views of resistance to change. Encountering opposition, we remain too ready to attribute it to the anxieties or competence levels of the individuals concerned. Often it is driven by the perceived relevance or feasibility of the proposed change, the way it has been developed or communicated. There may also be an element of change fatigue, based on frustration with previous "flavor of the month" programs.

> *People don't necessarily resist change. What they resist is having change imposed upon them.*

In a context of continuous transformation, we need to get beyond the symptoms of resistance and address its root causes. As Professor Kohlrieser puts it, "People don't necessarily resist change. What they resist is having change imposed upon them, change that they don't feel a part of. So for continuous renewal to work, employee engagement is really key."

Our collective capacity for change is the only enduring advantage in a chaotic environment. The transformation journeys we embark on deliver only temporary advantages, so we have to string these together to achieve more lasting competitive advantage.

The examples we have highlighted in each chapter may have got one journey right, but it is no guarantee of their enduring health. They have just built up their capabilities to keep exploring new territories. However successful our transformation journey, there is no end state, only a changed world and another journey to start. The quest is endless.

As global executives, we still occasionally need to step back and reflect on how far we have traveled, to celebrate these achievements, and to keep learning. Our challenge is to use our capacity for learning to create a better world. We need to carry this sense of responsibility on our next quest.

References

Introduction: The Quest for Transformation

[1] Etzioni, A. (1964). *Modern organizations*. Englewood Cliffs, NJ: Prentice-Hall.

[2] See http://inventors.about.com/od/timelines/a/Nineteenth.htm

[3] Rothkopf, D. (2012). *Power, Inc: The epic rivalry between big business and government – and the reckoning that lies ahead*. New York: Farrar, Straus & Giroux.

[4] Micklethwait, J. & Wooldridge, A. (2005). *The company: A short history of a revolutionary idea*. London: Phoenix.

[5] Jouko Karvinen interviewed by Paul Hunter (2013). "Looking to past values to get ahead of the curve," featured on IMD's exclusive Corporate Learning Network "Wednesday Webcast" series, January 13.

[6] Chanda, N. (2007). *Bound together: How traders, preachers, adventurers, and warriors shaped globalization*. New Haven: Yale University Press.

[7] Primo Braga, C. A. & Lehmann, J.-P. (2013). "The BRICS are here, but where is the mortar?" *Tomorrow's Challenges*, TC026-13, April. Lausanne: IMD.

[8] Steger, U., Amann, W. & Maznevski, M. (2007). *Managing complexity in global organizations*. Chichester, UK: John Wiley.

[9] Kotter, J. P. (1995). "Leading change: Why transformation efforts fail." *Harvard Business Review*, 73(2): 59-67.

[10] Vollmann, T. E. (1996). *The transformation imperative: Achieving market dominance through radical change*. Boston, MA: Harvard Business School Press.

[11] Miles, R. H. (1997). *Leading corporate transformation: A blueprint for business renewal*. San Francisco, CA: Jossey-Bass.

[12] Hooijberg, R. & Lane, N. (2013) "Transformational leadership." In E. H. Kessler (ed.) *Encyclopedia of management theory*. Thousand Oaks, CA: Sage.

[13] Denison, D., Hooijberg, R., Lane, N. & Lief, C. (2012). *Leading culture change in global organizations: Aligning culture and strategy*. San Francisco, CA: Jossey-Bass.

[14] Chakravarthy, B. & Lorange, P. (2008) *Profit or growth? Why you don't have to choose*. Upper Saddle River, NJ: Wharton School Publishing.

Chapter 1: The Quest for Global Presence

[1] Adel Al-Saleh interviewed by Preston Bottger and Paul Hunter (2008). "Leading in the top team: The CXO challenge," featured on IMD's exclusive Corporate Learning Network "Wednesday Webcast" series, November 26.

[2] Diffie, B. W. & Winius, G. D. (1977). *Foundations of the Portuguese Empire, 1415-1580*. Minnesota: University of Minnesota Press.

[3] Maddison, A. (2001). *The world economy: A millennial perspective*. Paris: OECD.

[4] Bergreen, L. (2004). *Over the edge of the world: Magellan's terrifying circumnavigation of the globe*. New York: HarperCollins.

[5] Barrera-Osorio, A. (2006). *Experiencing nature: The Spanish American Empire and the early scientific revolution*. Austin: University of Texas Press.

[6] Portuondo, M. M. (2009). *Secret science: Spanish cosmography and the New World*. Chicago: University of Chicago Press.

[7] Brotton, J. (2012). *A history of the world in twelve maps*. London: Allen Lane.

[8] Smith, R. C. (1993). *Vanguard of empire: Ships of exploration in the age of Columbus*. Oxford: Oxford University Press.

[9] Rosenzweig, P., Gilbert, X., Malnight, T. & Pucik, V. (2001). *Accelerating international growth*. Chichester, UK: John Wiley.

[10] Bartlett, C. A. & Ghoshal, S. (1989). *Managing across borders: The transnational solution*. Boston: Harvard Business School Press.

[11] Ichijo, K. & Kohlbacher, F. (2007). "The Toyota way of global knowledge creation: The 'learn local, act global' strategy." *International Journal of Automotive Technology & Management*, 7(2/3): 116-134.

[12] Fang, Y., Wade, M., Delios, A. & Beamish, P. W. (2007). "International diversification, subsidiary performance, and the mobility of knowledge resources." *Strategic Management Journal*, 28(10): 1053-1064.

[13] Rosenzweig, P. (2001). "International growth is everybody's business." In P. Rosenzweig, X. Gilbert, T. Malnight & V. Pucik *Accelerating international growth* (pp. 1-18). Chichester, UK: John Wiley.

[14] Henderson, J. & Bochukova, P. (2012). *ISS acquisition strategy (C)*. IMD case series IMD-3-2284.

[15] Malnight, T. W. & Keys, T. S. (2012). "Global trends for 2013: A top ten for business leaders." *The Economist*, November 26.

[16] Rosenzweig, P. M. (1994). "The new "American challenge." Foreign multinationals in the United States." *California Management Review*, 36(3): 107-123.

[17] For example, Fernandes, N. (2012). *Telefónica's bid for the mobile market in Brazil*. IMD case no. IMD-3-2320. See also, Ben-Hur, S. & Anderson, J. (2011). *Deutsche Telekom: A transformation journey*. IMD case no. IMD-3-2150.

[18] Lars Olofsson interviewed by Paul Hunter (2010). "Lessons from the top," featured on IMD's exclusive Corporate Learning Network "Wednesday Webcast" series, November 25.

[19] Cossin, D. & Keuleneer, L (2008). *Deal making in troubled waters: The ABN AMRO takeover*. IMD case no. IMD-1-0276.

[20] Sjöblom, L., Knecht, S. & Baumann, M. (2012). *The global logistics industry in 2012*. IMD case no. IMD-1-0331.

[21] Lane, H. W., Maznevski, M. L. & Mendenhall, M. E. (2004). "Globalization: Hercules meets Buddha." In H. W. Lane, M. L. Maznevski, M. E. Mendenhall, & J. McNett (eds.) *The Blackwell handbook of global management: A guide to managing complexity* (pp. 3-25). Malden, MA: Blackwell Publishing.

[22] Gilbert, X. (2001). "Stretching the business model globally: The outside-in approach and the learning intent." In P. Rosenzweig, X. Gilbert, T. Malnight & V. Pucik *Accelerating international growth* (pp. 167-188). Chichester, UK: John Wiley.

[23] Morrison, A. & Bouquet, C. (2011). "Are you giving globalization the right amount of attention?" *MIT Sloan Management Review*, 52(2): 15-16.

[24] Birkinshaw, J., Bouquet, C. & Ambos, T. C. (2007). "Managing executive attention in the global company." *MIT Sloan Management Review*, 48(4): 39-45.

[25] Bouquet, C. & Bryant, B. (2009). "The crisis is here to stay. Do you have the key to coping?" *Forbes.com*, April 21.

[26] Bouquet, C. & Birkinshaw, J. (2008). "Weight versus voice: How foreign subsidiaries gain attention from corporate headquarters." *Academy of Management Journal*, 51(3): 577-601.

[27] Bryant, B. & Wildi, J. (2008). "Mindfulness." *Perspectives for Managers*, no. 162, September. Lausanne: IMD.

[28] Bryant, B. & Jonsen, K. (2008). "Cross-cultural leadership: How to run operations in markets we don't understand." *Tomorrow's Challenges*, TC082-08, October. Lausanne: IMD.

[29] Fernandes, N. (2011). "Global convergence of financing policies: Evidence for emerging market firms." *Journal of International Business Studies*, Oct/Nov, 42(8): 1043-1059.

[30] Leleux, B. F., Turpin, D. & Brochier, T. (2008). *La Martina: Selling the passion*, IMD case series IMD-3-1971.

[31] Turpin, D. (2013). "Big global brands are now born everywhere." *Financial Times*, February 20: 10.

[32] Nie, W., Dowell, W. & Lu, A. (2012). *In the shadow of the dragon: The global expansion of Chinese companies – and how it will change business forever* (pp. 227-244). New York: Amacon.

[33] Lago, U., Fischer, W. A. & Liu, F. (2012). *Creating a customer-oriented company: ZZJYT at Haier*. IMD case no. IMD-3-2351.

[34] Rosenzweig, P. (2012). "Best business books 2012: Strategy." *Strategy & Business*, November 27: 21-25.

[35] Leleux, B. F. & Schuepbach, M. (2003). *Papyrus Laser (C): Going Vistaprint.com*. IMD case series IMD-3-0976.

[36] Yu, H. (2012). "Can China develop its own brand?" *Harvard Business Review China*, April 23.

[37] Morrison, A. J., Bouquet, C. & Beck, J. C. (2004). "Netchising: The next global wave?" *Long Range Planning*, 37(1): 11-27.

[38] Lane, H. W., Maznevski, M. L. & Mendenhall, M. E. (2004). "Globalization: Hercules meets Buddha." In H. W. Lane, M. L. Maznevski, M. E. Mendenhall & J. McNett (eds.) *The Blackwell handbook of global management: A guide to managing complexity* (pp. 3-25). Malden, MA: Blackwell Publishing.

[39] Steger, U., Amann, W. & Maznevski, M. (2007). *Managing complexity in global organizations*. Chichester, UK: John Wiley.

[40] Wade, M. & Büchel, B. (2013). "Anchored agility: The holy grail of competitiveness." *Perspectives for Managers*, no. 186, June. Lausanne: IMD.

[41] Wade, M. & Büchel, B. (2013). "Anchored agility: The holy grail of competitiveness." *Perspectives for Managers*, no. 186, June. Lausanne: IMD.

[42] Chakravarthy, B. & Henderson, J. (2007). "From a hierarchy to a heterarchy of strategies: Adapting to a changing context." *Management Decision*, 45 (3): 642-652.

[43] Bouquet, C., Birkinshaw, J. & DuBrule, A. (2010). *Global growth at Irdeto (B): A dual HQ strategy*. IMD case series IMD-3-2090.

44 Graham Kill interviewed by Paul Hunter (2010). "Lessons from the top," featured on IMD's exclusive Corporate Learning Network "Wednesday Webcast" series, July 3.

45 Narasimhan, A. & Daft, R. L. (2007). "What is the right organization design?" *Organizational Dynamics*, 36(4): 329-344.

46 Maznevski, M. L., Steger, U. & Amann, W. (2007). "Managing complexity in global organizations." *Perspectives for Managers*, no. 141, February. Lausanne: IMD.

47 Chakravarthy, B. (2010). "The sharing imperative." *Strategy & Leadership*, 38(1): 37-41.

48 Levy, O., Schon, B., Taylor, S. & Boyacigiller, N. A. (2007). "What we talk about when we talk about 'global mindset': Managerial cognition in multinational corporations." *Journal of International Business Studies*, 38(2): 231-258.

49 Lane, H. W., Maznevski, M. L. & Mendenhall, M. E. (2004). "Globalization: Hercules meets Buddha." In H. W. Lane, M. L. Maznevski, M. E. Mendenhall & J. McNett (eds.) *The Blackwell handbook of global management: A guide to managing complexity* (pp. 3-25). Malden, MA: Blackwell Publishing.

50 Black, J. S., Morrison, A. J. & Gregersen, H. B. (1999). *Global explorers: The next generation of leaders*. New York: Routledge.

51 Bryant, B. & Jonsen, K. (2008). "Cross-cultural leadership: How to run operations in markets we don't understand." *Tomorrow's Challenges*, TC082-08, October. Lausanne: IMD.

52 Black, J. S. & Morrison, A. J. (2010). *Sunset in the land of the rising sun*. New York: Palgrave Macmillan.

53 Nie, W., Dowell, W. & Lu, A. (2012). *In the shadow of the dragon: The global expansion of Chinese companies – and how it will change business forever* (pp. 99-124). New York: Amacon.

54 Hooijberg, R. & DiTomaso, N. (1996). "Leadership in and of demographically diverse organizations." *The Leadership Quarterly*, 7(1): 1-19.

55 Mendenhall, M. E., Jensen, R. J., Black, J. S. & Gregersen, H. B. (2003). "Seeing the elephant: Human resource management challenges in the age of globalization." *Organizational Dynamics*, 32(3): 261-273.

56 Ben-Hur, S. & Rutsch, A. (2012). *The corporate learning function and business transformation: The case of Capgemini*. IMD case no. IMD-4-0327.

57 Kettinger, W. J., Marchand, D. A. & Davis, J. M. (2010). "Designing enterprise IT architectures to optimize flexibility and standardization in global business." *MIS Quarterly Executive*, 9(2): 95-113.

58 Marchand, D. A. & Hykes, A. (2007). "The role of information in creating value efficiently." In U. Steger, W. Amann & M. Maznevski (eds.) *Managing complexity in global organizations* (pp. 169-189). Chichester, UK: Wiley.

59 Ichijo, K. (2007). "Enabling knowledge-based competence of a corporation." In K. Ichijo & I. Nonaka (eds.) *Knowledge creation and management: New challenges for managers* (pp. 83-96). Oxford, UK: Oxford University Press.

60 Marchand, D. A. & Peppard, J. (2013). "Why IT fumbles analytics." *Harvard Business Review*, 91(1): 104-112.

[61] Levy, O., Peiperl, M. A. & Bouquet, C. (2013). "Transnational social capital: A conceptualization and research instrument." *International Journal of Cross-cultural Management*, published online June 26, doi: 10.1177/1470595813485940.

[62] Anand, N. & Conger, J. A. (2007). "Capabilities of the consummate networker." *Organizational Dynamics*, 36(1): 13-27.

[63] Maznevski, M. L. & Shaner, J. (2011). "The relationship between networks, institutional development, and performance in foreign investments." *Strategic Management Journal*, 32(5): 556-568.

[64] Pulcrano, J., Shaner, J. & Fischer, W. (2008). "Your network balance sheet: What does it look like and where should you invest?" *Perspectives for Managers*, no. 160, July. Lausanne: IMD.

[65] Broeckx, P. V. & Hooijberg, R. (2008). "Nestlé on the move." *Perspectives for Managers*, no. 156, April. Lausanne: IMD.

[66] Fayard, A.-L. & Weeks, J. (2011). "Who moved my cube?" *Harvard Business Review*, 89(7/8): 102-110.

[67] Black, J. S. & Morrison, A. J. (2010). "A cautionary tale for emerging market giants." *Harvard Business Review*, 88(9): 99-103.

[68] Levy, O., Taylor, S., Beechler, S., Boyacigiller, N. A. & Peiperl, M. A. (2013). "Perceived global mindset: The effect of national social identities and demographic characteristics." Conference paper presented at the Academy of International Business (Istanbul, Turkey), July 3.

[69] Bouquet, C. & Birkinshaw, J. (2008). "Weight versus voice: How foreign subsidiaries gain attention from corporate headquarters." *Academy of Management Journal*. 51(3): 577-601.

[70] Rädler, G. & Steger, U. (1999). *The DaimlerChrysler Merger (A): Gaining global competitiveness*. IMD case no. IMD-3-0834.

[71] Rädler, G. & Steger, U. (2003). *DaimlerChrysler: Corporate governance dynamics in a global company*. IMD case no. IMD-3-1273.

[72] Vlasic, B. & Stertz, B. (2001). *Taken for a ride: How Daimler-Benz drove off with Chrysler*. New York: HarperCollins.

[73] Turpin, D. & Takatsu, N. (2012). *Japan's competitiveness in the age of globalization*. Tokyo: Nikkei Publishing.

[74] Tungli, Z. & Peiperl, M. (2009). "Expatriate practices in German, Japanese, U.K., and U.S. multinational companies: A comparative survey of changes." *Human Resource Management*, 48(1): 153-171.

[75] Woodford, M. (2012). *Exposure: From president to whistleblower at Olympus*. London: Portfolio Penguin.

[76] Turpin, D. (2013). "Global (non)competitiveness." *Tomorrow's Challenges*, TC001-13, January. Lausanne: IMD.

[77] Rosenzweig, P. (2006). "Learning from mergers and acquisitions: Beware of biases." *Tomorrow's Challenges*, TC070-06, December. Lausanne: IMD.

[78] Eban, K. (2013). "Dirty medicine." *Fortune* online, May 15.

[79] Caroline Firstbrook interviewed by Paul Hunter (2009). "A brave new world: Why nothing will ever be the same again," featured on IMD's exclusive Corporate Learning Network "Wednesday Webcast" series, November 18.

[80] Yasuchika Hasegawa interviewed by Dominique Turpin (2011). "Interviews with top leaders," December 8. See http://www.youtube.com/watch?v=ThpIufIxk0s.

[81] Hasegawa, Y. (2011). "Takeda eyes setting up overseas HQ." *Nikkei Report*, May 20.

[82] Hasegawa, Y. (2011). "Biggest challenge is decline in R&D productivity." *Pharma Japan*, October 31: 51.

[83] Turpin, D. (2013). "Why Japanese companies are falling behind the rest of the world." *ForbesIndia.com*, January 28.

[84] Jack, A. (2013). "A new corporate focus." *Financial Times*, February 5: 14.

[85] Black, J. S. & Morrison, A. J. (2010). *Sunset in the land of the rising sun.* New York: Palgrave Macmillan.

[86] The Nikkei (2012). "Japan pharma: Modern firms must be global and diverse." *Economist Intelligence Unit*, March 19.

[87] Transcript (2012). "Takeda Pharmaceutical earnings presentation," *CQ FD Disclosure*, October 31.

[88] Inagaki, K. (2012). "Takeda aims for top in vaccines." *Wall Street Journal Asia*, November 12: 28.

Chapter 2: The Quest for Global Value Generation

[1] Muhtar Kent interviewed by Paul Hunter (2008). "Lessons from the top," featured on IMD's exclusive Corporate Learning Network "Wednesday Webcast" series, December 17.

[2] McKendrick, N. (1970). "Josiah Wedgwood and cost accounting in the Industrial Revolution." *Economic History Review*, 23(1): 45-67.

[3] Salvatore Cantale interviewed by Paul Hunter (2011). "How business should talk to finance," featured on IMD's exclusive Corporate Learning Network "Wednesday Webcast" series, November 2.

[4] Porter, M. (1985). *Competitive advantage: Creating and sustaining superior performance.* New York: Free Press.

[5] Sjöblom, L. (2008). "The chief financial officer – a capital position." In P. Bottger (ed.) *Leading in the top team: The CXO challenge* (pp. 161-181). Cambridge: Cambridge University Press.

[6] Walsh, J., Woolfrey, A. & Coughlan, S. (2011). *The Coca-Cola Company.* IMD case no. IMD-5-0767.

[7] Chakravarthy, B. & Zintel, C. (2012). *Maggi noodles in India: Creating and growing the category.* IMD case no. IMD-3-2296.

[8] Enders, A., König, A., Hungenberg, H. & Engelbertz, T. (2009). "Towards an integrated perspective of strategy: The value-process framework." *Journal of Strategy and Management*, 2(1): 76-96.

[9] Enders, A., König, A., Hungenberg, H. & Engelbertz, T. (2009). "Towards an integrated perspective of strategy: The value-process framework." *Journal of Strategy and Management*, 2(1): 76-96.

[10] Fischer, W. & Henderson-Cohen, M. (2005). *Gutenberg's last laugh? Rethinking the book business,* IMD case no. IMD-3-1550.

[11] Cantale, S. & Coughlan, S. (2012). *Twitter: The struggle for value*. IMD case no. IMD-3-2271.

[12] Fernandes, N. (2013). *Finance for global managers*. In press.

[13] Fischer, W. A. (2010). *Dell Computers (A): 1984-2005*. IMD case no. IMD-3-2092.

[14] Fernandes, N. (2009). "The value of the long-term view: Balancing the shareholders' and stakeholders' priorities." *Tomorrow's Challenges*, TC083-09, November. Lausanne: IMD.

[15] Yaziji, M. (2008). "Time to rethink capitalism?" *Harvard Business Review*, November, 86(11): 27-28.

[16] Morrison, A. (2013). "Diversification key to global expansion: Proactive strategies for emerging market companies." *Tomorrow's Challenges*, TC035-13, May. Lausanne: IMD.

[17] Malnight, T. W., Keys, T. S. & Van der Graaf, K. (2013). *Ready? The 3Rs of preparing your organization for the future*. Switzerland: Strategy Dynamics Global.

[18] Killing, P. & Govinder, N. (2003). *Bharti: "Flying on the wings of others."* IMD case no. IMD-3-1115.

[19] Michel, S., Brown, S. W. & Gallan, A. A. (2008). "Service-logic innovations: How to innovate customers, not products." *California Management Review*, 50(3): 49-65.

[20] Ulaga, W. & Eggert, A. (2006). "Value-based differentiation in business relationships: Gaining and sustaining key supplier status." *Journal of Marketing*, 70(1): 119-136.

[21] Foster, G., Gupta, M. & Sjöblom, L. (1996). "Customer profitability analysis: Challenges and new directions." *Journal of Cost Management* (Spring): 5-17.

[22] Ryans, A. (2009). *Beating low cost competition: How premium brands can respond to cut-price rivals*. Chichester, UK: Wiley.

[23] Ryans, A. & Pahwa, A. (2006). *Ryanair: Defying gravity*, IMD case no. IMD-3-1633.

[24] Ryans, A. (2009). *Beating low cost competition: How premium brands can respond to cut-price rivals* (p. 57). Chichester, UK: Wiley.

[25] Cordón, C. & Nie, W. (2011). "Leverage the supply chain to improve your company's bottom line: Forming win-wins with suppliers in a post-financial crisis world." *Tomorrow's Challenges*, TC063-11, October. Lausanne: IMD.

[26] Ryans, A. & Pahwa, A. (2006). *Ryanair: Defying gravity*, IMD case no. IMD-3-1633.

[27] Marchand, D. A. (2007). "The chief information officer: Achieving credibility, relevance and business impact." In P. Bottger (ed.) *Leading in the top team: The CXO challenge* (pp. 204-22). Cambridge: Cambridge University Press.

[28] Marchand, D. A., Kettinger, W. J. & Rollins, J. D. (2001). *Making the invisible visible: How companies win with the right information, people and IT*. Chichester, UK: John Wiley.

[29] Marchand, D. A., Chung, R. & Paddack, K. (2002). *Global growth through superior information capabilities*. IMD case no. IMD-3-1081.

[30] Marchand, D., Nie, W. & Tsai, G. (2006). *Ping An of China: The making of an insurance giant and a leading Chinese integrated financial services group.* IMD case no. IMD-3-1663.

[31] Nie, W., Dowell, W. & Lu, A. (2012). *In the shadow of the dragon: The global expansion of Chinese companies – and how it will change business forever.* New York: Amacom.

[32] Boynton, A. & Fischer, W. (2005). *Virtuoso teams: Lessons from teams that changed their worlds.* Harlow, UK: FT Prentice Hall.

[33] Turpin, D. & Margery, P. (2011). *Havaianas: A Brazilian brand goes global.* IMD case no. IMD-5-0748.

[34] Michel, S., Brown, S. W. & Gallan, A. S. (2008). "Service-logic innovations: How to innovate customers, not products." *California Management Review,* 50(3), 49-65.

[35] Yu, H. (2011). "Rethinking strategy to escape commoditization: A lesson from Mickey Mouse." *Tomorrow's Challenges,* TC078-11, December. Lausanne: IMD.

[36] Stross, R. E. (1996). "Microsoft's big advantage: Hiring only the supersmart." *Fortune,* November 25, 134(10): 159-162.

[37] Strebel, P. (2011). "In touch boards: Reaching out to the value critical stakeholders." *Corporate Governance,* October 18, 11(5): 603-610.

[38] Manzoni, J.-F. & Barsoux, J.-L. (2008). *Strike at British Airways: Unavoidable or set-up-to-fail?* IMD case no. IMD-3-1736.

[39] Paul Strebel interviewed by Paul Hunter (2012). "Reaching out to value-critical stakeholders," featured on IMD's exclusive Corporate Learning Network "Wednesday Webcast" series, April.

[40] Kohlrieser, G. (2012). "Case study: Making allies out of opponents." *Financial Times,* July 17: 10.

[41] Narasimhan, A. & Dogra, A. (2011). Sula Wines: Creating a legacy (A), IMD case series IMD-3-2247.

[42] Bazerman, M. H. & Watkins, M. (2008). *Predictable surprises: The disasters you should have seen coming, and how to prevent them.* Boston, MA: Harvard Business School Press.

[43] Bris, A. & Cantale, S. (2012). "The right governance delivers real benefit." *Financial Times,* January 30: 1.

[44] All are IMD cases relating to problems of board oversight.

[45] Manzoni, J.-F. & Barsoux, J.-L. (2010). *Renovating Home Depot.* IMD case no. IMD-3-1907.

[46] Ben-Hur, S., Jonsen, K. & Kinley, N. (2010). "Why the best executive teams can make the worst decisions." *Forbes.com,* November 10.

[47] Strebel, P. (2011). "In touch boards: Reaching out to the value critical stakeholders." *Corporate Governance,* October 18, 11(5): 603-610.

[48] Strebel, P. (2011). "In touch boards: Reaching out to the value critical stakeholders." *Corporate Governance,* October 18, 11(5): 603-610.

[49] Cossin, D. (2012). "Corporate boardrooms are in need of education." *Financial Times,* January 9: 9.

⁵⁰ Nie, W. & Lennox, B. (2010). *Zappos: Keeping the wow post-Amazon.* IMD case no. IMD-6-0325.

⁵¹ Barwise, P. & Meehan, S. (2010). "The one thing you must get right when building a brand." *Harvard Business Review*, December, 88(12): 80-84.

⁵² Walsh, J. (2012). "Managing the connected consumer." *Tomorrow's Challenges*, TC002-12, January. Lausanne: IMD.

⁵³ Enders, A. & Ionescu-Somers, A. (2013). *One company's viral headache: Palm oil pressures (A)*, IMD case series IMD-2-0165.

⁵⁴ Walsh, J. (2012). "Managing the connected consumer." *Tomorrow's Challenges*, TC002-12, January. Lausanne: IMD.

⁵⁵ Yaziji, M. (2013). "Developing unique business models: Going beyond services/solutions." *Perspectives for Managers*, no. 184, May. Lausanne: IMD.

⁵⁶ Denison, D. & Lief, C. (2008). *IKEA: Past, present, and future.* IMD case no. IMD-4-0282.

⁵⁷ Michel, S., Brown, S. W. & Gallan, A. S. (2008). "Service-logic innovations: How to innovate customers, not products." *California Management Review*, 50(3), 49-65.

⁵⁸ Denison, D. & Lief, C. (2008). *Ikea: Past, present, and future.* IMD case no. IMD-4-0282.

Chapter 3: The Quest for Global Leadership Development

¹ Matti Alahuhta interviewed by Paul Hunter (2009). "Lessons from the top," featured on IMD's exclusive Corporate Learning Network "Wednesday Webcast" series, November 23.

² Briant, P. (2002). *From Cyrus to Alexander: A history of the Persian Empire.* Warsaw, IN: Eisenbrauns.

³ Axworthy, M. (2008). *Iran: Empire of the mind.* London: Penguin.

⁴ Farazmand, A. (1998). "Administration of the Persian Achaemenid world-state empire: Implications for modern public administration." *International Journal of Public Administration*, 21(1): 25-86.

⁵ Due, B. (1990). *The Cyropedia: Xenophon's aims and methods* (p. 237). Aarhus, Denmark: Aarhus University Press.

⁶ Nadon, C. (2001). *Xenophon's prince: Republic and empire in the "Cyropedia."* Berkeley: University of California Press.

⁷ Bottger, P. C. & Barsoux, J.-L. (2009). "Do you really want to be a leader?" *Wall Street Journal Europe*, November 30: 15.

⁸ Lane, H. W., Maznevski, M. L., Mendenhall, M. E. & McNett, J. (2004). *The Blackwell handbook of global management: A guide to managing complexity.* Malden, MA: Blackwell.

⁹ Bottger, P. C. & Barsoux, J.-L. (2011). "Leaders versus managers: Ending the debate on a dead-end distinction." *Forbes.com India*, November 1.

¹⁰ Toegel, G., Kilduff, M. & Anand, N. (2013). "Emotion helping by managers: An emergent understanding of discrepant role expectations and outcomes." *Academy of Management Journal*, 56(2): 334-357.

¹¹ Peiperl, M. & Jonsen, K. (2007). "Global careers." In H. Gunz & M. Peiperl (eds.) *Handbook of career studies* (pp. 350-372). Thousand Oaks, CA: Sage.

[12] Morrison, A. (2013). "BRICs' lack of effective global leaders." *The Business Times*, June 7.

[13] Haour, G., Billington, C. & Pahwa, A. (2008). *Infosys: Effectively leveraging global resources*, IMD case no. IMD-3-1814.

[14] Schwass, J. (2013). "Meet the family." *Tomorrow's Challenges*, TC043-13, June. Lausanne: IMD.

[15] Wood, J. D. (2011). "Why classic leadership teaching doesn't work." *Business Spectator*, January 20.

[16] Wood, J. D. (2011). "Why classic leadership teaching doesn't work." *Business Spectator*, January 20.

[17] Black, J. S. & Gregersen, H. B. (2008). *It starts with one: Changing individuals changes organizations*. Upper Saddle River, NJ: Pearson Education.

[18] Conger, J. A. & Toegel, G. (2003). "Action learning and multi-rater feedback as leadership development interventions: Popular but poorly deployed." *Journal of Change Management*, 3(4): 332-349.

[19] Hooijberg, R. & Lane, N. (2009). "Using multisource feedback coaching effectively in executive education." *Academy of Management Learning & Education*, 8(4): 483-493.

[20] Watkins, M. D. (2012). "How managers become leaders." *Harvard Business Review*, June, 90(6): 64-72.

[21] Peiperl, M. A. (2011). "Switch-hitters, virtuoso pianists, and leaders who learn: The importance of playing to your strengths and improving your weaknesses." *Fast Company.com*, October 15: 2.

[22] Fischer, W. & Boynton, A. (2005). "Virtuoso teams." *Harvard Business Review*, July/August, 83(7/8): 116-123.

[23] Büchel, B. (2008). "Facilitating groups to drive change: Overcoming obstacles to moving forward." *Tomorrow's Challenges*, TC069-08, September. Lausanne: IMD.

[24] Kohlrieser, G. (2006). *Hostage at the table: How leaders can overcome conflict, influence others, and raise performance*. San Francisco, CA: Jossey-Bass.

[25] Miles, S. A. & Watkins, M. D. (2007). "The leadership team: Complementary strengths or conflicting agendas?" *Harvard Business Review*, April, 85(4): 90-98.

[26] Bryant, B. & Sull, D. (2006). "More than idle chatter." *Financial Times*, April 7: 6.

[27] Bryant, B., Hooijberg, R. & Maznevski, M. (2006). "Engaging through conversation." *Tomorrow's Challenges*, TC047-06, October. Lausanne: IMD.

[28] Bryant, B. & Sull, D. (2006). "More than idle chatter." *Financial Times*, April 7: 6.

[29] Barwise, P. & Meehan, S. (2011). *Beyond the familiar: Long-term growth through customer focus and innovation*. San Francisco, CA: Jossey-Bass.

[30] Denison, D., Hooijberg, R., Lane, N. & Lief, C. (2012). *Leading culture change in global organizations: Aligning culture and strategy*. San Francisco, CA: Jossey-Bass.

[31] Ben-Hur, S. (2013). *The business of corporate learning: Insights from practice*. Cambridge: Cambridge University Press.

[32] Mahmood, I. P., Zhu, H. & Zajac, E. J. (2011). "Where can capabilities come from? Network ties and capability acquisition in business groups." *Strategic Management Journal*, 32(8): 820-848.

[33] Bottger, P. C. & Barsoux, J.-L. (2012). "Masters of fit: How leaders enhance hiring." *Strategy & Leadership*, 40(1): 33-39.

[34] Jonsen, K. & Bryant, B. (2008). "Stretch target." *People Management*, August 21, 14(17): 28-31.

[35] Kohlrieser, G., Szekely, F. & Nedopil, C. (2010). *Thinking outside the box in talent development: Intercompany employee exchange*. IMD case series IMD-4-0304.

[36] Watkins, M. D. (2009). *Your next move*. Boston, MA: Harvard Business Press.

[37] Bartolomé, F. & Weeks, J. (2007). "Find the gold in toxic feedback." *Harvard Business Review*, April, 85(4): 24-26.

[38] Peiperl, M. A. (2001). "Getting 360° feedback right." *Harvard Business Review*, January, 79(1): 142-147.

[39] Wood, J. (2008). "An effective coaching strategy." In B. Büchel, S. Read, A. Moncef & S. Coughlan (eds.) *Riding the winds of global change* (pp. 221-228). Lausanne: IMD.

[40] Jonsen, K. & Maznevski, M. (2006). *Volvo walks the talk*. IMD case no. IMD-4-0284.

[41] Toegel, G. & Barsoux, J.-L. (2012). "Harnessing personality differences in teams." To be published.

[42] Büchel, B. & Antunes, D. (2007). "Reflections on executive education: The user and provider's perspectives." *Academy of Management Learning & Education*. 6(3): 401-411.

[43] Ben-Hur, S. (2012). "The fragile state of talent management." *Tomorrow's Challenges*, TC072-12, October. Lausanne: IMD.

[44] Büchel, B. (2009). "Fear of failure: Is risk aversion hindering the impact of executive education?" *Tomorrow's Challenges*, TC021-09, May. Lausanne: IMD.

[45] Described in Ben-Hur, S. (2013). *The business of corporate learning: Insights from practice*. Cambridge: Cambridge University Press.

[46] Nie, W. & Zhang, L. (2009). Vanke (A): *Transforming from a diversified conglomerate to a focused property company*. IMD case series IMD-3-2112.

[47] See Pamela Thomas-Graham (Chief Talent, Branding and Communications Officer, Credit Suisse) interviewed by Sean Meehan (2011). "Lessons from the top," featured on IMD's exclusive Corporate Learning Network "Wednesday Webcast" series, March 23.

[48] Kinley, N. & Ben-Hur, S. (2013). *Talent intelligence: Finding and measuring the X-factor*. San Francisco, CA: Jossey-Bass.

[49] Ben-Hur, S. & Crawford, R. (2012). *Building the corporate learning brand: The story of Nike U*, IMD case no. IMD-4-0330.

[50] Kohlrieser, G., Goldsworthy, S. & Coombe, D. (2012). *Care to dare*. San Francisco, CA: Jossey-Bass.

[51] Antonakis, J. & Hooijberg, R. (2007). "Cascading vision for real commitment." In R. Hooijberg, J. G. Hunt, J. Antonakis, K. B. Boal & N. Lane (eds.) *Being there even when you are not: Leading through strategy, structures, and systems* (pp. 235-249). Amsterdam: Elsevier Science.

[52] Bottger, P. C. & Barsoux, J.-L. (2009). "What new general managers must learn and forget in order to succeed." *Strategy & Leadership*, 37(6): 25-32.

[53] Peiperl, M. A., Arthur, M. B. & Narasimhan, A. (2002). *Career creativity: Explorations in the remaking of work*. New York: Oxford University Press.

[54] Toegel, G. & Barsoux, J.-L. (2012). "How to become a better leader." *MIT Sloan Management Review*, 53(3): 51-60.

[55] Bryant, B. (2010). "Leading for the future: How we can prepare the next generation." *Tomorrow's Challenges*, TC038-10, May 26. Lausanne: IMD.

[56] Barsoux, J.-L. & Bottger, P. C. (2008). "The talent imperative." In P. Bottger (ed.) *Leading in the top team: The CXO challenge* (pp. 33-51). Cambridge: Cambridge University Press.

[57] Barsoux, J.-L. & Bottger, P. C. (2008). "The talent imperative." In P. Bottger (ed.) *Leading in the top team: The CXO challenge* (pp. 33-51). Cambridge: Cambridge University Press).

[58] Paddy Coyne (VP Enterprise Learning and Leadership Development, Shell International BV) interviewed by Paul Hunter (2012). "Refreshing leadership development at Shell," featured on IMD's exclusive Corporate Learning Network "Wednesday Webcast" series, November 7.

[59] Peiperl, M. A. (2011). "Global is the new normal." *Fast Company*, April 2: 41-43.

[60] Ben-Hur, S., Jaworski, B. & Gray, D. (2012). *Re-imagining Crotonville: Epicenter of GE's leadership culture*. IMD case no. IMD-3-2313.

Chapter 4: The Quest for Global Solutions

[1] Zhang Ruimin interviewed by Dominique Turpin (2013). "Reinventing business with a Chinese touch," featured on IMD's exclusive Corporate Learning Network "Wednesday Webcast" series, March 13.

[2] Wild, A. (2005). *Black gold: The dark history of coffee*. London: HarperCollins.

[3] Schultz, H. M. & Jones Yang, D. (1999). *Pour your heart into it: How Starbucks built a company one cup at a time* (p. 249). New York: Hyperion.

[4] Weeks, J. & Barsoux, J.-L. (2010). *Rebooting IBM*. IMD case no. IMD-4-0318.

[5] Ryans, A. B. (2009). *Beating low cost competition: How premium brands can respond to cut-price rivals*. Chichester, UK: Wiley.

[6] Ryans, A. B. & Sequeira, S. M (2007). *Orica Mining Services*. IMD case no. IMD-5-0725.

[7] Adrian Ryans interviewed by Paul Hunter (2009). "Cut-price rivals prosper in tough times: What you can do to slow them down," featured on IMD's exclusive Corporate Learning Network "Wednesday Webcast" series, February 11.

[8] Renault, C., Ulaga, W. & Dalsace, F. (2013). *Business model innovation: From selling tires to selling kilometers*. IMD case no. IMD-5-0793.

[9] Karsenti, G. & Ulaga, W. (2009). *Le business model des services*. Paris: Editions d'Organisation.

[10] Yu, H. (2012). "Rethinking strategy to escape commoditization." *The Jakarta Post*, January 21: 5.

[11] Levitt, T. (1960). "Marketing myopia." *Harvard Business Review*, July/August 38: 45-56.

[12] Bartiromo, M. (2006). "Google chairman and CEO interview: Part 1." CNBC/Dow Jones Business Video, May 22.

[13] Gilbert, X., Büchel, B. & Davidson, R. (2008). *Smarter execution: Seven steps to getting results*. Harlow: Financial Times Prentice Hall.

[14] Kashani, K. (2006). "Fighting commoditization: Strategies for creating novel customer values." *Perspectives for Managers*, no. 137, October. Lausanne: IMD.

[15] Manzoni, J.-F. & Barsoux, J.-L. (2007). *Renovating Home Depot: 2000-2006*. IMD case no. IMD-3-1907.

[16] Kashani, K. (2006). "Fighting commoditization: Strategies for creating novel customer values." *Perspectives for Managers*, no. 137, October. Lausanne: IMD.

[17] Kashani, K. (2006). "Fighting commoditization: Strategies for creating novel customer values." *Perspectives for Managers*, no. 137, October. Lausanne: IMD.

[18] Kashani, K. & Miller, J. (2003). *Innovation and renovation: The Nespresso story*. IMD case no. IMD-5-0543.

[19] Turpin, D. (2005). "How far can you stretch your brands?" *Perspectives for Managers*, no. 124, October. Lausanne: IMD.

[20] Ulaga, W. & Reinartz, W. (2011). "Hybrid offerings: How manufacturing firms combine goods and services successfully." *Journal of Marketing*, 75(6): 5-23.

[21] Gebauer, H., Fleisch, E. & Friedli, T. (2005). "Overcoming the service paradox in manufacturing companies." *European Management Journal*, 23(1): 14-26.

[22] Ulaga, W. & Loveland, J. M. (2013). "Transitioning from product to service-led growth in manufacturing firms: Emergent challenges in selecting and managing the industrial sales force." *Industrial Marketing Management*, in press.

[23] Michel, S. (2010). "From producer to service provider: Why some companies fail to make the transition." *Tomorrow's Challenges*, TC-028-10, April. Lausanne: IMD.

[24] Kashani, K. (2006). "Fighting commoditization: Strategies for creating novel customer values." *Perspectives for Managers*, no. 137, October. Lausanne: IMD.

[25] Michel, S., Brown, S. W. & Gallan, A. S. (2008). "Service-logic innovations: How to innovate customers, not products." *California Management Review*, 50(3), 49-65.

[26] Rubalcaba, L., Michel, S., Sundbo, J., Brown, S. W. & Reynoso, J. (2012). "Shaping, organizing, and rethinking service innovation: A multidimensional framework." *Journal of Service Management*, 23(5): 696-715.

[27] Michel, S. (2010). "From producer to service provider: Why some companies fail to make the transition." *Tomorrow's Challenges*, TC-028-10, April. Lausanne: IMD.

[28] Ulaga, W. & Reinartz, W. (2011). "Hybrid offerings: How manufacturing firms combine goods and services successfully." *Journal of Marketing*, 75(6): 5-23.

[29] Weeks, J. & Barsoux, J.-L. (2010). *Rebooting IBM*. IMD case no. IMD-4-0318.

[30] Bottger, P. & Barsoux, J.-L. (2013). "Fast trackers, specialists and unsung heroes: Understanding the three talent types." *Tomorrow's Challenges*, TC-025-13, March. Lausanne: IMD.

[31] Reinartz, W. J. & Ulaga, W. (2008). "How to sell services more profitably." *Harvard Business Review*, 86(5): 91-96.

[32] Steger, U. & Ramus, C. A. (2003). *Xerox and the waste free office*. IMD case no. IMD-3-0788.

[33] Michel, S. (2013). *Hilti fleet management: Strategically moving from products to B2B solutions*. IMD case no. IMD-3-2354.

[34] Killing, P. (1997). *Hilti Corporation (A) & (B)*. IMD case series IMD-3-0663.

[35] Johnson, M. W. (2010). *Seizing the white space* (p. 65). Boston: Harvard Business Press.

[36] Meehan, S. (2010). *Hilti: Full utilization of fleet*. IMD case no. IMD-5-0759.

[37] Langenberg, K. & Seifer, R. (2008). *Hilti (A): Gearing the supply chain for the future*. IMD case no. IMD-6-0313.

[38] Johnson, M. W. (2010). *Seizing the white space* (p. 68). Boston: Harvard Business Press).

Chapter 5: The Quest for Global Agility

[1] Peter Brabeck-Letmathe interviewed by Peter Lorange (2007). "Energizing and innovating to fuel growth," featured on IMD's exclusive Corporate Learning Network "Wednesday Webcast" series, December 5.

[2] Xinjiang, R. (2001). "New light on Sogdian colonies along the Silk Road: Recent archaeological finds in Northern China." Lecture at the Berlin-Brandenburgische Akademie der Wissenschaften (BBAW), September 20. Retrieved from: http://edoc.bbaw.de/volltexte/2009/1106/pdf/IV_01_Rong.pdf.

[3] Boulnois, L. (2008). *Silk Road: Monks, warriors and merchants*. Hong Kong: Odyssey Books.

[4] Enders, A. & König, A. (2010). "Adapt or die with technology." *The Times*, June 8: 17.

[5] Chakravarthy, B. (1997). "A new strategy framework for coping with turbulence." *Sloan Management Review*, 38(2): 69-82.

[6] Strebel, P. (2001). "High speed strategy in large companies." In S. Crainer & D. Dearlove (eds.) *Financial Times handbook of management* (pp. 269-279). London: Pearson Education.

[7] Chakravarthy, B. S. & McEvily, S. (2007). "Knowledge management and corporate renewal." In K. Ichijo & I. Nonaka (eds.) *Knowledge creation and management* (pp. 254-274). Oxford: Oxford University Press.

[8] Büchel, B. & Wade, M. (2013). "Balancing local flexibility with global efficiency: Five steps for competing in highly dynamic markets." *Tomorrow's Challenges*, TC020-13, March. Lausanne: IMD.

[9] IMD survey conducted with international executives attending the Orchestrating Winning Performance program in June 2013.

[10] Ben-Hur, S. & Anderson, J. (2011). *Deutsche Telekom: A transformation journey*. IMD case no. IMD-3-2150.

[11] Ben-Hur, S. & Anderson, J. (2011). "Case study: Deutsche Telekom." *FT.com*, June 1.

[12] Pacheco de Almeida, G., Henderson, J. E. & Cool, K. E. (2008). "Resolving the commitment versus flexibility trade-off: The role of resource accumulation lags." *Academy of Management Journal*, 51(3): 517-536.

[13] Anand, N. & Daft, R. L. (2007). "What is the right organization design?" *Organizational Dynamics*, 36(4): 329-344.

[14] Strebel, P. & Ohlsson, A.-V. (2009). "How to distinguish smart big moves from stupid ones." *Strategy & Leadership*, 37(2): 21-26.

[15] Chakravarthy, B. & Lorange, P. (2008). *Profit or growth? Why you don't have to choose*. Upper Saddle River, NJ: Wharton School Publishing.

[16] Chakravarthy, B. & Govinder, N. (2003). *Medtronic: Keeping pace*. IMD case no. IMD-3-1139.

[17] Cordón, C., Hald, K. S. & Seifert, R. W. (2012). *Strategic supply chain management*. New York: Routledge.

[18] Fischer, W. A. (2009). "Reinventing the managerial mindset: Keys to surviving and thriving in volatile times." *Tomorrow's Challenges*, TC039-09, June. Lausanne: IMD.

[19] Cordón, C. & Nie, W. (2012). "Leverage the supply chain to improve your company's bottom line." *Harvard Business Review China*, July.

[20] Nie, W. & Lennox, B. (2010). *Zappos: Keeping the wow post-Amazon*. IMD case no. IMD-6-0325.

[21] Nie, W. & Lennox, B. (2011). "Case study: Zappos." *FT.com*, February 16.

[22] Meehan, S. (2011). *Measuring customer satisfaction with net promoter score*. IMD case no. IMD-5-0772.

[23] Barwise, P. & Meehan, S. (2011). *Beyond the familiar: Long-term growth through customer focus and innovation*. San Francisco, CA: Jossey-Bass.

[24] Barwise, P. & Meehan, S. (2010). "The one thing you must get right when building a brand." *Harvard Business Review*, December, 88(12): 80-84.

[25] Barwise, P., & Meehan, S. (2010). "The one thing you must get right when building a brand," Harvard Business Review, December, 88(12): 80-84.

[26] Strebel, P. & Ohlsson, A. V. (2008). *Smart big moves: The story behind strategic breakthroughs*. Harlow: FT Prentice Hall.

[27] Manzoni, J.-F., Barsoux, J.-L. & Strebel, P. (2011). "Widening the lens: The challenges of leveraging boardroom diversity." *Rotman Magazine*, Spring: 65-69.

[28] Fischer, W. & Boynton, A. (2005). "Virtuoso teams." *Harvard Business Review*, Jul/Aug, 83(7/8): 116-123.

[29] Kohlrieser, G. (2006). *Hostage at the table: How leaders can overcome conflict, influence others, and raise performance*. San Francisco, CA: Jossey-Bass.

[30] Kirkpatrick, D. (2006). "Microsoft's new brain." *Fortune*, May 1: 56.

[31] Chen, G. & Loewe, P. (2007). "Update: Is Microsoft in the groove?" *Optimize*, March 1: 22.

[32] Boynton, A. C. & Fischer, W. A. (2004). "Deep dive!: A rigorous team process to drive innovation and execution." *Perspectives for Managers*, no. 110, June. Lausanne: IMD.

[33] Barsoux, J.-L. & Bottger P. C., (2006). "Can we really 'master' uncertainty?" *Financial Times*, March 17: 11.

[34] Davidson, R. & Büchel, B. (2011). "The art of piloting new initiatives." *MIT Sloan Management Review*, Fall, 53(1): 79-86.

[35] Büchel, B. (2010). "From blind spots to strategic intelligence: Ensuring growth options are exploited." *Tomorrow's Challenges*, no. TC031-10, April. Lausanne: IMD.

[36] Büchel, B. (2010). "From blind spots to strategic intelligence: Ensuring growth options are exploited." *Tomorrow's Challenges*, no. TC031-10, April. Lausanne: IMD.

[37] Bazerman, M. H. & Watkins, M. (2008). *Predictable surprises: The disasters you should have seen coming, and how to prevent them*. Boston, MA: Harvard Business School Press.

[38] Koenig, A., Kammerlander, N. & Enders, A. (2013). "The family innovator's dilemma: How family influence affects the adoption of discontinuous technologies by incumbent firms." *Academy of Management Review*, 38(3): 418-441.

[39] Gerstner, W.-C., Koenig, A., Enders, A. & Hambrick, D. C. (2013). "CEO narcissism, audience engagement, and organizational adoption of technological discontinuities." *Administrative Science Quarterly*, 58(2): 257-291.

[40] Robertson, D. (2009). *Innovation at the Lego Group*. IMD case series IMD-3-1978.

[41] Cordón, C., Seifert, R. & Wellian, E. (2009). *Lego: Consolidating distribution*. IMD case no. IMD-6-0315.

[42] Cordón, C., Seifert, R. & Wellian, E. (2010). "Case study: Lego." *FT.com*, November 24.

[43] Ward, A. (2011). "A brick by brick brand revival." *FT.com*, July 17.

[44] Jorgen Knudstorp interviewed by Paul Hunter (2009). "Leading from the top," featured on IMD's exclusive Corporate Learning Network "Wednesday Webcast" series, February 25.

Chapter 6: The Quest for Global Co-innovation

[1] Barbara Kux interviewed by Annie Tobias (2006). "Lessons from the top," featured on IMD's exclusive Corporate Learning Network "Wednesday Webcast" series, May 12.

[2] Sobel, D. (1995). *Longitude: The true story of a lone genius who solved the greatest scientific problem of his time*. New York: Walker and Company.

[3] Fischer, W. (2010). "Co-creation: The key to the best innovation." *Forbes.com*, December 15.

[4] Read, S. & Robertson, D. (2008). "What is the next big innovation in innovation?" *Tomorrow's Challenges*, TC076-08, September. Lausanne: IMD.

[5] Fischer, W. (2010). "Co-creation: The key to the best innovation." *Forbes.com*, December 15.

6 Denison, D. R., Hart, S. L. & Kahn, J. A. (1996). "From chimneys to cross-functional teams: Developing and validating a diagnostic model." *Academy of Management Journal*, 39(4): 1005-1023.

7 Nevo, S. & Wade, M. (2010). "The formation and value of IT-enabled resources: Antecedents and consequences of synergistic requirements." *MIS Quarterly*, 34(1): 163-183.

8 Ryans, A. & Sequieira, S. (2007). *P&G: Innovating out of a crisis*. IMD case no. IMD-5-0726.

9 Barwise, P. & Meehan, S. (2011). *Beyond the familiar: Long-term growth through customer focus and innovation*. San Francisco, CA: Jossey-Bass.

10 Cordón, C., Vollmann, T. E. & Vivanco, L. (2005). *Numico (A): Delivering innovation through the supply chain*. IMD case series IMD-6-0264.

11 Cordón, C. & Nie, W. (2011). "Leverage the supply chain to improve your company's bottom line." *Forbesindia.com*, October 19.

12 Read, S., Sarasvathy, S., Wiltbank, R., Dew, N. & Ohlsson, A.-V. (2010). *Effectual entrepreneurship*. New York: Routledge.

13 Read, S. & Robertson, D. (2008). "What is the next big innovation in innovation?" *Tomorrow's Challenges*, TC076-08, September. Lausanne: IMD.

14 Barsoux, J.-L. & Weeks, J. (2010). *IBM: The value of values*. IMD case series IMD-4-0320.

15 Von Hippel, E. (1986). "Lead users: A source of novel product concepts." *Management Science*, 32: 791-805.

16 Deschamps, J.-P. & Barnett-Berg, M. (2007). *Medtronic's deep brain stimulation: Turning a revolutionary therapy into "standard of care"*. IMD case no. IMD-3-1947.

17 Billington, C. & Jäger, F. (2008). *Innocentive: Open innovation platform*. IMD case no. IMD-6-0296.

18 Lafley, A. G. & Charan, R. (2008). *The game-changer: How every leader can drive everyday innovation*. London: Profile Books.

19 Fischer, W. (2012). "Don't relax constraints, embrace them." *Forbes.com*, January 9.

20 Mahmood, I. P., Chung, C.-N. & Mitchell, W. (2013). "The evolving impact of combinatorial opportunities and exhaustion on innovation by business groups as market development increases: The case of Taiwan." *Management Science*, 59(5): 1142-1161.

21 Chakravarthy, B. & Coughlan, S. (2010). *Tata Nano: Dilemmas in sustainable development*. IMD case no. IMD-3-1947.

22 Snyder, J. (2008). "After Africa, Southeast Asia, Europe could get the Nano." *Automotive News Europe*, 13(2): 22.

23 Fischer, W. (2010). "Co-creation: The key to the best innovation." *Forbes.com*, December 15.

24 Gillette, F. (2011). "The rise and inglorious fall of MySpace." *Bloomberg Businessweek*, June 27: 52-59.

25 Bill Fischer interviewed by Paul Hunter (2010). "Benchmarking innovation practices," featured on IMD's exclusive Corporate Learning Network "Wednesday Webcast" series, July 28.

[26] Bryant, B. & Sull, D. (2006). "More than idle chatter." *Financial Times*, April 7: 6.

[27] Lane, H. H. W., Maznevski, M. L., DiStefano, J. J. & Dietz, J. (2009). *International management behavior: Leading with a global mindset*. Chichester, UK: John Wiley.

[28] Büchel, B. (2003). "Managing partner relations in joint ventures." *MIT Sloan Management Review*, 44(4): 91-95.

[29] Michel, S., Brown, S. W. & Gallan, A. S. (2008). "An expanded and strategic view of discontinuous innovations: Deploying a service-dominant logic." *Journal of the Academy of Marketing Science*, 36(1): 54-66.

[30] Robertson, D. & Crawford, R. J. (2008). *Innovation at the LEGO Group*. IMD case series IMD-3-1978.

[31] Birkinshaw, J., Bouquet, C. & Barsoux, J.-L. (2011). "The five myths of innovation." *MIT Sloan Management Review*, 52(2): 43-50.

[32] Maznevski, M. & Athanassiou, N. (2007). "Bringing the outside in: Learning and knowledge management through external networks." In K. Ichijo & I. *Nonaka, Knowledge creation and management* (pp. 69-82). Oxford: Oxford University Press.

[33] Fayard, A.-L. & Weeks, J. (2011). "Who moved my cube?" *Harvard Business Review*, 89(7/8): 102-110.

[34] Ryans, A. & Sequieira, S. (2007). *P&G: Innovating out of a crisis*. IMD case no. IMD-5-0726.

[35] Cording, M., Christmann, P. & King, D. R. (2008). Reducing causal ambiguity in acquisition integration: Intermediate goals as mediators of integration decisions and acquisition performance." *Academy of Management Journal*, 51(4): 744-767.

[36] Lane, H. H. W., Maznevski, M. L., DiStefano, J. J. & Dietz, J. (2009). *International management behavior: Leading with a global mindset*. Chichester, UK: John Wiley.

[37] Read, S., Sarasvathy, S., Wiltbank, R., Dew, N. & Ohlsson, A.-V. (2010). *Effectual entrepreneurship*. New York: Routledge.

[38] Hald, K. S., Cordón, C. & Vollmann, T. E. (2009). "Towards an understanding of attraction in buyer–supplier relationships." *Industrial Marketing Management*, 38(8): 960-970.

[39] Hald, K. S., Cordón, C. & Vollmann, T. E. (2009). "Towards an understanding of attraction in buyer–supplier relationships." *Industrial Marketing Management*, 38(8): 960-970.

[40] Büchel, B. (2003). "Managing partner relations in joint ventures." *MIT Sloan Management Review*, 44(4): 91-95.

[41] Boynton, A., Fischer, B. & Bole, W. (2011). *The idea hunter: How to find the best ideas and make them happen*. San Francisco, CA: Jossey-Bass.

[42] Lumineau, F. & Büchel, B. (2013). "Business with partners: How to avoid escalating into legal disputes." (Under review).

[43] Cordón, C. & Vollmann, T. E. (2008). *The power of two: How smart companies create win-win customer supplier partnerships that outperform the competition*. New York: Palgrave Macmillan.

[44] Lumineau, F. & Henderson, J. E. (2012). "The influence of relational experience and contractual governance on the negotiation strategy in buyer–supplier disputes." *Journal of Operations Management*, 30(5): 382-395.

[45] Büchel, B., Davidson, R. & Ferro, K. (2003). *Ericsson Hewlett-Packard Telecommunications*. IMD case series IMD-3-1097.

[46] Lane, H. H. W., Maznevski, M. L., DiStefano, J. J. & Dietz, J. (2009). *International management behavior: Leading with a global mindset*. Chichester, UK: John Wiley.

[47] Manzoni, J.-F. & Barsoux, J.-L. (2006). "Untangling alliances and joint ventures." *Financial Times*, October 19: 12.

[48] Cordón, C. & Vollmann, T. E. (2008). *The power of two: How smart companies create win-win customer supplier partnerships that outperform the competition*. New York: Palgrave Macmillan.

[49] Birkinshaw, J., Bouquet, C. & Barsoux, J.-L. (2011). "The five myths of innovation." *MIT Sloan Management Review*, 52(2): 43-50.

[50] Birkinshaw, J., Bouquet, C. & Barsoux, J.-L. (2011). "The five myths of innovation." *MIT Sloan Management Review, 52(2): 43-50.

[51] Yu, H. & Shih, W. (2008). "ASUSTeK Computer Inc. Eee PC (B)" Harvard Business School case # 609052.

[52] Harryson, S. & Lorange, P. (2005). "Bringing the college inside." *Harvard Business Review*, December, 83(12): 30-32.

Chapter 7: The Quest for Global Sustainability

[1] Nandan Nilekani interviewed by Paul Hunter (2009). "India at the crossroads," featured on IMD's exclusive Corporate Learning Network "Wednesday Webcast" series, November 4.

[2] Carroll, S. B. (2010). "Tracking the ancestry of corn back 9,000 years." *New York Times*, May 25: 2.

[3] McGregor, N. (2010). *A history of the world in 100 objects*. London: Allen Lane.

[4] Fussel, B. (1992). *The story of corn*. Albuquerque: University of New Mexico Press.

[5] Mazutis, D. (2010). "Why zero is not one: Towards a measure of corporate social strategy." *Academy of Management Best Paper Proceedings*, Montreal, Quebec: Winner – Social Issues in Management Division Best Paper Award.

[6] See Ralf Boscheck's extensive work on the preoccupations of different industries, notably *Energy futures* (Houndmills: Palgrave MacMillan, 2007); *Strategies, markets and governance: Exploring commercial and regulatory agendas* (Cambridge: Cambridge University Press, 2008); and "Intellectual property rights & compulsory licensing: The case of pharmaceuticals in emerging markets," *World Competition: Law and Economics Review*, 35(4), December 2012: 621-634.

[7] Cordón, C. & Nie, W. (2011). "Re-evaluating the supply chain cost post-Japanese earthquake." *Tomorrow's Challenges*, TC025-11, April. Lausanne: IMD.

[8] Andreas Jacobs interviewed by Jim Pulcrano and Aileen Ionescu-Somers (2011). "Sustainable cocoa," featured on IMD's exclusive Corporate Learning Network "Wednesday Webcast" series, March 24.

[9] Yaziji, M. & Doh, J. (2009). *NGOs and corporations: Conflict and collaboration*. Cambridge: Cambridge University Press.

[10] Steger, U., Killing, P., Winter, M. & Schweinsberg, M. (1996). *Brent Spar platform controversy*. IMD case series IMD-2-0070.

[11] Steger, U., Ogunsulire, M., Ramus, C. & Hum, C. (2001). *Monsanto's genetically modified organisms: The battle for hearts and shopping aisles*. IMD case no. IMD-2-0086.

[12] Chun, R. & Duke, L. (2011). *Foxconn and blood iPhones*. IMD case no. IMD-3-2193.

[13] See John Elkington's presentation at IMD on http://www.youtube.com/watch?v=m_nUPI83lJA

[14] Seifert, R. W. & Comas, J. M. (2010). "Creating business opportunities through supply chain environmental management: Analyzing companies' best practice." *Tomorrow's Challenges*, TC065-10, September. Lausanne: IMD.

[15] Manzoni, J.-F. & Barsoux, J.-L. (2008). *Tesco: Delivering the goods* (B). IMD case series IMD-3-1956.

[16] Leleux, B. F., Schwass, J., Lavoie Orlick, A. & Diversé, A. (2009). *Coronilla: The quadruple bottom line*. IMD case no. IMD-3-1998.

[17] Schwass, J. & Lief, C. (2008). "About family, business and philanthropy." *Perspectives for Managers*, no. 165, November. Lausanne: IMD.

[18] Szekely, F. & Ionescu-Somers, A. (2013). "Innovation for sustainability: Business context and drivers." *Tomorrow's Challenges*, TC016-13, March. Lausanne: IMD.

[19] Braga, C. A. Primo & Lehmann, J.-P. (2013). "Getting the dynamics of global business right." *Businessworld*, February 23: http://businessworld.in/en/storypage/-/bw/getting-dynamics-of-global-business-right/791765.0/page/0

[20] Marchand, D. A. & Moncef, A. (2012). SMS for Life (A): *A public-private collaboration to prevent stock-outs of life saving malaria drugs in Africa*. IMD case series IMD-3-2168.

[21] Marchand, D. A. & Barrington, J. (2013). "Leveraging CIO expertise to create social value: Novartis' SMS for life initiative." *MIS Quarterly Executive*, 12(1): 37-47.

[22] See IMD/Burson-Marsteller report: http://burson-marsteller.eu/wp-content/uploads/2011/10/IMD-B-M-Corporate-Purpose-Impact-Study-2010.pdf

[23] Weeks, J., Ionescu-Somers, A. & Braga, T. (2011). "Revealing corporate DNA." *Tomorrow's Challenges*, TC071-10, December. Lausanne: IMD.

[24] Steger, U., Ionescu-Somers, A., Salzmann, O. & Mansourian, S. (2009). *Sustainability partnerships: The manager's handbook*. Basingstoke: Palgrave MacMillan.

[25] Cantale, S. & Eckardt, A. (2012). *The water challenge in Kenya: A challenge or an opportunity?* IMD case no. IMD-3-2340.

[26] Yaziji, M. (2011). "Going forward with tomorrow's sustainability approach: More can equal less thanks to industrial ecology." *Tomorrow's Challenges*, TC035-11, June. Lausanne: IMD.

[27] Cossin, D. (2005). "A route through the hazards of business." *Financial Times* (FT Mastering Corporate Governance), June 10: 4-5.

[28] Szekely, F. & Strebel, H. (2013). "Sustainability is actually good news: Three ways to change our mindset." *Tomorrow's Challenges*, no. TC031-12, April. Lausanne: IMD.

[29] Michel, S. (2010). *Grameen Bank*. IMD case no. IMD-3-2163.

[30] Read, S., Lepoutre, J. & Margery, P. (2012). *TerraCycle: Branded waste*. IMD case series IMD-3-2286.

[31] IMD Professor Stuart Read illustrates the point with the case of the Swiss start-up Freitag http://www.youtube.com/watch?v=DnGrcCVG8TE

[32] Szekely, F. & Ionescu-Somers, A. (2013). "Innovation for sustainability: Systems and leadership," *Tomorrow's Challenges*, TC021-13, March. Lausanne: IMD.

[33] For the views of several IMD professors see: http://www.imd.org/news/IMD-Professors-on-Responsible-Leadership.cfm

[34] Szekely, F. & Knirsch, M. (2005). "Responsible leadership and corporate social responsibility: Metrics for sustainable performance." *European Management* Journal, 23(6): 628-647.

[35] Bryant, B. (2007). "Be aware of your shadow." *Tomorrow's Challenges*, TC007-07, January. Lausanne: IMD.

[36] Yaziji, M. (2012). *Desso (A): A cradle-to-cradle business model*. IMD case series IMD-3-2349.

[37] Yaziji, M. (2012). *Desso (B): Making it happen – the implementation of a C2C business model*. IMD case series IMD-3-2350

[38] Mazutis, D. (2013). "Authentic leadership," in W. G. Rowe & L. Guerrero (eds.) *Cases in leadership* (pp. 295-339). Thousand Oaks: Sage Publications.

[39] Yaziji, M. (2004). "Turning gadflies into allies." *Harvard Business Review*, 82(2): 110-115.

[40] Yaziji, M. (2010). "Corporate-NGO collaboration: Co-creating new business models for developing markets." *Long Range Planning*, 43(2-3): 326-342.

[41] Seifert, R. W., Ionescu-Somers, A., Braga, T. & Strebel, H. (2011). *Unilever Tea (A): Revitalizing Lipton's supply chain*. IMD case series IMD-6-0327.

[42] Seifert, R. W. & Ionescu-Somers, A. (2011). "Making a leading brand sustainable: Unilever tries to choose the right partner." *Financial Times*, November 15: 16.

[43] Boscheck, R. (2008). "Competitive advantage and the regulation of dominant firms." *World Competition: Law and Economics Review*, 30(3): 433-448.

[44] Yaziji, M. (2008). "Shaping the regulatory environment: Why those who don't do politics get done by politics." *Tomorrow's Challenges*, TC071-08, September. Lausanne: IMD.

[45] Szekely, F. & Knirsch, M. (2005). "Responsible leadership and corporate social responsibility: Metrics for sustainable performance." *European Management Journal*, 23(6): 628-647.

[46] Ionescu-Somers, A. & Szekely, F. (2013). *Puma*. IMD case no. IMD-81499, work in progress.

47 Comas, J. M. & Seifert, R. W. (2012). "Assessing the comprehensiveness of supply chain environmental strategies." *Business Strategy and the Environment*, 22(5): 339-356. Seifert, R. W. & Comas, J. M. (2010). "Analyzing companies' best practice." *The Jakarta Post*, October 2.

48 Szekely, F. & Knirsch, M. (2005). "Responsible leadership and corporate social responsibility: Metrics for sustainable performance." *European Management Journal*, 23(6): 628-647.

49 Szekely, F. & Knirsch, M. (2005). "Responsible leadership and corporate social responsibility: Metrics for sustainable performance." *European Management Journal*, 23(6): 628-647.

50 Keys, T., Malnight, T. & Van der Graaf, K. (2009). "Making the most of corporate social responsibility." *McKinsey Quarterly*, December.

51 Barsoux, J.-L. & Bouquet, C. (2013). "How to overcome a power deficit." *MIT Sloan Management Review*, 54(4): 45-53.

52 Kohlrieser, G., Szekely, F. & Coughlan, S. (2010). *Playing to win: Leadership and sustainability at ESB Electricity Utility*. IMD case no. IMD-4-0302.

53 TEDx talk featuring Michael Yaziji (2012). "Rethinking the structure of corporations." Lausanne. http://www.youtube.com/watch?v=8eRwOM9iqVo.

54 Cordón, C., Hald, K. S. & Seifert, R. W. (2012). *Strategic supply chain management*. New York: Routledge.

55 Mazutis, D. (2010). "Why zero is not one: Towards a measure of corporate social strategy." *Academy of Management Best Paper Proceedings*, Montreal, Quebec: Winner – Social Issues in Management Division Best Paper Award.

56 Ionescu-Somers, A. & Szekely, F. (2013). "Innovation for sustainability: Implementation challenges." *Tomorrow's Challenges*, TC018-13, March. Lausanne: IMD.

57 Schwass, J. & Glemser, A.-C. (2013). *Ayala (A): Going beyond the sum*. IMD case series IMD-3-2315.

58 Anon. (2010). "Standouts in the Philippines." *Finance Asia*, August 15.

59 Ionescu-Somers, A. & Szekely, F. (2013). "Innovation for sustainability: Implementation challenges." *Tomorrow's Challenges*, TC018-13, March. Lausanne: IMD.

60 Ionescu-Somers, A. & Steger, U. (2008). *Business logic for sustainability: A food and beverage industry perspective*. Houndmills: Palgrave Macmillan.

61 See Ionescu-Somers, A. (2012). "What's stopping your sustainability schemes? You are." *Tomorrow's Challenges*, TC023-12, March. Lausanne: IMD.

62 Chakravarthy, B. & Santos, P. (2013). *Natura Cosméticos*. IMD case no. IMD-3-2375, in press.

63 Weeks, J. & Galunic, C. (2003). "A theory of the cultural evolution of the firm: The intra-organizational ecology of memes." *Organization Studies*, 24(8): 1309-1352.

64 Manzoni, J.-F. & Barsoux, J.-L. (2008). *Tesco: Delivering the goods (B)*, IMD case series, IMD-3-1956.

65 Kohlrieser, G., Goldsworthy, S. & Coombe, D. (2012). *Care to dare: Unleashing astonishing potential through secure base leadership*. San Francisco, CA: Jossey-Bass.

[66] Billington, C., Ionescu-Somers, A. & Barnett Berg, M. (2009). "The 5 Cs of going green: How to achieve responsible procurement." *Tomorrow's Challenges*, TC042-09, September. Lausanne: IMD.

[67] Strebel, P. & Rogers, B. (2012). *British Petroleum (C): Economic and environmental sustainability?* IMD case series IMD-3-2182.

[68] Steger, U. & Nedopil, C. (2006). *BP: Too rusty to continue?* IMD case no. IMD-3-1721.

[69] Marais, D. (2009) "The worst of the greenwashers." *The Star*, December 14: 7.

[70] Cossin, D. & Constantinou, D. (2011). *The Macondo blowout: Decision making in difficult times.* IMD case no. IMD-3-2186.

[71] Steger, U. (2004). *The business of sustainability.* Basingstoke, UK: Palgrave Macmillan.

[72] Yaziji, M. & Doh, J. (2009). *NGOs and corporations: Conflict and collaboration.* Cambridge: Cambridge University Press.

[73] Schuler, D. A. & Cording, M. (2006). "A corporate social performance-corporate financial performance behavioral model for consumers." *Academy of Management Review*, 31(3): 540-558.

[74] Leleux, B. F. & Scheel Agersnap, B. (2009). *Noir/Illuminati II (B): Greenwash and anorexic models.* IMD case series IMD-3-1910.

[75] Seifert, R. W. & Comas, J. M. (2012). "Have ecolabels had their day?" *Tomorrow's Challenges*, TC032-12, May. Lausanne: IMD.

[76] Hooijberg, R. & Van der Kaaij, J. (2007). "Moving the world: Corporate philanthropy at work." In B. Büchel, B. F. Leleux & A. Moncef (eds.) *Anticipating the future.* Lausanne: IMD.

[77] Peter Bakker interviewed by Paul Hunter (2009). "Responsible leadership summit," featured on IMD's exclusive Corporate Learning Network "Wednesday Webcast" series, February 2.

[78] See Peter Bakker 2009 presentation at IMD, Lausanne: http://www.youtube.com/watch?v=2ysmKJUcBcM.

[79] Anon. (2010). "TNT leads consortium to buy 3,000 electric trucks." *CEP Research*, July 16.

[80] Peter Bakker (2008). "TNT NV Earnings Conference Call." *Voxant FD (Fair Disclosure) Wire*, February 18.

[81] Confino, J. (2011). "Radical change and innovation is needed to meet the challenges ahead." *The Guardian*, November 9: 17.

[82] Peter Bakker interviewed by Paul Hunter (2009). "Responsible leadership summit," featured on IMD's exclusive Corporate Learning Network "Wednesday Webcast" series, February 2.

Conclusion: Learning from Transformation Journeys

[1] Igor Allinckx interviewed by Paul Hunter (2007). "Taking over at the helm," featured on IMD's exclusive Corporate Learning Network "Wednesday Webcast" series, April 25.

[2] Nie, W., Dowell, W. & Lu, A. (2012). *In the shadow of the dragon: The global expansion of Chinese companies – and how it will change business forever.* New York: Amacon.

[3] Primo Braga, C. & Lehmann, J.-P. (2013). "Brazil and China: Partners in constructing the new global architecture?" *Tomorrow's Challenges*, TC055-13, September. Lausanne: IMD.

[4] Kolesnikov-Jessop, S. (2005). "Did Chinese beat out Columbus?" *The New York Times*, June 25.

[5] Lehmann, J.-P. (2013). "China's global tectonic shifts: The dawn of a new era." *The World Financial Review*.

[6] Primo Braga, C. & Lehmann, J.-P. (2013). "Brazil and China: Partners in constructing the new global architecture?" *Tomorrow's Challenges*, TC055-13, September. Lausanne: IMD.

[7] Lehmann, J.-P. (2012). "The power of China in the new world: Have you embraced globalization?" *Tomorrow's Challenges*, TC037-12, May. Lausanne: IMD.

[8] Nie, W., Dowell, W. & Lu, A. (2012). *In the shadow of the dragon: The global expansion of Chinese companies – and how it will change business forever.* New York: Amacon.

[9] Lehmann, J.-P. & Lehmann, F. (2010). *Peace and prosperity through world trade: Achieving the 2019 vision.* Cambridge: Cambridge University Press.

[10] Manzoni, J.-F. & Barsoux, J.-L. (2006). *Prudential UK: Rebuilding a mighty business.* IMD case no. IMD-3-1674.

[11] Malnight, T. W. (2008). "Strategically engaging your organization: Assessing your current reality." *Tomorrow's Challenges*, TC029-08, March. Lausanne: IMD.

[12] Fry, J. N. & Killing, P. J. (1986) *Strategic analysis and action.* Englewood Cliffs, NJ: Prentice Hall.

[13] Crossan, M. M., Rouse, M. J., Fry, J. N., & Killing, J. P. (2013). *Strategic analysis and action* (8th ed.). Toronto: Pearson Prentice Hall.

[14] Killing, P. J., Malnight, T. & Keys, T. (2005). *Must-win battles.* London: FT Prentice Hall.

[15] Malnight, T. W. (2008). "Strategically engaging your organization: Challenging your ambition." *Tomorrow's Challenges*, TC031-08, April. Lausanne: IMD.

[16] Black, J. S. & Gregersen, H. B. (2008). *It starts with one: Changing individuals changes organizations.* Upper Saddle River, NJ: Pearson Education.

[17] Marina Gorbis interviewed by Paul Hunter (2012). "Generating foresight," featured on IMD's exclusive Corporate Learning Network "Wednesday Webcast" series, March.

[18] Black, J. S. & Gregersen, H. B. (2008) *It starts with one: Changing individuals changes organizations.* Upper Saddle River, NJ: Pearson Education.

[19] Denison, D., Hooijberg, R., Lane, N. & Lief, C. (2012) *Leading culture change in global organizations: Aligning culture and strategy.* San Francisco, CA: Jossey-Bass.

[20] Strebel, P. (2003). *Trajectory management: Leading a business over time.* Chichester, UK: Wiley.

[21] Kohlrieser, G. (2007). "How to take the pain out of change – and make it all happen." *Tomorrow's Challenges*, TC020-07, April. Lausanne: IMD.

List of Pictures

Cover: Tall ship and antique globe © Photonic 8 / Alamy.

Introduction: The first stock certificate (1288) © Stora Enso.

Chapter 1: Henry the Navigator (1394-1460) detail from the Polyptych of St. Vincent, c.1465 (oil on panel), Goncalves or Gonzalvez, Nuno (fl.1450-71) / Museu Nacional de Arte Antigua, Lisbon, Portugal / The Bridgeman Art Library.

Chapter 2: Manufacture of Porcelain: Hand Modelling & Moulding (w/c and gouache on paper), Chinese School, (19th century) © Peabody Essex Museum, Salem, Massachusetts, USA / The Bridgeman Art Library.

Chapter 3: Philosopher Xenophon © iStockphoto.com/traveler1116.

Chapter 4: Interior of a London Coffee House, c.1650-1750 (w/c on paper) © English School / Private Collection / The Bridgeman Art Library.

Chapter 5: Frescoes from Ancient Sogdian Penjikent at the National Museum of Antiquities in Dushanbe Tajikistan © dbimages / Alamy.

Chapter 6: The Board of Longitude © National Maritime Museum, Greenwich, London.

Chapter 7: Zapotec Corn god Oaxaca Museum Mexico © G. Tortoli/Ancient Art Architecture Collection Ltd. Ancient Art & Architecture Collection Ltd / Alamy.

Conclusion: Wall Painting of Chinese Ship of Admiral Zheng He or Cheng Ho (1371-1433) on Chinese Temple Shrine Penang Malaysia © Chris Hellier / Alamy.

Index

About the Authors

N. ANAND (anand@imd.org) is the Shell Professor of Global Leadership at IMD. He advises organizations on transforming their leadership capability. His research focuses on institutional change, organization design, social networks, and emotion in organizations and has appeared in publications such as *Academy of Management Journal, Annual Review of Sociology, Organization Science, Organizational Dynamics and Personnel Psychology.*

JEAN-LOUIS BARSOUX (jean-louis.barsoux@imd.org) is a senior research fellow at IMD. He is the co-author of books and cases on leadership, corporate transformations and cross-cultural management and he has published several articles in *Harvard Business Review* and *MIT Sloan Management Review.*